SCOTTISH THEOLOGY

IN RELATION TO CHURCH HISTORY SINCE THE REFORMATION

John Macleod

The Knox Press (Edinburgh)

THE KNOX PRESS (EDINBURGH)
15 North Bank Street, Edinburgh

*

© *Free Church of Scotland*
First published 1943
Second edition 1946
Reprinted jointly by the Knox Press (Edinburgh)
and the Banner of Truth Trust 1974

ISBN 0 85151 193 7

*

Printed in Great Britain by Offset Lithography by
Billing and Sons Ltd., Guildford and London

PREFACE

Early in 1938 the Senatus of Westminster Theological Seminary, Philadelphia, USA, did me the honour of asking me to give a course of ten Lectures dealing with Scottish Theology since the Reformation in the light of Scottish Church History. This volume contains the Lectures, which were delivered in April, 1939, just as the tenth year of the functioning of the Seminary was drawing to a close. The subject of these Lectures fitted in with the object which the founders of Westminster had in view—the maintenance of the well-known Princeton tradition in the loyal defence, and the unambiguous exposition and avowal, of the Reformed Theology. It has been my endeavour to handle my theme in a free and familiar fashion so as to avoid a coldly technical and stiff treatment of it, and to make it as instinct with human interest as the case permitted. This called for setting forth a theological discourse in a setting of real Church life. Thus, if there is so much of discussion and exposition in the Lectures, it is woven into a fabric of narrative; and repeatedly in the course of these pages American references occur which speak of the fact that the Lectures were meant for an overseas audience. I need hardly say that I write from the standpoint of one cordially attached to the faith and witness of the Reformed Churches. Though that faith is, for the time being, largely under an eclipse, its friends live in the hope that with a resurgence of Evangelical godliness in days of reviving it will have an ample vindication, so that its future will in glory and in power surpass the best and brightest days of its past. The cause of the Reformed Theology is one and indivisible in all the Churches of the Reformation, and it is by no means a petty thing with a mere parochial or provincial outlook.

Part of two of the chapters has already appeared in another form; and in the last chapter, I take it that the writer is not a plagiarist when he quotes from an article which he contributed to the *Princeton Theological Review*.

v

It was a refreshing experience to come in close touch with the staff and students of the Seminary, and to enjoy their gracious courtesy and hospitality. The Lecturer alone is responsible for the choice he has made of the material at his disposal, and for the estimates of values that he has ventured to put on record.

Edinburgh, *February* 1943   JOHN MACLEOD

PREFACE TO THE SECOND EDITION

It is a matter of gratification to me that a reprint of this volume is called for, indicating, as it clearly does, that interest in the Reformed Faith is still keenly alive on both sides of the Atlantic.

I feel indebted also to the kindness of the friends in Westminster Theological Seminary for the interest they have taken in a practical way to secure a substantial circulation of this book in the great constituency of America; and to my friend, Rev G. N. M. Collins, BD, for kindly seeing both editions through the press.

Edinburgh, *June* 1946   JOHN MACLEOD

PREFACE TO THE THIRD EDITION

The earlier editions of this book have long since been off the market, and the many enquiries which still reach the original publishers clearly indicate that a new edition is due. It was with great pleasure therefore that they decided to co-operate with the Banner of Truth Trust in producing it afresh. The errata of the earlier editions have been corrected, and the index has been completely redone by S. M. Houghton of Oxford.

The joint-publishers send out this new edition with the prayer, and in the hope, that it may bring enlightenment and strength to many earnest people who may be disturbed by the doctrinal confusion which is so deplorable a characteristic of present-day ecclesiastical life, and help towards the creation of a new interest in the Reformed theology of which Principal Macleod was so distinguished an exponent.

Edinburgh, *December* 1973   G. N. M. COLLINS

JOHN MACLEOD

Dr. John Macleod, the author of this book, was undoubtedly one of the most remarkable men of his generation. If he was not as widely known as his rich scholarship merited it was partly because he was guided in his choice of service by strong religious conviction and not by any considerations of self-advancement; and partly because his varied activities made so many demands on his time that he had little opportunity—and, it may be suspected, little inclination—to submit himself to the domination of the pen.

A native of the West Highland township of Fort William, Dr. Macleod distinguished himself in academic pursuits from his youth. He was only 18 years of age when he graduated in Arts at Aberdeen University with First Class Honours in Classics, adding to other distinctions the Simpson Prize in Greek, the Seafield Medal in Latin, the Jenkins Prize in Classical Philology, and the Fullerton Scholarship. His Professor in Latin, Sir William M. Ramsey, and Professor Harrower of the Greek Chair, urged him to take up a Ferguson Classical Scholarship that fell vacant in the year of his graduation, and proceed to Oxford or Cambridge to specialize in Classics. Sir W. M. Ramsay, indeed, invited him to become his associate in his archaeological researches in Asia Minor. But John Macleod had early become a disciple of Christ, and it was to His service in the Christian ministry that he consecrated his talents.

Mr. Macleod's record as a student in theology matched in distinction that of his Arts course, and it was as a scholar well-grounded in the Reformed Faith that he began his ministry. His first pastorate was that of the Free Presbyterian Church in Ullapool, Ross-shire, for he was one of the Free Church students who sided with the Free Presbyterian secession after the passing of the Free Church Declaratory Act of 1892. He was later translated to Kames, in Argyleshire; but when the

ix

remanent Free Church of Scotland, after the Union in 1900 between the United Presbyterians and the Free Church majority, repealed the Declaratory Act of 1892 he felt it was his duty to return to the Church of his youth. He was received into the Free Church in 1905, and in 1906 he was appointed Professor of Greek and New Testament Exegesis in the Free Church College, Edinburgh. In 1913 he accepted a call to the pastorate of the Free North Church, Inverness. During his ministry there his *alma mater* conferred the degree of Doctor of Divinity upon him in 1927, and in the same year he was appointed Principal of the Free Church College. In 1930 he was recalled to the teaching staff of the College as Professor of Apologetics and Pastoral Theology, a position which he held until his retirement in 1942.

To know Dr. Macleod was to become acquainted with the best school of Scottish Reformed Divines in whose succession he undoubtedly had his place. William Cunningham, John Duncan, Hugh Martin, George Smeaton, James MacGregor and James Gibson stood high in his list of Scotland's great theologians, as this book reveals, and he spoke of them from such full and detailed knowledge as almost to suggest that he belonged to their generation. Certainly their own contemporaries were not more thoroughly acquainted with their thinking than he was.

A quarter of a century has passed since Principal Macleod's homecall, but he is still remembered by the older generation of church folk in Scotland as a saint and a scholar. It is fitting that though dead he should, through the medium of the printed page, still speak. And modern Scotland will do well to hearken.

G. N. M. COLLINS

CONTENTS

I

INTRODUCTORY

SUFFER a few prefatory words. There is a course of the Cunningham Lectures which treats of Scottish Theology and Theologians. The author was himself a remarkably well-read and capable divine—James Walker of Carnwath. His Cunningham Lecture, which has seen two editions, is such a masterly work as to make it difficult for another to go over something like the same field and not invite a comparison with what is, in its own department, a classic. There is, however, in the title to the present course a phrase, which, if taken with a little latitude, will allow a measure of freedom to deal with the subject of Scottish Theology in a fashion less technical and academic than that of Dr Walker. There is thus no call to make an invidious comparison between our present course and the Cunningham Lectures for 1871. Any comparison indeed we deprecate.

We are to deal with Scottish Theology since the Reformation in relation to the history of the Church. That is to say, we propose to treat our subject in the light of its historical character and setting, and this leaves room as it comes our way to discuss the practical outcome of Theology as that is seen in the message of the pulpit and in the life of the Church. Or it permits of a more concrete and perhaps interesting presentation of the subject than a severely academic treatment of itself would. The setting in the life of the Church lends an element of personal interest to what might be exhibited in a shape which, if detached or abstract, orderly or scientific, would be more dry and formal and less attractive. The subject is shown in a more real and human light when it is handled in connection with its changing historical environment as various aspects of the Faith were brought into the foreground of the picture. Even if an anecdote is given to relieve strain on the hearer it seems to make more picturesque a tale that might otherwise be of a less inviting character.

Let me add that justice could hardly be done to the theme of the Lectures unless there were given more or less of an exposition of the principles which shaped the life, faith and worship of Reformed Scotland. And in this opening lecture we may before its close glance at matters that will meet us in historical connections as they were discussed in later days. It is not for the lecturer to magnify the value of his contribution to the discussion of his subject. Yet he may say that he has had an almost lifelong acquaintance, more or less thorough, with the field that he covers. He has never, however, looked upon himself as the possessor of the detailed and expert knowledge of such a specialist as he would covet to be; and though he prized and welcomed the honour of being asked to lecture on the subject proposed to him by the Faculty of Westminster Seminary, the request took him by surprise. He need hardly add that as he looks on his subject with his own eyes no one else is responsible for the judg-ments that he ventures to pass as an Old School Evangelical. He is, however, satisfied that the ancestral Theology of his country can be so set forth and exhibited as to teach needed lessons to the present generation, not only in Scotland, but far beyond its borders.

NATIONAL INDEPENDENCE AND WHAT CAME OF IT

Had the unifying and aggressive policy of Edward I. of England proved to be a lasting success there would have been no such country left as Scotland. It would have come to be but a subordinate province that served for the aggrandisement of England and its Norman crown. In the feeble hands, however, of his son and successor, the militant programme of the Hammer of the Scots ended in thorough discomfiture on the field of Bannockburn. The decision of that day of battle was one that had far-reaching results. Not the least important and significant of these are to be found in the region of Church History, British, and, I may venture to say, American also. For the independence of Scotland as a national unit finds its reflection and remote outcome in the specific difference which marks ou. the character of the Reformation of its Church, and in the type of ecclesiastical life and confession and tradition that we find in its history. These are the outflow of its distinction in nationality. The achievement of civil independence served to call out and foster a nationalism which extended to all classes of the population. In the Middle Ages the feudal system prevailed, and the common folk derived little good from a change of rulers. Yet a popular sentiment developed that was prepared to stand in defence of national independence; and this served to keep the Scots with a national identity of their own.

In the centuries that intervened between Bannockburn and the Reformation, Scotland, though it had national freedom, was an ill-governed country. It had a weak central executive, a turbulent aristocracy, a bloated Church, and a down-trodden commonalty. Its internal history is ,a record of feud and faction which secured for the strong hand the supremacy of the local tyrant. There was hardly a country in Europe that was more backward in civilisation, or one in which life and property were less secure. As a nation the Scots served in the old alliance with France as a pawn in the political game of the French kings as they contended with those of England. Their overflow of youth and energy found a field for the exercise of its activities in mercenary service as soldiers of fortune in European wars in the service of the French crown. At home, a clergy, who were at once licentious and rapacious, held in their hands wellnigh half the wealth of the land. And the looseness of their living was matched only by the ignorance that prevailed in their ranks. Such a country stood, if any did, in need of a Reformation. It needed above all such a Reformation as would bring in its train purity of life and morals. The likelihood that such a change would take place in the recognised order of things was a very remote one indeed. Yet this backward country came under the power of the mighty Reforming movement; and when this happened, it reaped the benefit of the independence for which it had fought so stoutly, and had so hardly won, and which had proved to be of such little value before. As a land that was independent of England it had a Reformation that was not of the Tudor order, but one that asserted and vindicated with the freedom of the Gospel the freedom of the Church of Jesus Christ. In the case of England, the autocratic spirit of a Tudor queen, who, in domineering masterfulness, took after her father, laid civil restraints on the policy and activities of her Reformers, who would, had they their own way, have reformed their national Church after a pattern very different from that which they were permitted to follow. It was in this connection that the national freedom of Scotland served to determine the distinction between the character of its Reformation when it came, and that of its sister country. Yet in the early stages of the Reforming movement in Scotland, it owed much to the help of England. Church and State were interlaced. Indeed, the policy of the Lords of the Congregation, as the Reforming Barons were called, the policy, too, of John Knox, seemed to work for the reversal of the traditional hostility of their country to its southern neighbour. And it made in the end for the virtual unification of Great Britain. In the first days of the Northern Reformation the influence of England and of the English Church told on the worship of the early Scottish Reformers as for some time they made free use of the Service Book of the Reformed Church of England. This might have issued in a settlement of religion that would have been an echo of the Anglican Reformation. But there came to be at the head of the Scottish Reforming movement a man who was the Reformer of a nation—John Knox.

KNOX

During the reign of Edward VI., Knox, as one of the great preachers of the Gospel in the kingdom, had been active in promoting the work of Reformation in the Church of England. This work he was engaged in when preachers like him were few, and when they were highly valued by those who aimed at furthering the Evangelical cause. But Knox was not only a mighty popular force by reason of his preaching power, he was a leader in the inner circle of the Protestant party. Such was the influence that he wielded that he secured the insertion in the English Communion Office of what got the name of the Black Rubric, which expressly disallows the worship of the consecrated elements in the Supper, and teaches that the posture of kneeling, on the part of the communicant, was not to be construed as an act of worship to the bread and to the wine. As Dean Weston puts it : " A runagate Scot did take away the adoration or worshipping of Christ in the Sacrament; by whose procurement that heresy was put into the last Communion Book; so much prevailed that one man's authority at that time." Knox was a man mighty in words, and not less mighty in deeds. Like Luther, it might be said to him—*Fulmina erant linguae singula verba tuae.* He had already done great things before his stay in Frankfort and Geneva, but it was his destiny to do greater things still, and the supreme work of John Knox's life was to be done, not in England, but in his native land.

The reign of Edward VI. of England soon came to an end; and he was succeeded upon the throne by his sister Mary, who reversed not only the policy of her brother and his counsellors, but also that of her father. When she became Queen, many of the prominent English Reformers sought safety for themselves by flight to the Continent of Europe. One of the refugees was Knox, and he found an asylum in the free city of Frankfort. To his stay in that German city may be traced the beginnings of the rift in the English Reforming movement which in the end resulted in the separation of Puritans and Conformists. To the English exiles in Frankfort the use of one of the city Churches was granted for their worship. Among them there were two classes. One of these, of which Knox was a leader, desired a more thorough Reformation than was embodied in the Liturgy of Edward VI. The other class, which was headed by Cox, who in after years became one of Queen Elizabeth's bishops, insisted on using the Prayer Book as it was, even though it was likely that, had Edward lived, it would have been reformed in the direction that Knox and his friends aimed at. In the course of the strife that began between these two parties, Knox was driven out of Frankfort and made his way to Geneva, where he became pastor of the exiled English who had found shelter in the city of John Calvin. In this city, the vigorous Scottish Reformer saw, as he thought, the most perfect school of Christ that was to be found on earth. And when he was called home to Scotland to lead the national Reforming movement, he carried with him the lessons of his exile in Geneva. So the Swiss Reformation left its mark on Reformed Scotland. For when Knox became the dominant figure and driving force of the Reformation in his native land, it accepted the principle which marked out the Swiss from the Lutheran and Anglican Churches. The leading English Reformers as a class, from Hooper downward, were of the same mind with Zurich and Geneva. Their endeavours to bring about a more thorough Reform in England earned for the most outspoken and militant of them what was meant to be a reproach, but became a badge of honour, the nickname of Puritans.

THE PURITANS

The Puritans, of whom Knox may well be admitted to have been the greatest, were the out-and-out Protestants of the British Reformation. As a class they have been made the victims of no end of caricature and misrepresentation. There were among them undoubtedly extreme men, but these were not typical specimens of the movement. Yet the sober, well-balanced men who were the leaders and the authentic representatives of the Puritans have been depicted as though they were more absurd and extreme than the most extreme of their party. In reality their aim was simple and clear; and their policy was unambiguous and straightforward. They aimed in their Reforming activities at getting down to bed-rock and, when they reached it, they sought to build upon it. They would not rest satisfied with a basis of Church life which was a compromise with a mere *jus humanum* when they might have a *jus divinum*. The goal for which they were making was a return of the Church to the Apostolic pattern. This they sought to reach all along the line not only in Faith but in Order and Discipline and Worship. In regard to Order and Worship they made what was quite a valid distinction between what was peculiar to the Apostolic age and what in the life of that age was normal and ordinary. The office of the Apostles themselves was a supernormal one and the charismatic element that entered into the worship of their age was peculiar to its foundation character for which it received the Pentecostal endowment. Apart from what in this way was supernormal and exceptional the Puritans sought to bring the life and practice of the Church back to the truly primitive model. They stood for the unabated avowal of the primitive Faith. This they endeavoured to hold fast and to hold forth. In respect of their aim they were of the school that paid full homage to Apostolic authority.

The opponents of Puritanism when Conformists tended to become Anglo-Catholics laid great stress upon the primitive character of the Faith and Order and Worship for which they contended. They were the professed champions and exponents of primitive Church Principles in regard to all these. It is worthy of note how they coupled together primitive Faith and Order. With them, however, primitive did not mean more than patristic. They made their appeal to the Fathers, and forgot that those Fathers were themselves but the children of the Grandfathers. So what had only the authority of the Fathers fell short of being truly primitive. Their appeal did not carry them far enough back as it built on what was only patristic and not Apostolic. And even at that, it might accept as of authority usages and developments which, though in a sense patristic, were only of late emergence, and as such far removed from the Faith and Practice of the Apostolic age. The principle, on the other hand, accepted by the Puritans was the recognition of, and the return to, the Scripture pattern in all the departments of Church life so far as this could be learned from the teaching and narrative of Holy Writ; and this reforming standard was accepted in Scotland.

The thoroughgoing Protestants held that the Church in its visible embodiment is the outward Kingdom of its Lord and Head. They held a positive doctrine of His Headship which became the word of Christ's patience in Scotland for the martyr Church in the next century. As they laid stress upon His Headship of the body, and His Lordship of the Church, they loved to think generous and kindly thoughts of His bounty in the liberal provision that He has made for the guidance of His people through the ages. They did not hold themselves to be competent to improve upon the teaching set forth by His authentic representatives. What He spoke in the years of His public ministry on earth is enshrined for all time in the record of the Gospels, and in its written form it has the same authority that it had when it was spoken. In its written form we have the abiding witness of those who saw and heard, and could tell of what they had seen and heard at first hand. What the Lord went on to speak as the Risen and Glorified Christ Who by His Spirit upon them and in them used His Apostles and Prophets to be His spokesmen is also on record, and equally with the rest of the New Testament Scriptures it bears the stamp of an authority from which our Reformers felt that there can be no appeal. The Lord spoke directly and indirectly. Whichever way He took to make His mind known, the Word that He gave is possessed of His authority, for it is His. From the witness and teaching of the Apostles we learn how the authority of their Lord is impressed upon Old Testament Scripture. And their teaching as we have it in written form is clad with the same authority which it had when spoken by Christ and His Apostles by word of mouth. The Scriptures that preserve such teaching, the Puritans, being good Protestants, treated as of final authority. And in this ultimate authority they rested. The Holy Books give us the Christian Faith in its authentic presentation. Such was the doctrine of what Scripture is that they learned from Scripture itself. And he is a very odd specimen of the Christian name that would, in the realm of Christian doctrine, find fault with the principle of accepting the absolute Divine authority and completeness of the written

Apostolic Deposit. But the return to Christ and His Apostles as the Masters of the Church in her Faith which marked the Reformation, and was the true " Back to Christ " movement, was carried out by the Puritan leaders of Reform not only in the realm of doctrinal truth but also in that of order and worship.

It is at this point that their fellows in Reform of a less thorough quality parted company with their out-and-out Reforming brethren. The latter held that in all departments of the Church's life, as well as in profession of faith, there has been given to us a sufficient and a Divine Directory. Whatever we have by way of precept or of pattern, of ordinance or of example, is ours that we may follow it. It was their conviction that the Head of the Church has given in His Word not only a correct but a comprehensive and sufficient pattern and model. When this position is guarded from being an extreme one by the avowal that there are " circumstances common to human actions and societies " which are to be determined according to the dictates of the light of nature and seemliness or Christian prudence, in the absence of precept or pattern or example that the Church is bound to follow, the Puritans showed how far they would go and where they stood. The proviso laid down and admitted was not to be stretched so as to admit anything that is not in keeping with the general rules of the Word which are on no account to be set aside. Such a principle to regulate the practice and worship of the Church is one that gives the Lord the credit of His own bounty. And when we look the matter fairly in the face we see how unseemly a thing it is to accuse Him of being a niggard in making provision for the needs of His Church. To take up such a position as suggests that He has failed in the liberality of His provision is to say, in effect, that we must come to His assistance and fill up from the wealth of our wisdom the blank that He has omitted to supply. When the matter is looked at from this angle, the Puritan contention is seen to fit in with the instincts of a free and loyal heart. On the other hand, it is not in keeping with such instincts to impugn the suitableness or sufficiency of the guidance which the Lord has supplied. The results of this attempt of the Puritans to give effect to their principle are freely spoken of as meagre and mean, as bald or bare and poverty-stricken. Those who venture on such a freedom of critical speech may perhaps forget that to justify their censure they should first make good the position that the materials for guidance in Holy Writ are either overlooked or insufficient. If they are overlooked, the Puritans' own principle has not been carried out. If they are held to be insufficient, the criticism is one that passes what looks like a censure on the Word and its Giver.

We have noted the fact that it is the Reformed principle emphasised by the Puritan school that helped to determine the history of the Scottish Reformed Church. It came under the sweep of the Second Commandment when, as our Catechism tells us, it forbids "the worshipping of God by images, or in any other way not appointed in His Word." To adopt the leading principle that calls for Divine Prescription is a challenge to its opponents. It is for those that would introduce into the plain and unadorned simplicity of New Testament worship what would alter that simplicity, to bring forward their warrant from the regulative Word. The whole motley array of indefinitely varied improvements on the Apostolic pattern that run riot in the practice of the Churches would have the way foreclosed upon them if only this clear-cut principle were acted upon. And it can hardly be called a healthy or a Christian instinct that quarrels with the plainness of the unadorned worship of believing men and women who follow the Puritan ideal as they meet together to worship in Spirit and in truth.

The application of the same principle, which so unmistakably puts honour on the Head of the Church and His Word, to the sphere of Government, secured for the Reformed Church of Scotland its Presbyterian model which it claimed to be one founded upon the Word and agreeable thereto. In the militant centuries of its history it did not hide its light under a bushel. It put forth its claim to a *jus divinum* for the order of Government which it recognised. And what held in the field of Government was equally true in that of Discipline. Indeed, Discipline was one of the salient marks of the Scottish Reformed Church; for its Confession, when it was drafted, gave this as one of the notes by which the true Church was to be known. And in the early days of the Elizabethan history of the Church of England it was one of the most outstanding features of the Puritan programme that it sought to revive the godly discipline of early times, so that it was one of the nicknames of the out-and-out Reformers that they were called Disciplinarians. They earned the honour of this nickname though they aimed only at restoring that discipline, the loss of which the English Prayer Book in its Commination Service annually bewails, but which for four centuries the Anglican Establishment has been content to do without. What the Calvinistic Reformers failed to do in England they achieved in Scotland.

In the Scottish Reformation, not only did the due place of Discipline find recognition in the Confession of Faith, it found practical illustration in the working of the Church. This it did from the first; for even before civil recognition was given to the Reformed Church, the Register of the Kirk Session of St Andrews bears witness to the exercise of its rod. It is one of the favourite themes of acid criticism that such a course was taken. The Records of Church Discipline show the seamy side of life. In doing so they let men see how much had to be done not only to evangelise the community but even to teach it the elements of morality. We are not called upon to maintain that the Discipline of the House of God was always administered with wisdom. Yet there is no mistake about two things that came out in its exercise. The Church was not afraid to apply its discipline to men in the highest ranks. There was a noble manliness in its administration. And though in the earlier days of the Reformed Church its exercise might seem at times to trench on the realm of the civil magistrate, yet in the absence of diligence on his part, the Discipline of the Kirk was one of the most potent instruments for bringing a hitherto turbulent and untamed community into some shape of order, decency

and civilisation. Then, also, the Discipline which dealt with
the highest and did not let them escape at the same time
did not forget the poorest. And all the while this discipline
sought not to humiliate men but to promote their highest
good. The fight that the Church put up for its rights in
this connection made it ultimately the tribune of the people
and the instrument for breaking the tyranny of the feudal
order. In this sense, those who thought it to be their
interest that that order should be preserved recognised in the
Reformed Church an enemy to their class. One can see from
this how natural it was in later days for the aristocratic
party, or the landed gentry, to take sides with the Court
against its freedom and Discipline. If what the Stuart kings
meant by a Free Monarchy was to be set up or kept on foot,
they felt that it was a case of no Kingship worthy of the
name without its attendant Episcopacy. And when Charles II.
said that Presbyterianism was no fit religion for a gentleman,
it was sufficiently obvious from his record and its record
that there must be a clash. It was no religion suitable for
the loose life of a licentious libertine such as he was.

In spite of opposition in high quarters, the strict Discipline
of the Reformed Church came to be such a recognised part
of the life of the country that even during the days of the
Second Episcopacy Synod Records show how a very Earl
was made amenable to its demand. The higher ranks, however, took it ill to be subject to a system that treated them
as equally exposed to the judgment of God against sin with
the lowest of their henchmen and dependents. Under the
Roman order they had been subject to discipline. That was
such as could be compounded for in terms of cash. Here,
however, were Church Courts which at times might prove
unfaithful, but on the whole maintained their integrity and
laid the foundation for the recognised freedom of each class
of society. To the heart of the snob and the flunkey such
a record seals the doom of the Discipline of the Kirk
of Scotland; and so it has had to run the gauntlet of an
unfriendly criticism.

An Unrealised Possibility

There was a possibility that the Scottish Reformation might take on a Lutheran or an Anglican complexion. The work and influence of Knox decided that this should not be so. The earlier leaders of the movement, such as Patrick Hamilton and Alexander Alane, laid stress upon the Lutheran *articulus stantis et cadentis ecclesiae*. Hamilton as a student on the Continent sat at the feet of Francis Lambert at Marburg, while Lambert was still a Lutheran, for it was only after the death of Hamilton that the Marburg Conference took place, as the result of which Lambert took the side of the Swiss Reformers on the sacramental question that was at issue between Wittenberg and Zurich. The question of Justification was the main problem in those early days of the new era. If Hamilton's life had been prolonged it is possible that he might have developed along the lines of the Lutheran rather than the Swiss Theology. In his day, however, the Lutheran doctrine of grace was thoroughly Augustinian. His literary contribution to his country's enlightenment is found in *Patrick's Places,* as his Theses were called. They are preserved in Knox's *History* and in Foxe's *Acts and Monuments.* In the Theses he deals with Law and Gospel and gives a vigorous statement of the doctrine of free Justification by Faith alone. The other contribution that he made by his courageous martyrdom did more to impress on his countrymen the meaning of his teaching than that teaching itself, fruitful though it was, availed to do. Hamilton was cut off while he was yet a youth, and, as we have said, the great issue of those days was the doctrine of Justification by Faith. Had he lived he might have developed doctrinally as his master at Marburg did, or possibly he might have gone on Lutheran lines, as his disciple Alexander Alane did. Alane, or Alesius, did his life-work mainly among the Lutherans in Germany. Had he come back to Scotland he might have guided the Reforming movement along the lines of the German Reformation so that the type of teaching which found a welcome in Scotland might have been other than it came to be. This would have affected the relations of Church and State, the teaching in regard to the Sacraments, their nature and efficacy, the character of the Incarnation, and possibly the Synergism to which Melanchthon gave place in his later years and which set aside the robust and definite Augustinianism of Martin Luther. On this last subject the witness of the Reformers in their early days was one. Indeed, the De Servo Arbitrio of the Saxon Reformer is at times more sweeping in what might be called its Calvinistic strain than the Institutes of John Calvin himself. As through the dark ages the Evangelical witness, when it made itself heard, spoke again and again in the tones of Augustine of Hippo, so the Reformation itself might be spoken of, and not incorrectly, as a resurgence of the Doctrine of Grace. That the Scottish Reformers were definite in their loyalty to that type of teaching made it easy for them when they were asked to make confession of their Faith to set it forth in terms expressive of the full gracious consciousness of the Churches of the Reformed order.

THE SCOTS CONFESSION

The time came in due season when the challenge was given to set forth the Faith that Knox and his brethren held. This was in 1560, and in a few days the Reformers gave in, as their answer to this challenge, the Scottish Confession. It took them less than a week to put in shape, though it may be that for a few weeks before they were gathering together the material which they arranged at such short notice. One of the leading ends for which such documents were drawn up and given to the world was to let friend and foe alike know what the truth was that was held. Thus the Confessors might clear up difficulties and give a careful and considered answer to misrepresentations that found currency in regard to their Teaching. The Scottish Confession was the manifesto of the Reforming party. It was, as we see, hurriedly adjusted; but it was the work of men who were at home in their subject. And though it is less technical and academic than many of its sister Confessions, yet it is drafted in a more free and familiar fashion than any one of them. There is a frank outspokenness about it that was quite in keeping with the character of the leader of the Reforming movement. Its strength lies in these things and not in the balanced accuracy with which it sets forth the faith of the men who drew it up. The very fact that none of them would be spoken of as a specialist in the positive or dogmatic statement of the proportion and value of the various truths confessed makes the Scottish Confession a very human document. The men who gave it in were capable working theologians, but they could not be classed as experts of the first rank with Calvin or Bucer, or Peter Martyr or Bullinger. Knox in his treatise on Predestination gives a good sample of his work. He shows, however, his native boldness at times as when in his *History* he disagrees with what Paul did on the occasion of his last visit to Jerusalem when he was at the expense of the service of purification of the four men that had a vow. The Confession, however, though it is often spoken of as his work, was that of his fellow-Reformers as well as of Knox.

In common with the other Confessions of the Reformed Churches the Scots Confession makes its appeal to Holy Writ and builds upon its teaching. It gives a chapter to the authority of the Scriptures. Yet its statements as to what Holy Scripture is are not by any means full. But there is no dubiety as to what they mean and were intended to cover. Thus in the 18th chapter we come across these words which come in, as it were, by the way : " The doctrine taught in our Churches contained in the written Word of God, to wit in the books of the Old and New Testaments, in those books, we mean, which of the ancient have been reputed canonical. In the which we affirm that all things necessary to be believed for the salvation of mankind are sufficiently expressed." This chapter goes on to speak of its interpretation and says : " When controversy then happens for the right understanding of any place or sentence of Scripture . . . we ought not so much to look what men before have said or done as unto that which the Holy Ghost uniformly speaks within the body of the Scriptures. . . . For this is a thing universally granted that the Spirit of God which is the Spirit of unity is in nothing contrarious to Himself." Then again we read in the Preface :

" Protesting that if any man will note in this our Confession any Article or sentence repugnant to God's Holy Word that it would please him of his gentleness and for Christian charity's sake to admonish us of the same in writing; and we, upon our honours and fidelity, by God's grace do promise to him satisfaction from the mouth of God, that is, from His Holy Scriptures, or else reformation of that which he shall prove to be amiss."

There is given in the Confession a sketch of the history of the promise or of the process of gracious revelation. Yet it has no elaborate statement of what the word is, the assured faith of which it teaches. It obviously, however, proceeds upon the acceptance of Holy Writ as being God's Word. In this respect it followed in the line of the Universal Church as well as of the sister Churches of the Reformation age. They accepted the New Testament Scriptures as the Divinely authoritative account of the witness borne by the Apostles to the truth of the revelation of the Everlasting Word. The Apostles had seen for themselves and heard for themselves and were competent first-hand witnesses, and their witness is on permanent record for the good of the Church. Those Scriptures which embody and perpetuate their witness convey with equal truth and authority the teaching which they give to open up the meaning of the Gospel facts, so that with the New Testament books in her hand the Church to the end of time is able to hear the voice of the witnesses and teachers whom the Lord appointed for her establishment in her New Testament, and final earthly, form. In thus accepting the New Testament in its witness and its teaching as authoritative and trustworthy the Reformed Confession echoed the witness to Holy Scripture which was a feature of the historical Church as a visible organisation. Taking their place at the footstool of their Lord and His Apostles, our Reformers handled the Scriptures of the Old Testament with the same reverence and submission with which both Christ and His Apostles treated them. The Scriptures, then, that they built upon were the whole Canon of the Old Testament, Moses and the Prophets and the Psalms with those

of the dispensation of fulfilment. To controvert or overthrow
their teaching they held that their opponents must first set
aside the teaching of Holy Writ. For it was on the Divine
Word that they built, and their teaching owed all the authority
that it claimed to the written Word which was its warrant.

Teaching that made such claims naturally met with
opposition from the Roman Communion. So in argument
with the Romanists the Reformers were called upon to answer
objections and clear up difficulties which were as fully relevant
when raised against Rome's own doctrine on the subject as
they were against that of the rest of Christendom. The
difficulties were as real for the one side in the dispute as
for the other. In taking the line of raising such objections
the Romanists were seeking to shut men in to a blind
submission to what they held to be the infallible judgment
of the teaching Church. To secure their end some of their
spokesmen did not shrink from serving the cause of specific
unbelief. In practice this procedure meant that it was lawful
for them to do evil that good might come. As a matter of
fact the claims which they put forth on behalf of the Church
they defended by the witness of Scripture as the Word of
God, while, by taking the course that they did, they were
busy sawing off between themselves and the trunk the branch
of the tree on which they were sitting. All Christians have
the benefit of the witness of the Church in its historic
continuity. And the value of this witness does not depend on
the acceptance by all parties of the Roman definition of what
the Visible Church is.

It was one of the weaknesses that developed since the
age of the post-Reformation discussions that many of the
Protestants came to lay less stress than was well warranted
by their own true principles on the testimony of the custodian
in whose hands the sacred books have been throughout the
ages. When we find an Apostle directing one of those books
to all that in every place call upon the name of Christ Jesus
our Lord we may see what holds of the rest of the New
Testament books, that wherever the profession of the truth
of the Evangel is made by calling on the name of the Lord

those who make it are not outwith the range and ambit of
the definition that tells what the Visible Church of God is.
That Visible Church in which they have a place bears witness
to Holy Writ which it holds in its hands.   It is a mistake,
then, to leave with Rome, as if it were her exclusive property,
the witness of the Visible Church to the Holy Oracles.   For
it is a witness in which the whole visible corporate Church
has a share, and it is needed for the full exhibition of the
Christian case.

Such a mistake our Reformers did not think of making,
however rashly at times Luther might speak.   They were
teased by their opponents with piffling questions of a critical
nature, but they held fast the Canon of historical Christendom
which was more than Rome did, when, at Trent, she canonised
so many of the Apocrypha.   As they stood fast by the witness
of Holy Writ they relegated to the minor and subordinate
place that belongs to it the whole range of mere critical
details.   There is no mistake about this, that it was not on
the authority of the Church that they believed the Scriptures.
But when she as a witness brought the holy books to their
notice and they discerned the decisive intrinsic marks that
they bear, marks that are inwrought into their very fibre, and
that testify to their Divine origin, they saw the sacred writings
shine in their own light.   With such a discovery of their true
and inner glory they could say to the Church as was said
to the woman of Samaria : " Now we believe, not for thy
saying, for we have heard Him ourselves and know that this
is indeed the Christ the Saviour of the world."   The discovery,
in the Gospel, of the Lord in His glory and truth carries
with it a recognition of the truth of the Word that sets Him
forth.   And if we acknowledge the truth of the Word we
accept its testimony as to the spiritual equipment of its writers.
We see, too, the Divine character that belongs to their word
as witnesses and teachers furnished by heaven for their work.
In regard to the place accorded to Holy Writ in the Theology
of Scotland, no great question was raised until the closing
quarter of the nineteenth century.

Quite in keeping with the haste with which it was put
in shape, the Scots Confession is not distinguished by that
deliberate order and consecution of parts that one prepared
in a more leisurely fashion might be expected to show. It
does not bear the mark of the dogmatic treatise or the handbook to Systematic Theology. Thus, for example, it is in
chapter III., which deals with Original Sin, that we find
its most definite statement in regard to Regeneration. This
reads : " Which regeneration is wrought by the power of the
Holy Ghost, working in the hearts of the elect of God an
assured faith in the promise of God revealed to us in His
Word, by which faith we apprehend Christ Jesus with the
graces and benefits promised in Him."

In a series of the chapters of the Confession there is
a narrative quality as they present in historical form the truth
that is confessed. It is a sketch before Jonathan Edwards'
day of the History of Redemption when the Confession treats
of the Revelation of the Promise in chapter IV., and then
in chapter V. the Continuance, Increase and Preservation of
the Church until the coming of Christ. This is followed by
chapter VI., which treats of the Incarnation, the great thing
to which the previous process was leading up. Such an
historical way of setting forth the truth in regard to the
onward progress of Divine Revelation is like an echo of what
is found in the Summa Doctrinae of John Alasco's Church
of the Strangers or Foreigners in London. Knox had come
into touch with this body both in London and in Frankfort.

As an illustration of how untechnical the Confession is
we have in chapter VIII. what we might look for in chapter
VII. The seventh chapter is entitled : " Why it behoved the
Mediator to be very God and very man." The next chapter
treats of Election, and there we read : ". . . It behoved
further the Messias and Redeemer to be very God and very
Man because He was to underlie the punishment due for our
transgressions and to present Himself in the presence of
His Father's judgment as in our person to suffer for our
transgressions and inobedience, by death to overcome him who
was the author of death. But because the only Godhead could

not suffer death, neither yet could the only Manhead overcome the same, He joined both together in one Person that the imbecility of the one should suffer and be subject to death which we had deserved; and the infinite and invincible power of the other, to wit, of the Godhead, should triumph and purchase to us life, liberty, and perpetual victory."

After the question why it behoved the Mediator to be very God and very man has been dealt with and the answer expanded under the caption of Election, there are three chapters which deal in order with the Death, the Resurrection, and the Ascension of Christ. From this the Confession goes on to acknowledge our faith in the Holy Ghost and in His work as that is seen in the good works of believers. Then in regard to good works, the question is taken up and handled of what their norm is. So the Law comes in for discussion, after which the Confession deals with the Perfection of the Law and the Imperfection of Men. It is in this chapter that its teaching in respect to Justification is given. This has no scholastic treatment accorded to it when we find it expressed in these terms: " And therefore it behoves us to apprehend Christ Jesus with His justice and satisfaction Who is the end and accomplishment of the Law by Whom we are set at this liberty that the curse and malediction of God fall not upon us albeit we fulfil not the same in all points. For God the Father beholding us in the body of His Son Christ Jesus accepts our imperfect obedience as it were perfect and covers our works which are defiled with many spots with the justice of His Son." In respect to the continued acceptance of believers we read again in chapter XXV. : " But such as with heart unfeignedly believe and with mouth boldly confess the Lord Jesus as before we have said shall most assuredly receive these gifts : First, in this life, remission of sins and that by only faith in Christ's Blood insomuch that albeit sin remain and continually abide in these our mortal bodies, yet it is not imputed unto us but is remitted and covered with Christ's justice."

Objection had been taken to such an account of Justification by Faith as not being the same as is taught in common by the Confessions of the Reformation. It is true it is not so distinctly or fully wrought out. There is no doubt, however, that our Scottish Reformers, though in the statements quoted they do not cover the whole field, were of one mind with their brethren in other lands in this matter. For we have to take note of the fact that as surely as they submitted their Confession they appointed Calvin's Catechism for the teaching of youth, and in 1566 cordially accepted the Second Helvetic Confession, apart from what it says in regard to holidays. And there is no dubiety as to where the Geneva Catechism and the Second Helvetic Confession stand on the subject of Justification by Faith. When the Confession speaks of "the end and accomplishment of the Law," Dr Mitchell of St Andrews aptly quotes to illustrate the meaning from Balnaves on Justification—Henry Balnaves was fellow-prisoner for the Faith with John Knox himself—"Christ is the end of the Law (unto righteousness) to all that believe, that is, Christ is the consummation and fulfilling of the Law and that justice which the Law requireth, and all they which believe in Him are just by imputation through faith, and for His sake are reputed and accepted as just." (Baird Lectures on *The Scottish Reformation*, p. 113, by A. F. Mitchell, D.D.) On this doctrine no one doubts that Knox was at one with his old comrade and partner in suffering and witness.

The Confession goes on to treat of the Church and its notes. In regard to these marks of the Visible Church it lays stress, as we have seen, on the exercise of godly discipline when it says (chapter XVIII.) : " Last, ecclesiastical discipline uprightly ministered as the Word prescribes, whereby vice is reproved and virtue nourished." In giving this note, the Confession stands among Symbolic documents pretty much by itself. It goes on then to deal with the Sacraments along the lines of Reformed teaching which restricts the good of them to the Elect, the people of God, the faithful. Particular stress is laid, and that at some length, on the Lord's Supper. There is a chapter treating of the Civil Magistrate which laid the foundations for the later teachings of the Church of Scotland in regard to the office of the supreme power in the

State and his duties *circa sacra* as *custos utriusque tabulae*. Without adverting further in detail to the chapters of the Confession, before we say a little in regard to the Sacraments, we might just mention a thing of which Dr A. F. Mitchell takes note, the extent to which its statements and expressions are an echo of Alasco on the one hand and Genevan documents on the other. There is in particular a number of close parallels between its way of putting things and the words of Calvin's Institutes in the first edition.

1. THE SACRAMENTS

In the first half-century of the Reformation movement, differences as to the doctrine of the Sacraments did more than anything else to break the unity of the Protestant front. There was no one in such a state of affairs among the Reformers that was disposed to go to greater lengths in an irenic interest than John Calvin. His overtures, if such they might be called, to make the peace met with more or less of a response from Melanchthon in his later years. The Preceptor of Germany came under suspicion in his own Communion of being a Crypto-Calvinist. This was suspected in spite of the fact that the Synergistic type of teaching which he came latterly to favour was quite out of harmony with the consistent supernaturalism of grace taught by Calvin and the Confessions of the Reformed Churches. In fact his Synergism was the precursor of Arminianism. In the acceptance that they accorded to teaching of this nature, the Lutheran Churches broke away not only from the Reformed wing of Protestantism but from the teaching of Luther himself and his fellows in the early days of the German Reformation. As to the process of the work of grace, the friends of Melanchthon did not at all approach an acceptance of Calvin's teaching; yet the Sacramental doctrine of the Genevan Reformer was a distinct move away from what goes by the name of Zwinglianism. One might detect in the Scots Confession an echo of this tendency in the twofold fact that it disavows with a strong emphasis the doctrine of those who found in the Sacramental elements only bare and naked signs,

while at the same time it strikes no positive discordant note
of criticism on the high Sacramental teaching of the Lutherans.
In this connection, it is possible that what is disavowed is
not so much the teaching of Zwingli and his school as that
of the naturalistic tendency at work in the thinking of the
early Socinians, which, though not by 1560 given openly to
the world as it was soon afterwards, would be matter of
whispered discussion in the Swiss Churches before Knox came
back to Scotland; for so many of the Italian refugees for
religion had found an asylum in Switzerland. The elder
Socinus was known already to hold disintegrating views on
Christian Theology though his nephew had not yet in 1560
formulated or published the teaching of their school. In 1566
the Assembly in Scotland gave, as we have seen, its
approval to the Second Helvetic Confession which represented
the consensus of the teaching of the Swiss Reformers, when
under the leadership of Bullinger the Divines at Zurich made
a close approach to the higher Sacramental doctrine of Calvin,
and by so doing showed that the tradition of Zwingli and
Zurich, in spite of some of Zwingli's more extreme statements,
was not so far away as it had been, by some Lutheran
polemics, represented to be from the more mystical view of
the Sacraments that was taught by the Divines of Wittenberg.
The acceptance of this Zurich Confession which met with
such wide approval in the Reformed Churches is a commentary
on the mind of the Scots Reformers. For the men who in
1560 drew up their Confession sealed in half a dozen years
with their approval the mature, unambiguous teaching of the
Helvetian Reformed Communion. They were not militant
against the leaders of the Zwinglian Churches. There had
been, of course, such a type of Sacramental teaching as goes
by the name of historical Zwinglianism; but except as a
bugbear for polemic Lutherans it had no place in the Reformed
Churches for the best part of a generation before 1560.

It is possible to lay too much stress on the fact that the
Confession of 1560 disclaimed the doctrine that the Sacraments
are but bare signs, while the Westminster Confession of 1647
is definite in its rejection of the Lutheran doctrine on the

subject. The opposition of the latter to the Lutheran teaching is found in chapter XXIX., section 7. This reads : " The body and blood of Christ being then not corporally or carnally in with or under the bread and wine; yet as really but spiritually present to the faith of the believer in that ordinance as the elements themselves are to their outward senses." We find also the words of the Westminster Larger Catechism to be equally opposed to any elemental change when it says in the answer to the 170th question : "the body and blood of Christ are not corporally or carnally present in with or under the bread and wine in the Lord's Supper, and yet are spiritually present to the faith of the receivers no less truly and really than the elements themselves are to their outward senses." Such repeated, distinct and definite repudiation of the Lutheran view of the Supper might be called for in particular by the upgrowth of high Sacramental doctrine in the Anglican school of Laud. This the Westminster divines were called upon to reject with no doubtful voice. For to meet and deal with the revival of Mediaeval teaching in England was really what called them together.

In recent years Anglican Sacramentarian teaching made an approach to the Lutheran position in the case of some leading ecclesiastics, as, for instance, Dr Frederick Temple when he was Archbishop of Canterbury put it forward as a half-way house of compromise with the avowed Tridentine doctrine of the Ritualistic faction. The attitude of the followers of Laud in the generation that preceded the Westminster Assembly is itself enough to account for the evident repudiation in its documents of the Lutheran type of teaching as one form of unduly high doctrine at the same time as they teach that the Sacraments are something more than significant institutions inasmuch as they are sealing ordinances which, with the blessing of God upon them, are effectual means for building up believers in their spiritual life.

The endeavour on the part of recent Sacramentarians of the Scottish Church Society to find in our Scottish documents a doctrine of what is in effect a virtue in the Sacraments *ex opere operato,* and, in particular, a doctrine of Baptismal

Regeneration, is about as signal an example as can be quoted of wrongheaded futility in facing a forlorn hope. It would put the Scots Confession outside of the Symbolic documents of Reformed Orthodoxy. For nothing can be clearer in the teaching of the Reformed Faith than that the good of Sacramental worship is confined to the believer and is his through the working of faith. The answer on the subject in the Shorter Catechism sets forth the common Faith of the Reformed Churches when it tells us that in the Sacraments, by signs perceptible to the senses, " Christ and the benefits of the New Covenant are represented, sealed and applied to believers." This means that it is believers in Christ that get the good of them. A statement of this kind leaves no loophole for the admission of a virtue intrinsic to the Sacraments that does good to those who are not already partakers of the faith that saves. The Catechism—Calvin's—that was meant to be used according to the First Book of Discipline asks in question 317 : " How and when is it that the Sacraments have this effect? " And the answer is : " When a man receiveth them in faith seeking only in them Christ and His grace."

The Sacramentarian teaching of the Scottish Church Society is very much a revival of the kind of doctrine to which, in certain fashionable circles, Edward Irving gave a vogue in his later years more than a century ago. Dr John MacLeod of Govan, who was the champion of the doctrine of Baptismal Regeneration, represented a strain of teaching that bore marked traces of this influence. There was about the year 1830 a reissue by Irving, with a laudatory preface, of the old Confession. This was in the interest of the Sacramentarian teaching which he and his followers had already adopted. His followers who accept the guidance of the Scottish Church Society programme make an appeal to the earlier Confession to find what support they can for their doctrine of Sacramental efficacy. They make this appeal alleging that for about a century the teaching of the Reformed Church of Scotland had the early Confession as its avowed and accepted standard. But no candid interpreter of its statements of doctrine can fail, if he is at all a competent theologian, to see how thoroughly its teaching represents the common Faith of Reformed Christendom. And even when in isolated expressions the later Confession was more cautious in its way of putting the doctrine of the Reformed Churches, it does no more than dot the " i's " and stroke the " t's " of its precursor. When at the epoch of the Covenanting struggle the place of the older Confession was taken as the Confession of the Church of Scotland by that of Westminster, the change-over took place on terms that were as honourable to the old standard as they were to the Covenanting Church. The later Confession was received as in nothing contrary to the received doctrine of the Church, which received doctrine, of course, means the Confession which the Church had so long recognised as her own. This action was taken without a dissenting voice; and the last authoritative doctrinal finding is the regulative one.

In the period of the Scottish Episcopacy—the reigns of Charles II. and his brother James—the old Scots Confession was for a time called back from the obscurity to which it had been relegated once the Westminster Confession had found acceptance. This was for no special love of the older standard. The Church that submitted at the royal dictation to the imposition of Episcopacy could hardly be said to be remarkable for its attachment to any definite Confession. The Vicar of Bray was well represented among its ministry. Nor could the King, in 1681, be regarded as much of an admirer of the old Confession of Knox and his brethren. Yet the Test Act which was passed in that year, and which was one of the culminating heights of Erastian supremacy and of Stuart tyranny, resuscitated the Confession of 1560 as one of the documents to which those who submitted to the Test bound themselves.

The anomalous condition of things during the days of cruel persecution comes out in the recognition by Episcopal Conformists of the General Assemblies of the Covenanting regime in the reign of Charles I. as Assemblies of the Church of Scotland. This is found, for example, in Robert Edward's little treatise in which he pleads for the use of the Doxology in connection with the Church's Psalmody. If the Assembly of 1645 which accepted the Westminster Directory for Public Worship is recognised by Edward, in spite of all that the Act Rescissory meant, as one of the Assemblies of his Church, there was no reason why that of 1647 which accepted the Westminster Confession of Faith should not meet with equal recognition. It is indeed less out of the way that a Conformist should acknowledge that of 1647; for the Assembly of 1645 was one of those at which there was no Royal Commissioner present. High Royalist Conformists in 1683 might well boggle at the recognition of such an Assembly; yet Edward recognised it. When that of 1645 is looked upon as valid no objection could be well taken to that of 1647. And as a matter of fact in those years of turmoil and disorder use was made of the Scots Confession at one time and of the Westminster at another.

Before we pass from the older Confession, which will always hold its place in the National Covenant, a word is in place in regard to two other matters which in one shape or another came into discussion in after years in the life of the Church—the one of them is the nature of the faith that saves, the other is the place of the Visible Church. In regard to these, the later Confession is much more mature and careful in the statements that it makes.

2. FAITH AND ASSURANCE

Between the years 1560 and 1647 there was much discussion in the schools of the Reformed Church. It was an age of controversy, indeed perhaps the greatest Theological age that the Church has ever seen. It is not fitted, then, to call forth surprise that in the clash of mind with mind in the warfare with Rome, with the Socinians and with the Arminians, the defenders of the Reformed Faith found reason to modify some ways of putting things that were current among their first teachers when in the early days of the Protestant Churches they, with one mind and voice, made common cause with one another in their teaching on the article of free Justification. This modification took place especially in the definition that was given of the Faith that saves. The early Reformers gave a place to an assurance of one's personal salvation as entering into it that involved them in difficulties for which their successors had to find a solution. In Calvin's Catechism, which was in current use after 1560, we find in answer to the question, "What is the right faith?" the definition that it is "a sure persuasion and steadfast knowledge of God's tender love towards us, according as He hath plainly uttered it in His Gospel, that He will be both a Father and a Saviour unto us, through the means of Jesus Christ." Here is a definition, not of saving faith at its lowest, but of faith set free from fetters and in lively exercise.

In the Reformation age itself there was much of an assurance of personal salvation enjoyed by a generation of believers on which the Gospel of the free grace of God in Justification burst in all its wonder as something altogether new. In that same age, however, there were cases that should have called a halt to all extreme statement. Our Scottish Reformer, for instance, had work to do as spiritual adviser in the case of godly Mrs Bowes, whose daughter Marjory was his first wife. There was a call upon spiritual casuistry so that the presence of the true faith of the regenerate was recognised even when a certainty of one's own salvation was very much a matter of debate. And as the flood-tide of spiritual fullness and assurance ebbed the teachers of the Reformed Church were increasingly called to minister to the questionings of many of their most godly and devoted hearers who could not, they felt, honestly claim that they had the possession of a full assurance of their good estate.

The emergence of the Arminian controversy had a bearing on this subject. For such a faith as was often called for by the Reformers of the first generation on the part of their hearers was one that could find a logical grounding only in a Universal Atonement which brought in its train a salvation equally universal. If saving faith was to be held to be a persuasion that Christ is mine and life and salvation through Him, the question arose as to who is warranted to cherish this persuasion—every hearer of the Gospel or those only who receive the Christ that the Gospel sets forth and commends. The more crude definitions of Saving Faith had to be revised and adjusted to the facts. One can find interesting side-lights on the problem as it had to be tackled among the Puritans of Essex and East Anglia in connection with the ministry of men like John Rogers of Dedham in Giles Firmin's *The Real Christian*, 1670. The glimpses that this writer gives are of the state of things that he saw in his youth fifty years earlier than his book saw the light, when the teaching of the Cambridge Divinity School was telling on that of the younger Puritan preachers. It was recognised that rightly enough the Reformers insisted on an assurance as to the facts of the Gospel which is essential to the faith that receives the good of it. But it came to be clearly seen that though the believer is assured as to the truth of Law and Gospel, his assurance of his personal interest in the provision of the Gospel could not be stronger than his certainty that he for himself received that provision, accepted the Lord and Saviour as his own, and took upon him His yoke as his own Redeeming Lord, or closed with the offer of Him as held out in the Gospel to be Prophet, Priest and Prince. It was felt rightly enough that no chain can be stronger than its weakest link, and so unless there was a clear witness of personal consciousness to the fact that the hearer of the Gospel on his own side was willing to have Christ as Saviour and Lord he could not have the persuasion that Christ was his and salvation in Him. It was one thing to be sure that He is a Saviour and is offered to me as such; it was another to be certain that I take Him as my own. It was recognised freely that the discovery of Who and what the Saviour is may be so clear and full and compelling as that the believer cannot but be satisfied that he has taken Him, and does take Him, as his own Redeemer and Lord. It was seen that in faith's closing with Christ there is truth and reality, and attending upon it the germ at least of the conviction that I indeed believe. It was felt, however, that in the life of godliness there may be times and cases where the pulse beats strong, and others where it indeed beats, but the beat is weak.

And with a sense of this spiritual phenomenon the question emerges as to the reality of faith when its heart beat is not strong. With the appreciation of the implications of this question it came to be plainly seen that there may be a real reception of the grace of the Gospel which is not to be rejected or set aside when men believe the truths of Law and Gospel and yet have to mourn over how little sense they have of a cordial, wholehearted acceptance of Christ as their own, and of the dedication of themselves to Him such as leads them to rejoice in Him as their own, and in the hope of everlasting life as their destiny. When these things were taken into account it was held that the assurance of personal salvation may accompany the faith that welcomes the Gospel, yet that it is not so knit to its conscious exercise as that there may not be much inward conflict experienced before the true believer who is indeed willing to be his Lord's disciple can reach a satisfying assurance that he for himself has believed or has passed from death to life. This view of the matter did not call in question the good assurance of those who so clearly closed in with Christ as their own as to be sure that they took Him as their Saviour and gave themselves to Him as their Lord. No more did this view call in question the reality of the faith of the godly man who feels the strong opposition of unbelief or who mourns over the palsied weakness with which he responds to the grace of the Gospel.

The danger was when our Reformed teachers came to acknowledge the reality of a faith that is weak and hard beset with opposition and difficulties that the pendulum should swing to the other extreme, and such an assurance as attends a tried faith and is arrived at only after a longer or shorter experience of conflict with besetting difficulties should come to be looked upon as the norm of attainment in the life of the Church. Step by step a type of teaching came to be common which laid out its strength in the discussion of the question : What are the marks of a regenerate state by the recognised possession of which one may warrantably conclude that he has passed from death to life? When this came to be in the ascendant and to give tone to the life and teaching of the Church there was a shifting of the centre of gravity from the place that assurance of salvation held in the early days of the Protestant movement, though such an assurance continued to be highly valued. In those early days the question that pressed with a primary urgency was one that dealt with the relative grace of the Gospel. Its imperious demand was : How shall a man be just with God? It found its answer in the provision of the Gospel which tells of the Lord our Righteousness. The primacy now lay with the question : How shall I be satisfied that I have indeed passed from death to life? This belongs to the region and category of real as distinct from relative grace. It has its place in the realm of that grace which rescues from spiritual death and enables the twice-born in newness of life to show that they are new creatures by the fruits of regeneracy that they bring forth in life and conduct. At both these stages it is clear that a high value is put upon a believer's assurance of his salvation. It is looked upon as a blessing that may be enjoyed and that is to be much desired. The outcome of the discussions that took place on the topic of Assurance we have in carefully guarded form in the chapter of the Westminster Confession that deals with it.

3. THE DOCTRINE OF THE CHURCH

There is scarcely any segment of the circle of Christian truth that has had more abundant heed paid to it in the Theology of Scotland than that which takes to do with the Church of God. In common with the prevalent strain of teaching on the subject among the Reformed the Scots Confession laid great stress upon the reality of the entity of the Church of God as it is in truth. Its treatment of the subject is such as to make clear that the Church as men see it, or the Visible Church, is not a body other than the Church as known to God. The Church of God is one, but God sees it as it is indeed, man sees it only according to the measure of his knowledge. As it is known to Him Whose it is, it consists of the whole Election of Grace. Thus it is made up of all who from the dawn of eternity have been given in the

counsel of peace by the Father to the Son to be His body
and His bride.   This countless company, looked at from the
viewpoint of the love of the Son and His undertaking on
their behalf, are, as the chosen of the Father, accepted by
His Son to be His clients for whom He came, whose burden
He took upon Himself, and for whom He won the life everlasting which is the reward of His service of love.   When
He came for them He was the true Israel Whose calling was
to be the Servant of the Lord and Who in pursuance of the
ends of that calling came under His Father's yoke to do
His will.   This same company when they reap the good of
the Saviour's work of love are made partakers of the fruit
of His mediation in their call by grace.   When they are thus
called they become members in truth of the Church of God.
Their effectual calling issues in the faith that unites them to
their Bridegroom and Head.   The Spirit Who in the Lord's
title works on them to bring them into oneness with Him
works in them once they have passed from death to life to keep
and perfect them unto the end.   The magnificent unity which
gives effect to God's thoughts of love as in His power He
carries out His purpose of grace is the Church in its essential
being or is the Church as it is known to God.   It is made up
historically of all that by God's call have been brought alive
from the dead, so many of whom have entered within the
veil and belong to the Church triumphant, while there is still
on earth a remnant who have experienced the power of the
same call and, as the Church militant, are wrestling on toward
heaven.

The Church of God, however, has not only a past and a
present which embrace all that God has called to the fellowship
of His Son.   It has a future; and that future embraces
all such as shall yet hear God's call and shall come in the
obedience of faith to His footstool.   They, too, are needed
to make up the fullness of the body of Christ so that the
Church in its ideal completeness shall not stand out as a
perfect unit until God makes up the number of His elect.
To this Church the promise of life everlasting is given and

made good. The Church thus looked at is the Bride, the Lamb's wife.

If we speak of the Church under another figure we may call it the Body whose Head our Lord is. He is the Head as the source of blessing and the seat of authority. As the source of blessing, having won life for His own whose place in Law He took, our Lord lives to bestow upon them what He died to win for them. So it belongs to Him to put forth His might to give effect to His right. And as the seat of authority, it is for Him to say what His ransomed ones ought to be and ought to do. Having all authority in heaven and in earth He can put it in exercise over all natural forces and they obey Him. They know the voice of their Lord. He has also all rational beings alike as units and as organised bodies under His sway. In His power over them He can bend their wayward will so that His purpose is carried out. They may as rebels refuse to bow to His Kingly Will as made known. So doing they set His rightful authority at defiance. Yet such is His sovereign control over all being that whether men will hear or will forbear He brings His counsel to pass and makes even His foes subservient to His will. Such, in brief, is the Scottish doctrine of the Church Invisible and of Jesus Christ its Head.

The Scottish doctrine of the Church Visible is in no salient feature different from the common faith of Reformed Christendom. And yet in Scotland it came to hold such a place of control as that it is largely in connection with the application and working out of this doctrine that the most remarkable struggles and discussions of national Church life have taken place. It regards the Church in its visible form as a Kingdom with a King of its own. The King is not a mere absentee monarch nor is He only a figurehead. He is looked upon as the Head of the Church as it is His acknowledged realm. The avowal on the part of His confessing subjects of His Headship, and so of their subjection to His authority, is of such a kind as to leave the Church in its corporate form as a recognised society under the obligation to accept His Word as the regulative authority that calls for its obedience. Thus His revealed will is its ultimate seat of authority on earth, and the true freedom of the Church is attained and enjoyed when it is subject to no sovereign will but His and finds delight in compliance with His behests. His Word it takes to be His, and in it is found the exhibition of His will and so the provision He has made for the guidance, instruction and obedience of His subjects. This it is for them alike in the duties of their private station and in those of their public relations. On this provision for making known the will of their Lord our Scottish fathers—Puritan as we have seen that they were—looked as one so ample and so generous that they held it to be an adequate guide to the Church in all departments of its activity. In Doctrine, in Worship, in Discipline and in Government it was regarded as so regulative as that, apart from "circumstances," to quote again from our Confession, which sets forth the Puritan principle on this matter, "common to human actions and societies" for which no specific guidance needed to be given, everything in the life of the Church is to be conformed to the pattern that is afforded by Apostolic precept or example, or that might be learned from the teaching of Holy Writ. This was but the leading principle of Puritanism, and Knox, as one of the Puritan leaders, was one of the most powerful exponents of this ideal. It gave tone and colour to Scottish Church life to a greater degree and on a wider scale than it told on any other section of British Christianity. It made for plainness and simplicity in worship. It made for fullness and care in doctrinal statement. It made for the conservation and defence of the rights of the individual. It made for a high standard of attainment in the purity of the Church's life. It has been spoken of as bigoted and narrow; and its fruits have been criticised as though its type of worship were bald and meagre, its doctrine needlessly detailed and minute, its government unduly rigid and, as over against civil government, too self-assertive, while its Discipline was found fault with as one that laid uncalled-for restraints upon the joy of living. But we need not go over again the counts of the oft-repeated indictment. There are many to speak against it.

for they feel that it is against them. It had, however, in hand the making of a nation; and it had in the end of the day something to show for its work. It believed thoroughly in the sufficiency of its rule of faith and its pattern of practice, and its works went to justify its faith.

In regard to the Reformed Church of Scotland, there is no doubt about the sympathy with which it looked upon the more thorough Reformers in England apart from the radical Independents. In the later sixteenth century it held in highest honour the leaders of English Puritanism. It looked upon them as leading the right wing of the Protestants in the Church of England in what was the real conflict of the age— the war with Rome. Thomas Cartwright was invited to a Scottish Chair. John Udal was welcomed as a visitor, and when he met his untimely end even King James, though himself no Puritan, either in speech or in policy, could say: " By my sal, the greatest scholar in Europe is dead." It has been left in these last times for the representatives of the Anglicising school in the Scottish Presbyterian Church to resuscitate the term Puritan as a name of reproach and to confound those to whom of right the name belonged with the radical Separatists or the Brownists. They have adopted this way of speaking from the vocabulary of the conforming sycophantic school of Sharp and Spottiswoode and the militant Jacobite Non-jurors of the disestablished Episcopal hierarchy. It was the spirit of the subservient underling that was at work in the Erastianism which was content to transfer the usurped headship of the Papacy to a new usurper. What Henry VIII. of England succeeded in doing when he carried out his theory of Caesaro-Papalism was a model embodiment of the claim to ecclesiastical supremacy put forward by the civil power not only in the sphere of the Lutheran Reformation, but to a large extent also in that of the Calvinistic movement. That movement, however, in its doctrine of the Visible Church and its Headship had at work in it a principle that was creative of the ordered civil liberty of more modern times. This wrought powerfully in Scotland and produced a conscience of duty on the part of the rank and file toward the

Church's one Head that made them jealous of any invasion
of His crown-rights. The Reformed doctrine of the Headship
of the Visible Church told mightily as a formative force in
the civil history of Britain and the States deriving from it.
Both sides of the Atlantic have felt it.

It was one of the artifices of the Erastian polemics to
make a free admission of the truth that our Lord is the
Head of the Church as His mystical Body while they refused
to own Him as Head and King of the Church Visible. The
Headship or supreme government of this in its corporate
capacity as a body ecclesiastic in the midst of the body politic
of the State they assigned to the Christian Magistrate in
Christianised lands. To recognise the organised Church as
a free corporate unit in the realm while it was not in its
special functioning subject to the king they held to be the
recognition of an *imperium in império*. And with the old
jealousy of societies or clubs or organisations which exercised
an intrinsic self-government, a jealousy that came down from
the tradition of Roman imperial policy, they gave a supremacy
to the civil authority which subordinated the administration
of the affairs of the Church to the Magistrate and thus
virtually set aside the ordinance of Church Government which
was instituted by the Head of the Church Himself. It was
not to be wondered at that the Erastians were in a very marked
way the latitudinarian wing of the Church. They found it
easy to conform to the pattern of things that was favoured
by the Court. The legal mind, too, gravitated towards
the acknowledgment of a civil supremacy over the Church,
especially in regard to its Discipline, and this was the rock
on which the Parliamentary Puritan Revolution in England
made shipwreck. The Long Parliament was decidedly of an
Erastian complexion. Indeed, England as a whole, though
it had a strong Puritan party in its Church, was not ripe
for a Puritan Reformation.

The stand made in Scotland against the encroachments
of the Crown and on behalf of the exclusive kingly rights
of its Head and Lord to appoint the conduct of the government of the Visible Church as His professed kingdom on

earth is what more than anything else accounted for the
stormy conflict which lasted so long and was so often renewed
in the Church history of the country. With the setting aside
of the sole Headship of Christ and the obligation to recognise
its range of claim and submit to it there went a laxity as
to what was lawful for the Church to do in the whole realm
and region of its organised activities.

The refusal of our Reformed Church to allow the intrusion
of a mundane authority within the sphere of the holy things
of the house of God was held to be perfectly consistent with
the recognition of an obligation lying upon kings and rulers
to yield homage to the King of kings and Lord of lords and,
as they did so, to further by all means competent to them
the security and welfare of the Church. The Church is His
special realm, and the civil power, when it professes submission
to His sceptre, is called upon to honour His revealed will in
regard to the administration of what is His Kingdom on earth.
The duty that it thus held to lie upon the supreme civil
ruler to do what is in his power to further the cause of
the Kingdom of God was not held to invest him with the
keys of that Kingdom. Thus, in his independent sphere, the
Magistrate for his guidance in respect to his duty to the
Church and truth of God was fully entitled to exercise his
own judgment as to what he ought to do. At the same time
he was bound to have regard to the intrinsic authority that
inheres in the institute of government which the Head of
the Church has appointed and ordained in His visible kingdom.
It is easy to see how a despotic tendency at work in the
State could abuse its function and encroach on and tyrannise
over the Visible Church. At the same time it is equally
easy to see how an ambitious Church policy could refuse to
give due respect to the judgment of its co-ordinate authority.
Two ordinances, both of them of Divine origin, ought to live
in harmony and each of them ought to hold itself within the
bounds of its own special province. Unhappily, however,
this was not always done.

The claim put forward by the Church to have the
exclusive Headship of its Lord honoured and kept inviolate

was not to be confused with an aggressive self-assertion that has only too often been found in the policy of its rulers in the seat of authority who failed rightly to distinguish between self-will and loyal homage to Him Whom they claimed to represent and to serve. History has many a concrete example to show how fond the churchman is of power. There was, however, a deep conviction that animated the Reforming school in the Scottish Church in regard to the Lordship of Christ and the regulative authority that resides in His Word as the Statute Book of His Kingdom. And it is only when the Word is faithfully honoured as the revealed will of the Lord that the self-government of the Church succeeds in holding fast the lawful freedom that belongs to it as the Kingdom of God. When men leave this authority out of view and go as they please there may be a very riot of self-will, and that is the freedom of the rebel who takes the throne as his own and leaves the King out of his reckoning. When, however, the Church and its rulers are faithful to their profession and to their trust the Word is honoured, and so the will of the King is done, as it is made known. The achievement of this, however, is, of course, a thing of degrees. But when a righteous relation holds between the Church and the Word with which it is put in trust, there is an honest and serious effort made to do the will of the Lord and to show in doing so that His subjects are obedient children. And as such obedience prevails in the personal life of the people it will be their endeavour to do justice to the corporate responsibility that lies on the Church as a whole. The endeavour of the healthy Christian and of the healthy Church will ever be to do the will of the Lord on earth as it is done in heaven. Love to Him and loyalty to His will tell with effect on the life of the general and wider communal environment in the bosom of which the Church has her lot cast.

The conflict between the Church and the civil power began almost as soon as the Reformation took place. The type of statesmen that found treasure trove in old Church lands and tithes and titles and rights, and that sought to make

the Church a convenience for their own ends, tried their best
by means of nominal bishops and titular abbots to hold for
themselves and their friends a substantial share of the old
ecclesiastical wealth. The record of the self-seeking Scottish
great families is not a clean one. And when James VI. began
to reign on his own account he made the most of the loot
that was still at his disposal. He aimed at autocracy, but
he found that there stood in his way a barrier in the public
sentiment and conviction generated by the spiritual freedom
of the Reformed Church. What to him was a free monarchy
was for the Kingdom freedom to do what pleased him as
king. He was booted and spurred and ready to ride in the
saddle as an autocrat. The tyrannical policy followed by
his son and his grandsons was but a heritage that he left
them. They were only pursuing the despotic ideal that he
set before them. It was part of the family tradition.

With the breakdown of the Mediaeval order there had
been a steady growth of royal claims. This was not peculiar
to Scotland. The Stuart monarchs shared in it with the
Tudors and others. And James VI. had his heart set on the
aggrandising of the monarchy. In his attempts to bring about
this end, as he found that the Presbytery which prevailed
in Scotland was in the way of his ambitions, he put his
judgment of the case in the words that Presbytery and
monarchy agreed as well as God and the devil. His experience
in Scotland was crystallised in the saying, " No Bishop, no
King." With his determination to strengthen the crown he
aimed at having a restored hierarchy that would be submissive
as the creatures of the Court and obsequious to the royal
will. Such exalted functionaries would put no obstacle in
the way of the tortuous policy which he pursued in national
and international affairs, and at the same time would serve
as a gag for an outspoken Church. He found that the wide-
awake guardians of the Reformed Faith and Polity would
not be his tools in furthering his secular aims. They did not
have their price, for they were not for sale, or he would
have bought them. Those men were more than the guardians
of the Church; they were the tribunes of the people and

the champions of civil freedom. It was in defence of the rights of the Church's Head that they fought their stern and long-drawn-out fight. In the course of this struggle they enlisted on their side, what their teaching and witness may be said to have brought into being, the loyal and enlightened support of the common folk who are the ultimate constituents of both Church and State. A people instructed, interested, and evangelised proved the anvil on which the hammers of royal absolutism and oppression rained their blows in vain.

II.

THE SUCCESSORS OF KNOX

I.

THE MEN OF THE REFORMATION CENTURY

1. ANDREW MELVILLE

KNOX was honoured to be the leading man among the instruments who achieved the Scottish Reformation. If his words took concrete form in things, he left to his successors an accomplished fact. And yet there was much to be done before the Reformation could be said to be at all complete. The foundations, however, were laid. The Confession of the Reformed Church was published to the world. The lines along which the movement was to go were marked out. There was a programme sketched, the carrying out of which was the task of those who had something to build upon and were not called to start from the very beginning. The Reformed Church, though still in its infancy, let the world know what it held, what it stood for and what it aimed at. Yet when the Reformer laid down his armour in 1572 he left behind him in the Scottish ministry no outstanding man to carry on his work. The work, however, was not of man and it was to be carried on, and if a man was needed to champion the good cause the Scottish Church had not long to wait for him. The times called for a man of grit, and a man of grit came forward. This was Andrew Melville.

With George Buchanan, Melville stood in the front rank of Scottish humanists. The two, however, were more than scholars of the humanistic Renaissance. They were Reformers; and they led the Reforming movement along the lines that in after years were to be characteristic of the stand made by the Reformed Church in defence of its Faith and freedom against the encroachments of royal supremacy.

41

Buchanan's *De jure regni apud Scotos* was the forerunner of the *Lex Rex* of Samuel Rutherford, and *A Hind Let Loose* of Alexander Shields. The principles that were in those works set forth and expounded and defended set limits before the authority of the Crown that were not at all to the liking of the Court and its partisans. But in the end of the Constitutional struggle these principles were vindicated, and in spite of men in high places and their obsequious tools, they were accepted by the nation. They set forth the essential system of Constitutional liberty.

Melville, who was Buchanan's younger contemporary, after a sojourn of about ten years overseas, came back to his native land two years or so after the death of Knox. He had studied in France. He had taught in the Academy of Geneva. He was the friend of Beza on whom rested the mantle of John Calvin. And when he came back to Scotland, still a young man not yet thirty years old, he brought with him a reputation for learning that won for him the academic posts at Glasgow and St Andrews Universities that he was fitted to adorn. The Jesuit reaction to the Reformation was in full flood, and as the strength of the early Reforming movement was to be found largely in the ranks of those who were conversant with the Greek culture of the Revival of Learning, the Jesuit leaders laid themselves out to capture the blue riband of scholarship that the Church might have at its call men who would outshine the scholars who had wrought such havoc on the Mediaeval system. This policy of theirs called for every effort on the part of the Reformers to maintain their ground and to train a generation of educated men who could speak to the enemy in the gate. It was in this field of polemic activity that Andrew Melville found his first and fundamental task when in the two oldest of his country's Universities he was entrusted with the work of adjusting the curriculum to current needs, levelling up the standards of learning, and bringing the Colleges of Glasgow and St Andrews abreast of the scholarship of the Continental schools. He met with conspicuous success in this academic work, so that students from the lands overseas to which his countrymen had been wont to resort began to frequent the Scottish seats of learning.

The impetus that Melville gave to sound scholarship was felt not only in the ministry of the Home Church, but in the standing that Scots came to enjoy in the Colleges of Huguenot France which then were second to none in the Reformed world. Besides, his work told on a line of his pupils who, while they responded to the stimulus of his learning and example, were not prepared to stand at his side or take up his place in the defence of the spiritual freedom of the Church against the policy of King James. Thus, though Patrick Forbes of Corse became a Conformist and died Bishop of Aberdeen, he owed his scholarship to the teaching and influence of Melville. As Bishop, Forbes was instrumental in founding the Aberdeen school of Theological Scholarship of which his eminent son John was the most distinguished ornament. Indeed, in the field of Patristics and Church History John Forbes was the finest scholar that Scotland has yet produced. His great, but unfinished work, *Instructiones Historico-Theologicae* was still referred to in the Theological schools of Europe a century and a half after his death. The Aberdeen doctors, though they were so thorough in their Erastian Conformity to Court measures, were thus in their learning the product at the second remove of the work done in his St Andrews days by Melville.

Mighty, however, and beneficent as the influence was that he wielded in College and Educational life, the great work done by Andrew Melville was his masterly guidance of the Church in her contendings with secular aggression. He led in the fight for the maintenance of Presbyterianism as the government of the Reformed Church. He was at the head of his fellows as they stood for the intrinsic freedom· that resides in the Church of God to do the will of her Head as He has made it known in His Word. It was in the *Second Book of Discipline* that the banner of the freedom of the Church was definitely unfurled. This historic work was produced in the early years of Melville's effective leadership in the Courts of the Church. To say that he and not Knox was the father of the Puritan and Presbyterian tradition in the Church of Scotland would be to speak very wide of the mark. Knox was as surely both a Presbyterian and a Puritan as Melville was. For any temporary departures from the practice of pure Presbytery for which his example is pleaded, such as the place given to Superintendents and the modified acknowledgment of an Episcopacy in the Leith agreement which was reached shortly before his death, were but concessions to the dire need of the times. It was no honorific sinecure to be a Superintendent in Knox's days. It meant a real increase of work and responsibility and when it was all done the Superintendent was subject to the oversight, the authority and the censure of the ministry and the eldership met in their General Assembly. With parishes not half staffed, and when staffed provided often only with lay readers, there was room for special measures by way of itinerant preaching and visitation on the part of the Superintendents. Again, the type of Bishop to be recognised after the Leith Convention was more or less of a legal figment whose name as a Church official was needed for the legal tenure of the lands which had belonged to the Mediaeval Bishoprics and were not yet alienated by royal grants to secular holders. His office was more or less of a sinecure. He was a convenient liaison officer to pass on to laymen the fruits of ecclesiastical endowments, but it could hardly be said that the sinecure of a Tulchan Bishop was honorific. Presbytery was the undoubted government of the Reformed Church.

The practical difficulties that confronted the leaders of the Reformation would account for their resort to the device of having Superintendents. And when the proposals of the Convention of Leith were discussed on the floor of the General Assembly, Knox made quite clear his opposition to the introduction of even a titular episcopate whose powers were as limited as those of the Superintendents. He saw what the possible developments were that might be looked for from such an interim restoration of the old hierarchy in name.

In spite of all that he did, the fact remains that what the wily Lethington spoke of as a devout imagination did not mature in Knox's life, and his *First Book of Discipline* for which he has been so often praised, and rightly so, as a Christian statesman was more an ideal than an achievement as far as the successful carrying out of his programme was concerned. He had to deal with a greedy set who saw to it that of the patrimony of the Church the third part should be divided between the Court and the Reformed ministry. Two-thirds were to go to the "outed" priests. It was of this arrangement that the Reformer said: "Two parts were given freely to the devil, and the third part was to be divided between God and the devil." Those in power saw to it that as far as they could bring it about they would keep the Reformed ministers poor. The battle, however, that Knox fought did not end with his death, and when Melville's time came, he led the fight that issued in the definite establishment of the Reformed Faith and Church in Scotland. The issue of this conflict told on the whole future record of the country. In particular, it secured that a doctrine of Church and State came to be recognised as what might be called the distinctively Scottish doctrine on the subject.

The Scottish doctrine of Church and State is one that sets itself over against, on the one hand, that Erastian system which would make the government of the Church but a department of civil management, and, on the other, the scheme of Indifferentism that aims at putting no difference by the nation as such between one form of religious profession and another. In regard to the former of these contrasts, the Scottish Church had its long warfare to wage with the Court party and the feudal ideas that were entrenched in the privileges of the landed aristocracy. In regard to the latter, the opposition of the Indifferentism of the voluntary system came to be active as it wrought for the subversion of the alliance that the Reformers aimed at between the Divine ordinances of Civil Magistracy and Church Government. This opposition, however, did not need to be taken into account until the eighteenth century had accustomed men to look upon the Visible Church as no longer an unbroken unit.

Dissent and Separation and Secession had, by that time, changed the earlier face of National Church unity.

The ideal of the Reformation and Puritan ages was that there should be one " Face of Kirk " in the nation. With such an ecclesiastical unit confronting the civil unit, it was easier then than it is now to see how there might and should be a friendly alliance between Church and State, an alliance in which each of the contracting units recognised its own duty and that of the other, its own bounds and those of the other. With one Church over against one Kingly throne, Melville, in resisting the invasion of the province of the Church by the aggressive policy of the King, could use his oft-quoted words as he dealt with the aggressor. It was a private interview. Calling the King " God's silly vassal " and taking him by the sleeve, he spoke the words that lose nothing by being quoted again : " Sir, we will always humbly reverence your Majesty in public; but since we have this occasion to be with your Majesty in private, and since you are brought into extreme danger both of your life and crown, and along with you the country and the Church of God are like to go to wreck, for not telling you the truth and giving you faithful counsel, we must discharge our duty or else be traitors both to Christ and you. Therefore, Sir, as divers times before I have told you, so now again I must tell you, there are two kings and two kingdoms in Scotland : there is King James, the lord of this commonwealth, and there is Christ Jesus, the King of the Church, whose subject James the Sixth is, and of whose Kingdom he is not a King, nor a lord, nor a head, but a member. We will yield to you your place, and give you all due obedience, but again I say, you are not the Head of the Church; you cannot give us that eternal life which we seek for even in this world, and you cannot deprive us of it. Permit us, then, freely to meet in the name of Christ, and to attend to the interests of that Church of which you are a chief member. Sir, when you were in your swaddling clothes Christ Jesus reigned freely in this land, in spite of all His enemies; His officers and ministers convened for the ruling and welfare of His Church, which was ever for your welfare, when these same enemies were for your destruction. And now when there is more than extreme necessity for the continuance of that duty, will you hinder and dishearten Christ's servants and your most faithful subjects, quarrelling with them for their convening, when you should rather commend and countenance them as the godly kings and emperors did?" It took grit to beard kings who aspired to be tyrants. But whatever was not to be found in the manful and heroic figures of our Scots Worthies, this grit was not wanting. They would without fear and without favour speak to kings the Word of God.

Melville has met with much unfriendly criticism for the freedom that he took with his sovereign. But it is only to the soul of the flunkey that such outspoken manliness is repulsive. The encroachments of the monarchy invited such candid speech on the part of the defenders of the freedom of the Church of God. And we find the roots of the free constitutions of our day in the spirit that could deal thus faithfully with the highest in the land. What had in it the potency of such free and frank speech to kings served to make the holders of feudal superiorities make common cause with the Crown in the endeavour to keep down the spirit of freedom. This will help to make clear what was so often and so long the attitude of the nobility and the landed classes toward the spiritual independence of the Kingdom of God in their midst.

The doctrine in regard to the Church of God for which Melville and his followers were honoured to make a stand, became in later days the word of their Lord's patience for witnesses in all ranks of society who loved not their lives to the death. They believed it to be the truth of God that their Lord is the Head of His own Church, and to preserve this truth and pass it down to later ages intact they were willing to lay down their lives for it. And such is the revenge that the whirligig of time brings with it that the Scottish Episcopacy, which in its days as the State Church could not be too obsequious or courtly in bowing to the royal prerogative, has swung round from its old Erastianism and may be heard putting in the claim that the intrinsic rights of the Church should be conserved from the unholy hands of secular domination. The burden and heat of the day, however, in making a stand for these rights was borne by the men of the Knox and Melville tradition; and the ages are the heirs of the liberties for which they fought so strenuously and, in the end of the day, with such success. It was a long-drawn-out battle before it came to a definite issue, and, ere it ended, Scotland became a land not only of Covenanters but of Confessors and Martyrs.

We owe it to the vivid, naïve and picturesque diary of James Melville that we have such a clear and consecutive account of the long fight in which his uncle Andrew was the leader. Uncle and nephew were in affection and years like a pair of brothers, and a champion such as Andrew Melville was has seldom had such a trusty henchman as his brother's son proved to be. In his quiet, resolute way, the younger Melville was no unworthy second to his uncle. To be a leader a man needed to have a following, and there were in that generation faithful ministers who stood side by side with Melville. Among these were a few good Theologians who carried on the best traditions of the Reformed Theology. In this group were such men as John Welsh of Ayr, John Craig, Robert Bruce of Edinburgh, Robert Rollock and John Davidson. As the almost Apostolic ministry of Bruce lasted with interruptions until the fourth decade of the next century, he may be left to find his special place as a link with the men of the following generation. Welsh of Ayr, to whose work we shall now look, also lived until the third decade of the seventeenth century, but the last fifteen years of his life he had to spend in exile, so that his work in Scotland belongs to the generation of Knox's successors.

2. JOHN WELSH

John Welsh was the son-in-law of John Knox; and his wife was the worthy daughter of such a father and the worthy wife of such a husband. Among the scholarly saints of the Kirk, none held a higher place in the esteem of the godly than did Welsh. There is a biography that does justice to his work and memory from the pen of James Young who in his literary and historical work wrought in the vein of the McCrie tradition. But when we look for early traditional information about this worthy minister, we should seek it in quarters like John Livingstone's Characteristics where we find authentic traces of the glory and the afterglow of the great days of the Gospel that marked his brief but prayerful and powerful ministry in Ayr. His work there was done in the compass of three years. Yet the memory of it has persisted as one of the brightest times of spiritual enlargement that the Church of his land ever enjoyed. The monuments that survive of that ministry are about forty or fifty sermons which used to be in great demand in the reading of the peasant patriarchs of rural Scotland.

Welsh was well versed in the early Protestant theology, both practical and polemical. Of the latter kind there exists to show his quality his volume of controversy with Gilbert Brown, a Romanist polemic. This was published at the beginning of his ministry in Ayr in 1602, reissued as edited by Matthew Crawford in 1672, and reissued yet again as recently as 1878 under the oversight of Dr Moir Porteous, who gave it the title of *The Morning Star*. Its title, or at least the first words in Matthew Crawford's title, are " Popery Anatomised." The title-page to the first edition styles it, " A Reply against Mr. Gilbert Brown, Priest." This work lets one see that our early Scottish preachers were not at a loss when they were challenged to stand up for the faith that was in them. It is one of the first fruits of the teaching of Rollock in the University of Edinburgh, for the writer was one of the very earliest students that took their academic course at the new seat of learning in the capital city.

Welsh, for the part that he took in the Aberdeen Assembly, which was held in defiance of the King's embargo, was silenced, imprisoned and exiled. After years of service among the Huguenots he and his wife made their way to London to seek leave from the King for a dying man to go home to breathe his native air. Mrs Welsh presented her petition. The King asked who her father was. When he was told that

Mrs John Welsh was the daughter of John Knox, he said: "Knox and Welsh! the devil never made such a match as that." "It's right like, sir," was her reply, "for we never asked his advice." When the King enquired about her father's family and was told that there were only three daughters, James, lifting up his hands, said: "God be thanked, for if they had been three lads, I had never enjoyed my three kingdoms in peace." When the royal buffoon asked what her petition was and she told him that she sought for her dying husband leave to go home to breathe his native air, the answer she got was surly and unkingly: "Give him his native air! Give him the devil." "Give that to your hungry courtiers," was the rejoinder. Then, as if relenting, James said that if her husband would be submissive to the bishops he might go to Scotland. Lifting up her apron and holding it out to the King, she answered: "Please, your Majesty, I'd rather kep his head there."

Such is the tale of a king when face to face with the rugged and stubborn Scots who were not prepared to truckle to him when he put forth his secular claim to spiritual supremacy over the Reformed Church. The son of those devoted parents was one of the men so highly honoured in the Evangelical awakening of Northern Ireland where, as yoke-fellow of Robert Blair of Bangor and John Livingstone of Killinchy, Josias Welsh did his share at Templepatrick in founding that Presbyterian Church which more than the mother Church in Scotland helped to build up Presbyterianism of a believing, orthodox type in the States of America. His son in turn was the second John Welsh who was, at the Restoration of Charles II., driven from his charge at Irongray, and who, with his comrade in arms, John Blackader of Troqueer, was among the first of the "outed" Presbyterians to take to the fields to hold there the conventicles which did so much in the dark days of the despotism of the later Stuarts to keep alive in Scotland the witness of the Church for the Headship of her Lord. The tale of his hair-breadth escapes which brought it to pass that, uncaptured to the end, he was able to keep the blue banner of the Evangel flying on the moors of the southern

uplands of his country is one of the most picturesque stories
in the romantic history of his persecuted Church.

3. John Craig

John Craig, who once was a monk, was converted in Italy
by reading the Institutes of John Calvin. He made his way
home to Scotland and was one of the leading successors of
Knox to keep alive the Reformed witness. It fell to him to
draft the first National Covenant, or as it was called, " The
King's Confession." This document forms the first part of
the Covenant as drafted and buttressed and punctuated by
Henderson and Wariston, which rallied the nation to its
standard in 1638. What they did issued in the downfall of
Laud and the convening of the Westminster Assembly and
all that the Assembly of Divines stands for in the Reformed
Churches of Britain and America. John Craig was the author
also of a Catechism which was widely in use in the sixteenth
century and which is to be found in Dr Horatius Bonar's
Collection of Catechisms of the Scottish Reformation. This
handbook of the faith is remarkable for the clearness and
pith, the point and the brevity of its answers. Its author
had a place among the mighties who carried on the work of
Reformation.

4. Robert Rollock

Nor should we forget the place held among the successors
of the great Reformer by the first Principal of the Town's
College of Edinburgh. This was the first Protestant University
founded in Scotland. It dates from ten years after the death
of Knox. It was built in troublous times. The councillors of
the capital city did not show themselves backward, however,
in the institution of this seat of learning, and they found in
their first preceptor a competent divine who excelled in his
gift of exposition. Some of his discourses are to be found in
the two volumes of his work which the Wodrow Society issued
a century ago, where we have also translated from his Latin
original his accurate and careful treatise on Effectual Calling.
It does credit to the standard of Theological learning of the

Scotland of his day. In discussing the question as it is put in its Latin wording, " *Qui constet Scripturam esse Verbum Dei?* " he strikes no uncertain note as he asserts the self-evidencing light to be found in the Scriptures which bears witness to the divinity of their origin. This was the common teaching of the Reformed schools. They resolved the question of the divine warrant of Christian faith into the witness of the Holy Ghost in the heart of the believer bearing witness to the evidence of the sacred books themselves which contain in their body and framework the token of the fact that they have come from God's own hand as their supreme Author. Rollock is also the author of a Latin commentary on the Gospel according to John, several of Paul's Epistles and the Book of Daniel. This latter work might be thought to speak in particular of the polemical interest that our early Protestants took in hunting down the Papacy as the Antichrist. Their historical method of expounding the seventh chapter of the book of the statesman Prophet often discovered the Roman Antichrist in the Little Horn whose look was more stout than his fellows and who had a mouth that spake great things and who made war with the saints and prevailed against them. Our Reforming fathers were well assured, as Knox had been from the days of his first preaching at St Andrews and his disputation with the Romanist staff of the University, that the identity of the Man of Sin and the great Antichrist was a matter as to which there did not need to be any doubt. In his Latin commentary on the Thessalonians, the teaching of Rollock cannot be misunderstood. On this topic, as one that was part of the burning controversy of the times, he would be diligent in teaching his young men. Yet in dealing with Daniel vii., he finds in the Little Horn Antiochus Epiphanes. He was an eminently sober teacher. And one that trained such a preacher and champion as John Welsh for the work of his office could not be said to have laboured in vain. In the public conflicts of his age he took a less share than some of his fellows, but in respect of sound Theology he did his part in training a race of divines who did credit to his instruction and oversight. He was a faithful man who was able to teach others also.

5. JOHN DAVIDSON

Another of the godly succession from Knox, and by no means the least striking of the company, was John Davidson of Prestonpans. From his own time onward he always had a place in the mind of his Presbyterian countrymen as one of the noted Scots Worthies.

If it was said of James Renwick, the last of the martyrs of the Covenant, that he was of old Mr Knox's principles this might equally be said of John Davidson. There is not much by way of literary output to be ascribed to his pen. But the unflinching faithfulness of his ecclesiastical record marked him out as one worthy to be classed with the Melvilles as an unbending and unfaltering champion of the spiritual freedom of the Church. There was a scene that was long kept in memory when in 1596 he preached to the conscience of the General Assembly so that his hearers' hearts were moved as the heart of one man and the place was a veritable Bochim. One of his publications should not be overlooked. It was a Catechism which continued to be quoted for more than a century after his death as an authentic specimen of how the early Reformers set forth the doctrines of the Faith and in particular the nature of that faith which saves. Thomas Boston, for instance, in his notes on the Marrow of Modern Divinity, a reissue of which he published in 1726, quotes Davidson as an authority of weight about a dozen times altogether.

The doctrine of saving faith which laid stress as an element which enters into it of an assurance of one's own good state in Christ came into his definition of faith, though at the same time, and almost in the one breath, he speaks of it as a receiving of Christ. In his days there was the beginning of the process that issued in greater care on the part of the Protestant divines in their statement of what saving faith is. The assurance of personal salvation that was so common a feature of the inner life of the Reformers was not the universal and undisturbed attainment in experience of many of the best of their disciples and successors, so that in dealing with the trials that Christians met with on the ground of their want of the assurance of conscious salvation they had to learn to use greater care in the way in which they expressed themselves. They needed to be more guarded in their definitions that they might shun casuistical difficulties which they met with in the course of their pastoral work, difficulties that arose from the high place that they assigned to the assurance of personal salvation as necessary to the working of saving faith. They were not called upon to lower their doctrine of assurance so as not to find a place for it at least in a germinal form, wherever faith is present and at work. They did not need to deny that the beginning of a true assurance is found in all true faith of the Gospel. But they felt that they were shut in to look upon it as only rudimentary or seminal in the earlier and weaker exercises of saving faith in the case of many whom they could not refuse to look upon as true believers. It is of interest to observe how Davidson, 1549-1604, and his strict contemporary, William Perkins of Cambridge, 1558-1602, gave the alternative definitions of faith which without being identical were equivalent.

The selfish and greedy nobility of Scotland and its mean and grasping Court would have turned the Reformed Church of their country into a convenience, a mere engine of state-craft and mercenary exploitation. They would have made it only a feeble copy of the Erastianised Establishment of the Anglican Church as Reformed. It would have been at the mercy of secular schemers. And in the course of their many intrigues they might easily have driven things to such a pass as that the power of Rome would have been restored and so the work of the Reformation would be undone. Were it not for the open-eyed watchfulness of the Reforming leaders of the Church and the stand that was taken by them, the work of the Counter-Reformation might have met with success, and Scotland, as the catspaw of the Papacy and the French and Spanish Courts, would have been used as an instrument to overthrow the Reformation in England and elsewhere. The work of Davidson and his compeers was thus of first-rate, even of cardinal, importance in securing the maintenance of our Reformation and in laying the foundation on which the ordered civil liberties are built, that have been since the Reforming and Covenanting struggles the inheritance of the free peoples of the British race. Indeed the whole course of world history since the sixteenth century has been, as we may venture to say, determined by the results of their faithful witness. And it is but right that those who enjoy such a goodly heritage as constitutional freedom should not forget the men of heroic soul and temper to whose vigilance and faithfulness it is under God's hand due that the plots and schemes and intrigues of Popes and potentates, kings, princes and nobles were successfully met.

II.

THE MEN OF THE SUB-REFORMATION AGE

1. ROBERT BRUCE OF KINNAIRD

Those who may be called the men of the sub-Reformation age link the successors of Knox with the men of the Second Reformation. Robert Bruce we have reserved for this category though he was the age-fellow of John Welsh and much of his life's work was done before the end of the sixteenth century. He was, however, the most outstanding of the preachers and witnesses of the first third of the seventeenth century. He owed his position of pre-eminence alike to his personal qualities and to the great work that he had done in the course of his ministry in Edinburgh. From his post in the capital he was driven by the mean and malicious tyranny of the petty despot who held the throne. The King did his worst to put out of action as a minister the man who had shown himself to be his own best friend and the best friend of his country as he held the reins of power in the King's own absence. He was, however, a man who would not bow to the caprice of the royal will. And as he would not bend, he must be broken. So his ministry in Edinburgh came to an abrupt end. Yet in his exile at Inverness—it was exile in those days to be sent from the south to the north—his mouth was opened and he did a work, the remote fruits of which may be traced after the lapse of three hundred years. When he was allowed to go to his own house of Kinnaird near Stirling, he found an outlet for his calling as a brother helping his brethren at their Communion services. When it was known that Bruce was to preach, the people of the country around would flock together to hear him. So his ministry came to be very fruitful in various parts of Scotland that most likely would not have heard his message were it not that in his own charge his voice was silenced. The popularity of such preaching as his was one thing that helped to originate the great Communion gatherings that came to be such a marked feature of later Scottish religious life. It was on the occasion of one of these casual opportunities that he had of preaching that his word was blessed to the conversion of Alexander Henderson who was destined to be the leader of Scotland when a long-suffering people were at last goaded to defy the tyranny of the mitre and the crown. Bruce is said to have been the means of converting several thousands of souls. His influence was that of the holy life and of the spoken word clothed with power. There is a volume of his pulpit work in print. It belongs to his early ministry and gives seventeen of his discourses. These let us have an idea of what and how he preached. They were written in standard Scots. The sermons, however, that deal with the Sacraments were issued by Dr Laidlaw in the past generation in an English dress and so are accessible to the English reader. There had been a previous reissue of the seventeen Sermons in Scots in the volume of the Wodrow Society devoted to Bruce. This was edited by Dr William Cunningham. The Sermons on the Sacraments have been looked upon as being as accurate and clear an exhibition of the Reformed teaching in regard to the Sacraments as any of the Reformed Theologians of Scotland ever produced. The life of the author in Cunningham's edition is from the pen of the indefatigable Wodrow. There appeared also about thirty years ago a life of Bruce by D. C. MacNicol who was the son of a worthy Free Church minister and the son-in-law of Dr Horatius Bonar. It is quite a careful and sympathetic account of the life and work of one of Scotland's truly great men.

Among the contemporaries of Bruce there were some Conformists whose works come within the ken of the curious, such as Patrick Forbes of whom we have already spoken, and William Cowper, Bishop of Galloway, and Dr John Weemse of Lathocker, and William Nairne and David Lindsay. Another of the Conformists of his day was Walter Balcanquhal who attended the Synod of Dort. He was Dean of the Diocese of Ross and he held the Evangelical orthodoxy of the National Church of his day. As yet the Arminian influence of Laud had not begun to tell on the Scottish Conformists. Indeed, the Confession of Faith that was drawn up by the Assembly of Aberdeen in 1616—said to have been the work of Principal Howie of St Andrews who had been one of the wandering Scots that had studied in the Rhineland—is definitely Augustinian in its doctrine of grace. It was a document, however, that could hardly be spoken of as one of great authority, for the Aberdeen Assembly which adopted it was one of those that were set aside in 1638, and the successors to those who at that time were the Episcopal Conformists were little inclined to be positive in their avowal of the Reformed Faith. Yet it is plain that in the first part of the seventeenth century they were as definite in their profession of the Calvinistic Faith as they came to be hazy and indefinite on the subject of doctrine in later days. Indeed, from the days of Queen Anne they made no attempt to hide their Arminianism as over against the Calvinism of earlier days.

2. DAVID CALDERWOOD

Among the contemporaries of those Conformists who drafted the 1616 Confession there were noteworthy upholders of the purest strain of the Reformed Faith who preserved its tradition and passed it on. In the field of literary activity none of them was greater than David Calderwood, the historian and the defender of the Church of Scotland and its Worship and Order. He was silenced and exiled for his loyalty to his

principles; but he lived to see the vindication that they met
with in the Second Reformation. He is known as the historian
of the Church. Yet, though his history is a most valuable
work for the documents that it embodies, it is not by any
means the most learned or finished production of his pen.
The history appeared in 1678 as a folio but in a much shorter
form than it found when the Wodrow Society functioned and
issued it in full in eight substantial octavo volumes. The
work, however, by which the author of the history was better
known was one of his polemical pieces called forth by the
determination of the King to impose a thorough Anglican
model on the Church of Scotland. In this connection, also,
Calderwood wrote in criticism of the Articles of Perth which
innovated on the Reformed principle of worship; and he was
the author of a vigorous pamphlet entitled *Pastor and Prelate*.
Neither of these works, however, was his chief contribution
to the defence of his Church and its government and
worship. His *magnum opus* appeared bearing his name in
an anagram. David Calderwood, Davidus Calderwodius, had
become Edwardus Didoclavius. This work was published in
the Netherlands. It bore the title *Altare Damascenum*. In
its own department it was held in about as high esteem in
Holland as in Scotland itself as a solid and sufficient defence
of the Reformed ideal of the Church and its worship. It got
its name from the Bible story which tells how Ahaz, King of
Judah, saw at Damascus an altar that took his fancy, and on
his return to Jerusalem he set aside the brazen altar of the
house of God and put in its place a replica of the altar that
he had seen in Syria. Here was a parallel that hit off the
Scottish situation. An alien model furnished the pattern after
which the Church of Scotland was to be modelled. The King's
authority prescribed the pattern and conforming Churchmen
accepted it. In this work, which was looked upon in Reformed
circles as a masterly statement of the doctrine of the Church,
its ministry and worship, Calderwood gave to the world a
monument which bore witness to his thorough acquaintance
with the controversy in which he took such a vigorous

share. It contained a whole armoury of argument for the Presbyterian cause.

3. ROBERT BOYD

Among the Scots divines who were the contemporaries of Calderwood, two of the greatest note, though for a time they taught in their home land, did most of their work in the service of the Huguenot Church and its Colleges. These were Robert Boyd of Trochrig and John Cameron. Each of these was for a while Principal and Professor of Divinity in Glasgow University. Of the two, Boyd was the less inclined to fall in with the King's policy of aggression on the Constitution of his native Church. Indeed, though he was not such an opponent of Episcopacy and its claims as either his bosom friend John Welsh or David Calderwood, he was too far from being a hearty Conformist with the Court model to be at all a favourite with the King. James loved to have scholars in his Colleges, and Boyd was one of the most erudite Theologians of his age. But, if the King loved to have the Chairs of the Colleges filled by scholars, he loved also to have them tamely subservient to his own will; and Boyd was not sufficiently supple and compliant. So he did not long remain in his Scottish academic posts. Yet he did good work in training as theological scholars some young men who were in after years among the most eminent of the bright lights of the next generation. Robert Blair and John Livingstone and Robert Baillie were of the men that the Glasgow school which he influenced produced. His pupils who learned from him were imbued with a love of sound learning. Boyd's Latin Folio Commentary on the Epistle to the Ephesians remains as a monument of his sacred erudition. Like many of the massive commentaries of the two great Theological centuries, this volume is much more than a commentary. It contains elaborate discussions of the Theological questions of the age and these show how sound and ripe his judgment was as a Reformed divine. Boyd was one of the aristocracy of his native county of Ayr, being the cousin of Lord Boyd. He was cousin at the same time of the quaint if crabbed Zachary

Boyd of Glasgow, who, like himself, served for some time in
the ministry of the French Reformed Church. It was a
veritable blue riband of the Theological schools to be called to
teach in one of the chairs of Sedan or Saumur or Montauban
or Diez. And not a few of the Scots scholars shared with
Andrew Melville in this honour. There were, for instance,
Andrew Ramsay, who came back to be a minister in Edinburgh,
as well as Boyd and John Sharp, who was the fellow in
exile of John Welsh and John Forbes of Alford.

4. John Cameron

There was another, however, who drew to himself more
attention than all the rest. This better-known Scot was John
Cameron. For one reason or another, his name came to be
more noted than that of any other of those that we have just
named. This was the case not because he was a finer scholar
or a better divine than the rest of his countrymen who served
overseas. Celebrity and notoriety are not quite synonymous.
Cameron was a scholar of the scholastic type of post-
Reformation days. For some years he was a minister of the
Reformed Church at Bordeaux, and he served in professorial
chairs at Saumur and Montauban. Restless and speculative,
with a dash of ambition in his nature, and more or less, too,
of the brilliant about him, he became a man of significance
from the fact that he led a school of thought. He tried to
steer a middle course of his own between the Calvinism of
the Synod of Dort and the Arminianism which it condemned.
So he became a leader of innovation in the Huguenot body.
On one side he carried on the tradition of the teaching of
Piscator. Among those that followed him were a number of
the ablest men of the next generation in the ministry of the
French Church. Claude, for example, and Dallaeus and
Testard and Blondel were his followers, and above them all
was Moses Amyraut who was so prominent that he gave his
name to the tendency that derived from Cameron's teaching.
John Cameron came back from France to Scotland to serve
for a few years in the University of his native town, for he
was born at Glasgow. He seems, however, to have been

not at all satisfied with his position there, although he was
sufficiently flexible to be a fit agent for carrying out the policy
of the King. Robert Wodrow, in his rich legacy of material
bearing on the Church of Scotland, gives the fullest account
of his life and to some extent of his teaching that one can
easily find. For half a quarto volume each from his pen is
given in the books of the Bannatyne Club to the life of
Cameron and to that of Boyd.

The influence of Cameron's teaching did not tell to any
marked degree on the doctrine held in his native country until
a century after his death it came into vogue as it was developed
and moulded by the work of his followers in France and in
England and much later as developed in New England. In
England Richard Baxter assimilated the teaching of what went
by the name of the New Method in France and his influence
told powerfully in modifying the older Calvinism of Scotland
from the first quarter of the eighteenth century onward. It
was John Cameron, however, that set the tendency in motion
which in different lands has tried to mediate between the
consistent scheme of the Reformed Faith and the Arminianism
which was set aside by the findings of the Synod of Dort.

The type of teaching which sprang from Cameron's attempt
to improve upon the earlier Calvinism without committing the
Church to the Arminian teaching which the consensus of the
Reformed Churches had condemned went by the name of
Hypothetical Universalism. It taught, among other things, an
Atonement of universal extent with a definite saving reference
in the issue to God's elect people. In other words, though the
Atonement was universal in its range, yet, as being such, it
was not held to be an effectual Atonement at all. For had it
been effectual it would have issued in the salvation of all for
whom it was made. It was limited in its effective result by
the purpose of God to save His own. In such a case this
purpose lay open to the charge of being on its negative side
an intention to punish for their sins those whose sins on
Cameron's hypothesis have been atoned for already and thus
put away. The question of what the Atonement is comes
clearly up for discussion at this point, as well as that relating

to the field which it covers. It is obvious to anyone who sees
that our Lord's redeeming work in obedience unto death effects
the end at which He aimed that it issues in the salvation of
His redeemed ones. He came to redeem them from death and
He did this by dying their death out and out, and winning
life for them. This life He lives to bestow when He calls
them to His fellowship. On Cameron's teaching the work
of redemption did not save the lost so that his Universal
Redemption was one that did not secure life and salvation
for the redeemed. And in the case of those whom he
acknowledged to be chosen and called and saved he could not
ascribe their life from the dead to the sacrificial work of Christ
as their Redeemer. Thus his teaching went to evacuate the
work of the Redeemer of intrinsic saving virtue and merit and
content.

Redemption, however, was not the only subject in which
his work as an innovator produced confusion. The issues of
his mongrel compromising teaching were far-reaching. The
Church of his adoption felt the effect of his teaching to such
an extent as that the Theology of the later Huguenots was to
a large extent revolutionised. Their influence in turn told on
Richard Baxter and on all the varieties of teaching that can
be traced back to his type of doctrine. It affected the thinking
of New England; and as a return tide on its way back over the
Atlantic it determined the teaching of the English Edwardians,
both Independent and Baptist. The force of the current that
was thus changing the older Calvinism beat at last on the
Reformed teaching of Scotland in circles other than those of
the Neonomians. It found more channels than one in which
to flow. New England Revivalism did its share of the
work; and the influence of modern Calvinism in English
Nonconformity also contributed its quota. Along with the
disintegrating work of the New Light movement, which was
of home growth and which spoke of an uneasy spirit of
dissatisfaction with long accepted truth and of a restlessness
that was in quest of something new, the various streams of
influence that derived remotely from Cameron are responsible

for the collapse of the Confessional orthodoxy which had for
ages found a home in his native country.

III.

THE CONFORMISTS WITH THE ROYAL POLICY

The leading men as far as weight of character went who
conformed to the policy of the Court were the family of Forbes
of Corse in Aberdeenshire. John Forbes of Alford, however,
the brother of the future Bishop, was one of the sturdy
witnesses that were exiled for their opposition to the King's
plans. Yet his brother Patrick, the Laird of Corse, was a
Conformist. He was, as we have seen, one of the young men
that sat at the feet of Andrew Melville in his St Andrews
days. As his pupil, he imbibed a love of sacred learning and
was a convinced Protestant though he did not follow his
master and relative in his anti-Erastian militancy. As parson
of Keith in Banffshire, he made a more than local name for
himself so that he was not long in the ministry before he was
appointed Bishop of Aberdeen. In this function he was
perhaps the most exemplary of the Episcopal bench and used
the influence that he derived from his position not only for
the ordering of his diocese but for the promotion of education in
his See. Aberdeen, which was the seat of his diocese, had two
Colleges, each of which was looked upon as a University. The
older of them was King's College, which was the last founded
of the pre-Reformation Universities in Scotland. The other
was founded as a Protestant College about ten years later than
that of Edinburgh. Its founder was the Earl Marischal
after whose title it was called Marischal College. The Earl
Marischal had been himself one of the wandering Scots
students who, like Melville, had spent some time at Geneva.
On his return to his country he set up in Aberdeen the new
College which still goes by his name. Under Bishop Patrick
Forbes the two seats of learning in Aberdeen and Old
Aberdeen felt the touch of a kindly fosterage. But the type
of men and scholars that as a class were the product of this
influence were such as the Aberdeen Doctors of Covenanting

days. They, owing to their loyalty to their Erastian ideal, showed themselves the leaders of the opposition to the great movement that roused the rest of Scotland in defence of the independence of the Church. There was, along with the five Doctors who stood up against Henderson and Dickson, another of the school who went further than the rest in his conformity to the policy of Laud and the Court. This was William Forbes, who became the first Bishop of Edinburgh and who was one of the most definitely Arminian and Mediaeval of the conforming clergy. In these respects he was in marked contrast to his clansman, John Forbes of Corse, the son and heir of the Bishop of Aberdeen, who, though a strong Erastian partisan, was neither an Arminian nor a high Prelatist. Of John's *Instructiones* we have spoken already. That monumental work of historical and doctrinal learning appeared from the Elzevir Press in 1645 when its author was an exile in the Netherlands. He was there owing to his loyalty to Charles I. in his usurping Church policy which would make the king in Scotland what he was in England, the Supreme Governor in the Church. Dr Forbes' Erastianism kept him from taking the Covenant, although the popular leaders did what they could by patience and considerateness to win him to their side. He was a man of weight, but he was a stubborn royalist.

In defence of the royal policy which made for the adoption of the Anglican principle that regulates alike the Order and the Worship of the Church, John Forbes wrote his *Irenicum*, which is one of the ablest presentations of the case in whose defence it was written. It called forth as a reply to its teaching in regard to the Church's worship the first work of George Gillespie; and the first book of it has had the distinction of being reissued within our own time, edited by Dean Selwyn, as an Anglican classic. Forbes' treatment of sacramental doctrine has also been analysed from his *Instructiones* and his teaching set forth by Dr W. L. Low of the Scottish Episcopal Church. This publication is significant, as John Forbes was by no means a High Sacramentarian while the Scottish branch of the Anglican Communion is noted for its extreme teaching

on the Sacraments. Dr Forbes was ordained in his early days
in the Netherlands as a Presbyterian and was never Episcopally
ordained so that the most learned champion that Scottish
Episcopacy has produced was in striking contrast in regard
to his orders and to his doctrine of the Sacraments to the
present-day Episcopal body that claims him as one of its chief
ornaments. Indeed, with the present anti-Erastian movement
in the circles of High Anglicanism it has quite broken with
what was the salient and regulative feature of the Church
Principles of the Forbes family. At the same time as Dr
Forbes was a Reformed divine, definitely Augustinian in his
doctrine of grace, he held on the subject of imputation of our
Lord's active obedience with that wing of Rhineland Calvinism
which followed the lead of Piscator or Wendelinus. In this
he diverged from the accepted Scottish teaching of his day.
Rutherford, in his letters from his exile in Aberdeen, seems
to make the Aberdeen Doctors out to have been Arminian.
Yet it could hardly be made good of Dr Baron, and certainly
it was not the case with Dr Forbes, that they were Arminian
in their doctrine. The influence of Patrick Forbes made the
family policy one that told for long years on the north-east
of Scotland and kept it out of sympathy with the stand that
the Covenanters made for the intrinsic freedom of the Church,
as a visible kingdom of our Lord. The sounder class who
came under this influence might be spoken of as Evangelical
or mystical Erastians, such as Henry Scougal or, in another
circle, Robert Leighton. Others, however, were clearly
Arminian in their sympathy, and they paved the way for the
unmitigated Moderatism of later days. This latter type was
for a while mystic also in its tendency, and the teachings of
Antonia Bourignon found a champion in Dr Garden who
edited the collected works of John Forbes. His Jacobite and
Episcopal tendency ended in the removal of Dr Garden from
his chair at Aberdeen. The mystical stage, however, was only
a half-way house of Latitudinarianism that prepared its guests
for the cold unbelief of the Moderate falling away from the
Evangel of the Protestant Confessions.

THE SECOND REFORMATION GALAXY

THERE are great times in which a crop of great men is raised up. In one sense all times are great by reason of the opportunities which they offer and the duties for which they call. Men in quiet times, however, live in an age that tells on the more stirring times ahead and their influence will contribute to the stir and bustle of those times when they come. The quiet times see the stream of life running a more smooth and less exciting course. They may be said to be the days of the average man or of the leading man that is distinctly small. The days of the Second Reformation were not of the tame and uneventful kind. They were days when things happened that are not forgotten and great men appeared on the field and had the chance to show their quality. The leader of the Church of Scotland in those days was not one of the creatures of the court exalted to dignified office above his brethren. There were such men with honours thrust upon them—yet not against their will—strutting their petty hour upon the stage. They were, however, but the puppets and tools of royal policy. The leader who emerged when the call for his work came was the minister of a quiet country parish in Fife where he had almost as his next neighbour the Archbishop of St Andrews. The Archbishop was Spottiswoode, and the minister was Alexander Henderson.

1. ALEXANDER HENDERSON

Henderson in early life had left his University with a high academic record. But in the first years of his ministry he was an easygoing Conformist to the royal absolutism of the Stuart kings. In those days that absolutism was riding rough-shod over the liberties of the Reformed Church. Learning that Robert Bruce of Edinburgh was to preach within reach of his home, the minister of Leuchars, led by curiosity to see a man with such a record, went to hear him. That day was the turning point of his career. He not only became a lively Christian; he studied the Constitution of his Church, became an out-and-out Presbyterian by conviction, and when the days of crisis came he stood out as the wise counsellor, the prudent leader, the far-seeing statesman, and the firm patriot that the time called for, so that the mantle of the great Reformer seemed to rest upon his shoulders. He was a man of counsel and action more than a writer of books. His record is in the deeds of his later years. But though he did not write much for the press, he was a fine specimen of the learned and humble and patient divines that his Church was honoured to produce. In his own day, apart from his State papers, only a few pamphlets from his pen and some fugitive sermons saw the light. His pamphlet, however, expository of the Church government in Scotland is a document of importance. It was from a master's hand. It is in its pages that the statement is found that has often been referred to as descriptive of the properties of Government and Order in the Reformed Church: "Here, then, is a superiority without tyranny. . . . Here is a parity without confusion and disorder. . . . And, lastly, there is a subjection without slavery." About seventy years ago there was published a good-sized octavo volume of his sermons and prayers. The prayers, as they are given in this work, are of great interest as specimens of the exercise of public prayer while the old Book of Common Order was still in use; and the sermons, though not prepared by himself for the press, as they are but a hearer's notes, give a good idea of his doctrine and his preaching power. The wise counsellor was a man of an orderly, capacious, and vigorous mind whose thought was, in quality, as solid and substantial as its range was comprehensive. It is not, however, as a preacher or a theological thinker that his name has lived, but as a leader of men and a man of action in one of the greatest crises of the Reformed Churches.

2. SAMUEL RUTHERFORD

One of the names that live in the memory of the Evangelical
Churches in the English-speaking world is that of the pastor
of Anwoth, the exile in Aberdeen, the Westminster divine,
the professor at St Andrews. In his early ministry he took
a vigorous part in opposition to Arminianism. This was not
what was fitted to attract the favourable notice of the hierarchy
of the days when the Scottish bishops were eager to stand
well with William Laud. So Samuel Rutherford was driven
away from his country parish of Galloway to ward in the
city of Aberdeen where he was at the very heart of the district
in which conformity to court fashions in Faith and to the
Episcopal model in Government was strongest. When confined
to this city and shut out from his loved work in his quiet
country parish by the Solway, he wrote the most remarkable
series of devotional letters that the literature of the Reformed
Churches can show. The fervid piety, the burning zeal, the
love to his Lord, the loving response to his Lord's love, and
the lively figurative dress given to all these in the Letters
exhibit the workmanship of a spiritual genius whose branches
ran over the wall. The luxuriant wealth of his words marks
him out in his own line as a writer of the first order. The
style may be untamed, but the writer handed out his gems
in rich profusion. There is something seraphic and unearthly
in the fire that burns in his words. Not a Bernard in his
holiest and most exalted raptures can excel the devotion of
these Letters. They have made their most telling appeal to
those of most kindred spirit. Thus Charles Haddon Spurgeon
put on record his estimate of Rutherford's Letters. When he
should be no more, he said that he would like the world to
know that in his judgment these Letters were the nearest
thing to inspiration to be found in the range of Evangelical
literature. They are a religious classic which, appealing as
we have said to kindred spirits, finds its warmest welcome
where zeal for God's glory and love to the Lord Jesus Christ
are a most vehement flame. When exception is taken to them
on the ground that they use so freely the language of nuptial

love, the critics, to be justified in their fault-finding, ought first to expunge from Scripture the Song of Songs, the 45th Psalm, and much of the language in the Prophets and in the New Testament which speak of the Lord as espoused to His Church and of the Church as His Bride. Hearts that have never been melted and drawn out in the fervency of a living sense of the love of God in Christ, in the experience of a consuming, overmastering love which is the echo to God's love, will fail to prize the meaning and value of the emotional overflowing of a heart that tasted abundantly the sweetness of the comforts of the Gospel. It was to him a furnace experience to be cut off from the preaching of the Word which was his delight. He might have little solace in his exile from the friendly fellowship of men; yet his Lord was with him as he walked at liberty in the fire and was enabled to glory in tribulations. He seemed to accept them as so many tokens of love from his Lord, assurances indeed that it was for faith and a good conscience that he was passing through such an experience. His pen during his exile was able to do more for his Church and for a wider constituency in later times and in many lands than his unsealed lips might do, so that the things that befell him turned out for the furtherance of the good cause for which he was an ambassador in bonds.

It was in 1636 that the ministry of Rutherford was interrupted and he was banished to his exile in Aberdeen. A change, however, was at hand. The tighter a withe is bound the nearer is it to the breaking-point and the sooner will it yield. So it was with the bonds of the crowned and mitred tyranny that lorded it over the oppressed Church of Scotland. Its policy reached the breaking-point beyond which it could not further go. A fire was lit that soon set Britain ablaze. With the change in 1638 Rutherford was restored to his loved Anwoth. He was not, however, long left there. Edinburgh wanted him for the pulpit. But the claims of the capital were overruled; and St Andrews, the old ecclesiastical metropolis, secured him in 1639 for a Professor's Chair. This he held in conjunction with a charge in the Town Church, and St Andrews was his home for the rest of his life, except that during the sitting of the Westminster Assembly, to which he was sent as one of his Church's representatives, he spent some years in London.

Rutherford was an indefatigable worker. In spite of the strain of poetry and sentiment that was in his nature, he was the very reverse of a day-dreamer. He did not spare himself. The warm devotion of the writer of the Letters went hand-in-hand with the scholastic passion for definition and discussion so that in his one person he seemed to combine more persons than one in a multiple personality. He was the keen school-man, the seraphic preacher, the patient pastor, the diligent Catechist, the militant Churchman and the mystical man of God all in one. As a divine he drew the attention to his quality of the Theological schools of the Netherlands, then in their golden age, and he was invited more than once to take his place there as a Professor in a Theological Faculty. To be colleague with a man like Voetius of Utrecht was the same as to be admitted to the inner circle of the leaders of Reformed thought. It is just possible that it was the fact that he was a Supralapsarian that got for him the invitation to go to Utrecht, for though Supralapsarianism was not the common doctrine of the Dutch schools, it was strongly held by Voetius, who did not hide his light under a bushel. This he did neither at the Synod of Dort, where he was one of the few that expressed this view, nor in later life when he carried on a vigorous controversy in regard to it with Maresius. In Rutherford's time the higher and more speculative doctrine of the decree was widely held in Scotland. Indeed, it seems to have been part of the offence taken at the Dictates of Principal Strang of Glasgow that he was not a Supralapsarian. The tendency to lay what looks like an undue burden on the absolute Sovereignty of God was one in which a daring thinker like Rutherford indulged. Thus, in regard to the necessity of the Atonement, if sinners were to be saved, the speculative position that he took up laid him open to the serious critical animadversions of John Owen among his contemporaries, and of William Cunningham in the 19th century. Owen himself, at an early stage, held pretty much the same view as Rutherford

did, but came to see his mistake, and in his defence of
Punitive Justice as rooted not in the bare will but in the very
nature of God, he has left what one might call the classical
work of British Theology dealing with the subject. If on
the one hand Twisse and Rutherford and Owen in his early
years held that it trenches too much on the freedom which
we ought to attribute to the Sovereignty of God to hold that
it is only by way of Atonement that God can forgive sin,
yet, on the other hand, just as righteousness would have been
by the law if a law could be given that might give life, the
fact that God sent to save His people none less than His own
Son in their nature that He might take their place and satisfy
on their behalf seems to point in the direction that it was
because it could be secured in no other way, or at no less
a cost, that forgiveness is mediated by the expiatory blood
of the Cross. It is doubtful what following Rutherford had
in Scotland in his teaching in this connection. Fraser of Brea
we find appealing to him on the subject.

But apart from his Theological works properly so called,
Rutherford was the author of a work which has left its mark
upon the world. The tradition of Scottish Reformed teaching
in regard to the obedience that the people owe to the civil
power was to the effect that the power of the king
is restricted and that his authority has bounds within which
it ought to be kept. Knox and Buchanan and Melville had
not taught in vain. Stuart tyranny might fume and fret.
It usurped a place to which it had no right. There were laws
that set bounds to royal rights. Of this teaching, the best
known document that there had so far been was Buchanan's
De jure regni apud Scotos. Now, however, in the strenuous
days of the Covenanting struggle, while the English Parliamentary war was on, and the Westminster Assembly was
in session with Rutherford as one of its members, his
monumental work, *Lex Rex*, or *Law is King*, saw the light.
This treatise, which deals with a man's duty as a citizen or
subject and the magistrate's right to exact obedience, is one
that handles questions on the boundary line of ethics, natural
rights, civil law and Christian obedience and service. It

strikes a note by no means uncertain, and with the return of despotism at the Restoration of Charles II., it was made ground for a charge against its author. He was summoned to Edinburgh to answer for it. But there came another summons in the name of a higher than any earthly king that the accused must first obey. He was called home to his rest ere the court met that was to try him. His book, however, shared with George Buchanan's *De jure regni* the honour of being consigned to the flames by the public hangman. It was one thing to burn its pages. It was another thing to refute its teaching, or to keep the friends of freedom from giving effect to it. And the ordered liberties of the English-speaking world are to this day the outcome of that teaching in regard to civil rights and obedience to which the Reformed tradition in Scotland led the writer of *Lex Rex*. To the same teaching it led in other days the writers of *Jus Populi*, *The Informatory Vindication* and *A Hind Let Loose*. Stewart of Goodtrees and James Renwick and Alexander Shields carried on in these works the Whig teaching which was vindicated at the Revolution of 1689 and which is behind the history of your American Revolution. In your case it has told directly through the teaching of John Witherspoon in old Nassau Hall, and indirectly, with a more pagan strain, through the teaching of John Locke and those French philosophers who went crazy over liberty and the idealised Revolution Constitution of England. Jefferson was of this school.

Stuart absolutism held that a free monarchy is that of a king who is above the law and not bound by any bonds of constitutional obligation. Such a king would be free to modify or override, to dispense with or to set aside, the law. On such a reading of things the words of Robert Burns about Edinburgh would be true in a sense that he did not mean them to bear : " Where oft *beneath a monarch's feet* sat Legislation's sov'reign powers." This was the very place that James I., King of Great Britain, would assign to Parliament and law alike, And it would leave the people the place of being so many dumb, driven cattle. It was this kind of theory that

Scotland, as well as England, was up against. It was in
opposition to such a scheme that *Lex Rex* maintained that
Government, while it is from God and by His authority,
rests as a last resort, as among men, in the will of the people.
It is for them to choose the special form it will take. " The
aptitude and temper of every commonwealth to one form rather
than another is God's warrant and call to determine the will
and liberty of the people to pitch on monarchy or democracy
or aristocracy," though all three are from God. It is then
for the people to say what the limits are of the power with
which they entrust their rulers, to resume that power if need
be, and to hold it within the bounds of law so long as the
trust lasts. The king then had no irresponsible lordship. He
is put in trust, by the people's own choice, of the power that
God gives him in Providence. He holds his place of power
to conserve and not to override or dispense with the law;
and his judges are the servants of the kingdom rather than
of the king. They owe a duty in their office to the Supreme
Monarch which is paramount to that which is due to their
earthly king. Absolute power it is irrational and tyrannical
to claim and it is beyond the right of the people to grant it.
For they have all to answer to the King of kings. And such
power cannot be entrusted to Parliaments or to Senates or to
Congresses or to Dictators. The freedom of a constituency
of responsible rational beings is not a thing to be bought or
sold or sacrificed or trodden under foot. Such lessons are
not so antiquated or old-fashioned as not to be called for
in these days of ours. Our old Scots Whigs were true
conservatives of Divine rights and claims and not illiberal
teachers of human rights and duties in the realm of civil
government and citizenship.

As an authoritative writer on Church questions, or rather
as one the weight of whose teaching has made him to be
looked up to as a man that spoke with authority, Rutherford
ranks among his country's ecclesiastical writers second only
to his younger contemporary George Gillespie. He was a
man who feared no foe in the arena of discussion on Church
principles. He could fight on two fronts, Erastian and

Sectarian, at once. The Romanist, the Prelatist and the
Independent all knew where to find him. He and his age-
fellow Baillie were the candid critics of the New England
" way," however sympathetic they were with the godliness
of early Massachusetts and Connecticut. They recognised
that the American brethren by adopting Independent views
were not the authentic successors of the long-suffering
Puritans of the reigns of Elizabeth and James who aimed at
a Reformation of the old conservative Calvinistic kind. These
men, the fathers and founders of Puritanism, had their
genuine representatives in the divines who drew up the
Westminster documents. Over and above his polemic writings
in his later life, in which he held his ground against the
innovating views of the radical Independency which underlay
the hydra-headed Sectarianism that was rampant in the
England of Cromwell's days, Rutherford produced an
elaborate criticism of Arminianism. It runs to about 700
pages, and along with his critical handling of the Sectaries
gives what might be the body of his prelections in his academic
chair. He wrote many other books too, devotional and
doctrinal. Yet in his polemic against Arminianism his
Theological militancy ended in the field where it began.

It is interesting to see how he looked in the eyes of one
of his later students who became a conforming Episcopalian,
and who naturally had not too much sympathy with his
professor's standpoint. " Rutherford," says he, " was confused
in his notions and method of teaching, applying himself wholly
to the writing of books against the Sectaries then most in
vogue." This Episcopal critic gives a thumb-nail sketch of
his professor whom he describes as " of such a bizarre temper
that his very beard pricked up to his lips." Yet he allows
" that he was a person of great piety and free of covetousness."
The only portrait that professes to give Rutherford's likeness
shows him as a full-faced, clean-shaven man. From this
contemporary Episcopal source we learn that he wore a beard.
We may not be quite sure what he looked like, but from his
works we may still learn how he wrote and what he had to
say and how he still makes his appeal.

Rutherford lives in his Letters. It was only two or three years after his death that the first edition of them saw the light. In the early edition, the little volume in which they appeared went by the name of *Joshua Redivivus*. Their writer brought to the folk in the wilderness a good report of the land. They soon found a public that valued them. In many questions of Christian truth his contemporary Richard Baxter and he did not see eye to eye. But in regard to these Letters, Baxter was ungrudging in his assessment of their value as he put it to William Carstares. " Hold off the Bible, such a book as Mr Rutherford's Letters the world never saw the like." But the heavenly strain of warm and living fellowship with his Lord which so often is met with in them is to be found richly also in his other practical writings. One cannot read much of his *Trial and Triumph of Faith* without meeting it and without coming across the source of many of the expressions that have received classical currency in Mrs Cousin's *Last Words of Samuel Rutherford—The Sands of Time are Sinking*. In his gift of expression he had a mint and coinage of his own. So it was little wonder that the man who could preach Christ with the genius and the unction of his preaching should be looked upon as being in the front rank of preachers in a great age of popular preachers. As examples of his style we may take two or three passages, which may be taken as characterised by distinctive marks of his way of putting things. The first we find in *Christ Dying and Drawing Sinners to Himself*.

" Would sinners but draw near, and come and see this King Solomon in His chariot of love, and behold His beauty, the uncreated white and red in His countenance, he would draw souls to Him. There is omnipotence of love in His countenance, all that is said of Him here are but created shadows; ah! words are short to express His nature, Person, office, loveliness, desirableness. What a broad and beautiful face must He have Who with one smile and one turning of His countenance looks upon all in heaven and all in the earth, and casts a heaven of burning love east and west, south and north through heaven and earth, and fills them all; . . .

If it be so that death finding so precious a surety as Christ's princely and sinless soul, did make Him obey the law of the land, ere He escaped out of that land, what wonder that we die, who are born in the land of death? All things under the moon must be sick of vanity and death when the Heir of all things, coming in amongst dying creatures, out of dispensation, by law must die. If the Lord's soul and the soul of such a Lord die and suffer wrath, then let the fair face of the world, the heavens, look like the face of an old man full of trembling, white hairs and wrinkles—then, let man make for his long home, let time itself wax old and grey-haired. Why should I desire to stay here, when Christ could not but pass away? And if this spotless soul that never sinned was troubled, what wonder then many troubles be to the sinner? Our Saviour Who promiseth soul-rest to others, cannot have soul-rest Himself; His soul is now on a wheel sore-tossed. And all the creatures are upon a wheel and in motion; there is not a creature since Adam sinned sleepeth sound. Weariness and motion is laid on moon and sun, and all creatures on this side of the moon. Seas ebb and flow, and that's trouble; winds blow, rivers move, heavens and stars these five thousand years, except one time, have not had six minutes' rest; living creatures walk apace towards death; kingdoms, cities, are on the wheel of changes, up and down; mankind run, and the disease of body-trouble and soul-trouble is on them, they are motion-sick, going on their feet, and kings cannot have beds to rest in. The great All of heaven and earth, since God laid the first stone of this wide hall, hath been groaning for the liberty of the sons of God. The figure of the passing away world is like an old man's face full of wrinkles and foul with weeping; we are waiting till Jesus shall be revealed from heaven and shall come and wipe the old man's face. Every creature here is on its feet, none of them can sit or lie. But Christ's soul now is above trouble and rests sweetly in the bosom of God. Troubled soul, rejoice in hope."

Or, take again a passage from his *Trial and Triumph of Faith*: " There is not a rose out of heaven but there is a blot and thorn growing out of it, except that one only Rose of Sharon which blossometh out glory. Every leaf of that rose is a heaven, and serveth for the healing of the nations; every white and red in it is incomparable glory; every act of breathing out its smell, from everlasting to everlasting, is spotless and unmixed happiness. Christ is the outset, the master-flower, the uncreated garland of heaven, the love and joy of men and angels. But the fountain-love, the fountain-delight, the fountain-joy of men and angels is more; for out of it floweth all the seas, springs, rivers and floods of love, delight and joy; Christ cannot tire or weary from eternity to be Christ; and so He must not, He cannot but be an infinite and eternal flowing sea, to diffuse and let out streams and floods of boundless grace. Say that the rose were eternal; the sweet smell, the loveliness of greenness and colour must be eternal. Oh! what a happiness for a soul to lose its excellency in His transcendent glory! What a blessedness for the creature to cast in his little all in Christ's matchless all-sufficiency. Could all the streams return into the fountain and first-spring, they should be kept in a more sweet and firm possession of their being, in the bosom of their first cause, than in their borrowed channel that they now move in. Our neighbourhood, and retiring in, to dwell for ever and ever in the fountain-blessedness, Jesus Christ, with our borrowed goodness, is the firm and solid fruition of our eternal happy being. Christ is the sphere, the connatural first-spring and element of borrowed drops and small pieces of created grace. The rose is sweet in being, in beauty, on its own stalk and root; let life and sap be eternally in the stalk and root, and the rose keep its first union with the root, and it shall never wither, never cast its blossoms nor greenness of beauty. It is violence for a gracious soul to be out of his stalk and root; union here is life and happiness; therefore the Church's last prayer in Canonic Scripture is for union. 'Amen, even so come Lord Jesus.' It shall not be well till the Father and Christ the prime Heir, and all the weeping children, be under one roof in the palace royal. It is a sort of mystical lameness that the Head wanteth an arm or a finger; and it is a

violent and forced condition for arm and finger to be separated
from the Head. The saints are little pieces of mystical Christ,.
sick of love for union. The wife of youth, that wants her
husband some years, and expects that he shall return to her
from overseas lands is often on the shore; every ship coming
near shore is her new joy; her heart loves the wind that shall
bring him home. She asks at every passenger news : ' Oh!
saw ye my husband? What is he doing? When shall he come?
Is he shipped for a return?' Every ship that carrieth not
her husband is the breaking of her heart. The Bride, the
Lamb's wife, blesseth the feet of the messengers that preach
such tidings, 'Rejoice, O Zion, put on thy beautiful
garments, thy King is coming.' Yea, she loveth that quarter
of the sky, that being rent asunder and cloven, shall yield to
her Husband, when He shall put through His glorious head,
and shall come riding on the rainbow and clouds to receive
her to Himself."

The very Oriental luxuriance, incoherence, in a sense, and
vividness of such speech tells that it is a dialect by itself. It
is Rutherford. Here he is again refuting beforehand the
modern charge against those who look for the latter-day glory
before the advent of the Lord that they cannot look or long
for His coming. " O when will we meet? O how long is
it till the dawning of the marriage day! O sweet Jesus, take
wide steps! O my Lord, come over mountains at one stride!
O my Beloved, flee as a roe or young hart upon the mountains
of separation! O, if He would fold the heavens together like
an old cloak and shovel time and days out of the way and
make ready in haste the Bride for her Husband! . . . O
heavens, move fast! O time, run, run, and hasten the marriage
day! for love is tormented with delays! Look to the east;
the day-sky is breaking. Think not that Christ loseth time or
lingereth unsuitably. . . . The Lord's bride will be up or
down, above the water swimming or under the water sinking
until her lordly and mighty Redeemer and Husband set His
head through the skies, and come with His fair court to rid.
all these pleas and give them the longed-for inheritance."

3. George Gillespie

We have coupled the names of Rutherford and George Gillespie as the two best known by their writings of the Church divines of the era of the Westminster Assembly. George Gillespie was one of the marvels of an age that was itself sufficiently marvellous. At the age of 23 he was already the author of a most able and thorough discussion of the Church ceremonies such as the Stuarts were seeking to force on an unwilling and reclaiming Church. The Church as a whole was not willing to submit to the royal and prelatic impositions, for it held firmly to the Calvinistic and Puritan principle that regulates what is lawful and what unlawful in the worship of God. The problem that Gillespie handled was the burning question of the hour, and his treatment of it brought him at one bound into the forefront of the polemic divines of his age. The Puritan controversy had dragged its long length between Conformists and Nonconformists on both sides of the Border before he stepped into the arena. Whitgift and Hooker, Morton and Forbes, had written among the leaders on the side of the court. Cartwright and Travers and Ames and Calderwood were leaders in defence of a strict reading of the Reformed principle. Gillespie when he intervened showed himself a master of his material and dexterous in wielding his weapons. The vice of current controversial method, however, cleaves to his course of argument. He answered his opponents in detail. Instead of grouping as one all the champions of what was in substance the one line of argument and dealing with their principle once for all, he followed them into minutiae and then he virtually fought all his battles over again and thrice he slew the slain. This, however, was a fault of the method of his age and it did in his case only what it did in that of others—it made for redundancy and prolixity. His first book, however, made his name, and by the time that Gillespie was 30 he was sent as one of the divines of Scotland to represent his Church in the Assembly at Westminster. There he distinguished himself as a defender of the Reformed ideal of the Church in conflict with the leading Erastians, Selden and Coleman. He excelled as a ready debater. It was during the years that this Assembly sat that the youthful divine produced his masterpiece in defence of the freedom of the Church to carry out the will of its Head and Lord. This learned treatise goes by a name that bears the hallmark of the age. It is *Aaron's Rod Blossoming*. In it we have an exhaustive discussion of the questions at issue between the Erastians and the Orthodox. It is the recognised classic of Scottish Reformed Theology in its own department. The writer was also the author of what might be called a State paper in the Church's service, CXI. Propositions on Church Government, a work that was called for by the General Assembly in Scotland a year or two before his early death. His Treatise of Miscellany Questions covers a more various field, and it has in it some of his best writing. The writer was a master of swordplay with his rapier. The type of mental clarity, though not with quite the same lucid style, that one finds in Francis Turrettine is found also in George Gillespie; and he did his lifework in the short space of 36 years. As a supreme defender of the Reformed doctrine of the Church he was equally firm with Rutherford but less inclined to take up extreme positions. Though so much of his writing was of a polemic complexion, yet there was in his discussion of such a spiritual topic as assurance of salvation a wonderfully gracious touch. He was one of the mighties of his age which was so fertile in massive and heroic figures in the field of Evangelical Christian Theology. He filled well his place at Westminster.

4. Robert Baillie

The history of the Church of Scotland is deeply in debt to writers of diaries, first-hand memoirs, and personal letters. What should we know of the Scottish Reformation were it not for the lively narrative that we have of it from the pen of its foremost figure and leader? Then the Autobiography of James Melville keeps us in close touch with the Church's battle for freedom as that raged around his uncle as its storm-centre. For the period of his literary activity we have, at a later stage, the Letters of Robert Wodrow. For an authentic piece of self-portraiture that is also the picture of his class and the movement that it represents we have the Autobiography of Alexander Carlyle, where we can read the record of Moderatism, naked and unashamed, as it is set down by a not unfriendly hand. Wodrow's contemporary, too, in the previous generation gives us an illuminating account of much that was best in the life of his generation when we look into the pages of Thomas Boston's Autobiography. For the period of the Second Reformation we have the priceless letters of a prince of letter-writers and of gossiping special correspondents in the three volumes of the Letters of Robert Baillie. The writer was a man who kept in touch with public affairs and was himself often at the heart of the leading transactions of Church business that he put on record.

Baillie was one of the most scholarly men of his day in Scotland. He was not by nature disposed to take up with extreme views or to act upon them. His tendency was rather to take things as they were and to avoid making a fuss; for he had in him a very decidedly sluggish and conservative strain and he was a good party man. All this has to be taken into our reckoning when we look at things through his eyes. Had it not been for the extreme policy promoted by Laud and pressed upon a reluctant people he might have passed a life of cultured contentment and pastoral diligence in his Ayrshire charge of Kilwinning, varied with visits now and then to academic circles in Glasgow and possibly a transfer to a Theological Chair in the University whose Principal he came to be. But his lot fell in strenuous days and Baillie, the Reformed divine, did more justice to the Reformed strain that was in him in such days than he might have done in more peaceful times. He was a good Presbyterian; yet unless he was provoked to fight for Presbytery he might have been a kind of half-hearted Conformist to the royal will. As this was his natural build all the more credit attaches to him for the part he took in the great events of his days. As a party man, when he was put to it, he became a vigorous opponent of Episcopacy when that was the leading issue at stake. And then in turn he did battle with Independency. In his later days he became an equally keen Resolutioner; and he could not endure the stubbornness of his former brethren who, as Protesters, refused to be parties to what they looked upon as the betrayal of the cause of the Covenant by the action of the majority of Assembly which passed the Public Resolutions. To him the Protesters were the villains of the piece in the years of conflict that tore the Church asunder in Commonwealth times. And one is tempted in reading his pages, as he retails the faulty carriage of his former friends, to take with a grain of salt, or it may be more grains than one, the criticism that he passed on contemporaries that did not go all the way with him. Party feeling gives one a relish for small gossip that is not free from a spice of malice and jealousy. Thus he shows himself disposed to carp at Hugh Binning, who was one of the special stars of the pulpit of his brief day, for Binning was a Protester. So he is censorious of another Protester, Andrew Gray, a twin star with Binning. Gray died at the age of 22 and Binning was only 25 when he died. Binning came under Baillie's censure for adopting a new method of sermon-building; and he took the line that was also taken by Robert Leighton of using a more English and less Scottish style of speech.

Yet when he found that the trusted agent of his Resolutioner friends had deceived them all and came back to Scotland from his Church agency in London as the Archbishop of St Andrews, the old letter-writer became less bitter in his judgment of the Protesters; and in his conversation with James Wodrow not long before his death, when he gave him the pamphlets on both sides of the controversy, he left his old pupil to form his own judgment on its merits. As one of the Westminster divines he will live in the memory of all who feel an interest in the rich and full and careful exposition that the standards which they drew up afford of the Reformed Faith in its matured expression. The letters that he wrote from London while the Assembly was in session keep us abreast of its discussions. The fact also that he and some of the other older conservatives fell in with the Directory for Public Worship when it quietly set aside a few

Scottish practices that were rooted in their lives shows how far they were willing to go to carry out the great plan of having a single Reformed Church in Great Britain and Ireland. It was left for such disintegrating and honeycombing bodies as the Scottish Church Service Society to gird at the changes introduced by the Directory by ascribing them to the working of a Brownism which was largely alien to the great Puritan tradition. It is true that Brownism, in the work of its successor Independency, shut out the possibility of achieving the programme of the Covenanters. But the Independents formed only an almost negligible fraction of the men who drafted the Westminster documents. Baillie and his fellows had no sympathy with Independency, while they cordially sought to achieve the ideal that had brought the Parliamentary divines to the Jerusalem Chamber and then brought them into the Solemn League and Covenant.

5. DAVID DICKSON

Though the names of Rutherford and Gillespie as writers, particularly on Church questions, have left more of a mark on the page of history than that of David Dickson, and though Baillie from his Letters is in a sense more important for our purpose than he, yet in his own time there was no man who was held in higher esteem or carried greater weight than Dickson did in the councils of the Church, nor was there anyone that did more useful work in spreading the Faith of his Church and giving it popular and permanent form. In the early days of his ministry he was favoured to see a great awakening among his people and in the district about Irvine where his charge was. He was afterwards Professor of Divinity successively in Glasgow and Edinburgh. Before he left Irvine he had his share in the same honour that was bestowed upon Bruce and Welsh and Rutherford and Calderwood. He was silenced and banished by those who held the reins of power. In the later years of his life he, with Robert Douglas, was one of the leaders of the party that formed the majority of the ministry which was thoroughly royalist in sentiment and which was disposed to stretch its

loyalty to the Covenant to such a point as to be willing to
preserve the civil unity of the nation by winking at the holding
of high office by men who would not be looked upon as
true friends of the Covenanting cause. This majority of the
Assembly carried to a high pitch their doctrine of Church
authority in their attempt to suppress the protest of their
brethren who were not prepared to consent by the voice of
the Church to let potential traitors hold key positions in the
management of national affairs. In this sad business Dickson
was to some degree estranged from his best friends. For
among the Protesting minority were men like Rutherford and
Livingstone and Wariston and the two Guthries, James and
William. Along with Dickson were to be found ranged as
Resolutioners Douglas and Baillie and Hutcheson and Wood,
while men like Durham and Blair did what they could as
peacemakers to mediate between estranged brethren. The
Reformed Church never got over the bad results that can be
easily traced back to this schism which rent its unity in the
days of the Commonwealth.

David Dickson is the author of the first commentary on
the Westminster Confession that set itself in a sympathetic
and comprehensive way to open up its teachings and to
analyse its propositions. It is true that Parker's unfriendly
discussion of the teaching of the Confession preceded it.
That, however, has no weight as an exposition or a criticism.
The title given to Dickson's commentary is *Truth's Victory
Over Error*. This work came out more than a score of years
after the author's death. It was translated and published by
George Sinclair, who was one of the Regents or Tutors of
Glasgow University. This academic authority on Satan's
Invisible Kingdom in issuing Dickson's work gave no
indication as to who the author was. For anything that the
book shows it might have been Sinclair's own work. This
commentary, though a valuable one, was not Dickson's most
important Theological work, which was his *Therapeutica
Sacra*, the first issue of which saw the light in 1648. One
who had so much experience as the writer of this work had
in dealing with awakened sinners and with tried and exercised

believers was well fitted to deal with practical problems in therapeutics or in case divinity. His handling of the Federal Theology at such a date shows the vogue that it had already attained to as a systematic way of setting forth the leading teachings of the Word of God in regard to sin and salvation. We might also here draw attention to the exposition he gave of the Covenant Scheme in his careful address on doctrine at the great Glasgow Assembly of 1638. It was his method before the star of Cocceius had risen above the horizon. At any rate Scottish Covenant Theology could never be spoken of as Cocceianism. The Covenant Categories as the lines of doctrinal schematising were recognised and used in the previous century and did not begin only in the 17th century to be employed as the framework of Christian teaching. The *Therapeutica Sacra* appeared in the same year as Cocceius' *Summa*.

Along with his young friend and ministerial disciple, James Durham, Dickson was also the author of *The Sum of Saving Knowledge,* which, though without authority from the Church, has been often printed in the same volume as the Westminster documents. This solid and valuable piece is an expansion of some sermons preached by Dickson at Inveraray when he was Argyll's guest there; it was the means of the conversion of the amiable and eminent Robert Murray M'Cheyne. These were very great services that Dickson did to the Church. But perhaps most valuable of all was his work by way of writing commentaries on books of Scripture. In this line he not only took action, he stimulated others to like action. So the series of Scottish commentaries from his pen and from those of Fergusson and Hutcheson and Durham and Nisbet is as valuable a legacy of practical exegesis as has come down from the Puritan age. Along with these writers one might put Brown of Wamphray in his exposition of the Epistle to the Romans, though this is somewhat later than the Dickson series and indeed was not published for almost ninety years after the writer's death, when another worthy John Brown, his namesake of Haddington, saw it through the press. Nor should we forget, though it was not of the Dickson series, Robert Leighton's admirable commentary on I. Peter.

In regard to the commentaries which Dickson wrote or inspired, Spurgeon in his *Commenting and Commentaries* can hardly say enough in their praise. They were the work of writers after his own heart. Thus he says of Dickson on the Psalms : " A rich volume, dropping fatness. Invaluable to the preacher. Having read and reread it, we can speak of its holy savour and suggestiveness. We commend it with much fervour." So of Dickson on Matthew he says : " A perfect gem. The work is to men of our school more suggestive of sermons than almost any other we have met with." So again in commending Fergusson on Paul's Epistles, he says : " The author handles his matter in the same manner as Hutcheson and Dickson, and he is of their class—a grand, gracious, savoury divine." The works of this series tell of the warm piety and the sanctified learning of the divines of the Covenanting age. These works are :— Dickson on the Psalms and on Matthew and on Paul's Epistles and on the Hebrews, Durham on the Song of Solomon, Fergusson on Paul's Epistles, Hutcheson on Job and the Minor Prophets and the Gospel according to John, Nisbet on Ecclesiastes and I. and II. Peter. There is also a Latin Commentary by Dickson on the Epistles. From these volumes men may see what good work was the outcome of the old Scottish habit of lecturing in order through the books of Scriptures. This method of pulpit instruction was based on a careful exegesis of the text and it interwove into its fabric the doctrine and the connections of doctrine that were brought to light by the exposition of the passage. The Church is debtor to David Dickson for initiating and giving an impetus to this exegetical and expository movement which was meant to bring to the common man in the pew and at the hearth the ripe fruit of academic work so that in the best sense the learning of the study might be made popular. The ages that have followed him have been enriched with so many treasures of sound and wise and gracious teaching. The memory of the man who set this movement agoing and contributed so much to it should not be forgotten.

6. HUTCHESON AND FERGUSSON

The names of these two eminent expositors have been before us already as two who collaborated with Dickson in his project to furnish the religious public with so many handy expositions of books of the Bible. These volumes were to be based on a competent acquaintance with the work of the learned, but they were to be pitched on such a key as would make an appeal to the unlearned. Let the enterprise but succeed and the unlearned would be unlearned no more, but would be well grounded in the truth of the Gospel as it is set forth in the sacred books themselves. George Hutcheson and James Fergusson were both of them ministers in Ayrshire. They were of the class for whom Spurgeon, as we have seen, had so high an esteem. Hutcheson in the early days of his ministry was settled at Colmonell. In those days he was one of the strictest for applying the rule for worship which was accepted in the Reformed Church. He scrupled at the singing of the doxologies that were in common use which were sung at the close of the singing of the Psalms. This was a usage that passed with the adoption of the Westminster Directory, so that it was not the Directory that raised questions about it. The question had been keenly discussed before the Directory was drawn up. All that the Directory did was to make no provision, in the uniformity of use that it aimed at, for this old Scottish custom. There was no obvious connection between Brownism and the position taken up by Hutcheson and his friends. Baillie was to begin with strongly in favour of continuing use and wont, yet when the Directory was adopted he honourably accepted its guidance and ruling. Now Baillie was not a Protester, much less a Brownist. And no more was Hutcheson. When the strife between Resolutioners and Protesters was on foot he was not only not a Protester, he was militant on the other side. Indeed he was one of the chief pamphleteers in the controversy on the side of the Resolutioners. He became one of the ministers of Edinburgh, and it was during his Edinburgh days that he wrote his admirable commentaries. It was he who, when the great persecution began, accompanied to the scaffold the Marquess of Argyll, who was the first of the Covenanting martyrs. Now Baillie and Hutcheson saw very much eye to eye in their Church politics. They both alike were loyal to the ideal accepted in the Westminster documents, and though Baillie could charge his opponents with undue compliance with the Sectaries, yet he and they were at one in loyalty to the uniformity of Faith and Worship at which the Covenant aimed. The use made of Baillie's name in giving colour to the charge that the Protesters were tainted with Brownism and that they were responsible for the plainness of the type of worship that from Covenanting days was the common Scottish pattern is one of the disreputable things that belong to an innovating propaganda that is not marked by the high standard of honour shown in advancing its cause. It is convenient for this school of innovators to forget that the type of worship which abjured the lax principle of Anglicanism was undeniably the type for which both sides in the schism over the Public Resolutions stood. They were honest men who might differ on the questions that were at issue between them, but who were of one mind in holding the Reformed principle of worship and in accepting the Directory as part of the Covenanted uniformity of the British Churches.

In his later years Hutcheson as an " outed " minister accepted the position of the Indulged minister at Irvine and by so doing was criticised for yielding so far to the Erastianism of the day. It was during his years of service there that he produced his valuable exposition of the 130th Psalm. He thus ended his ministry in the same county in which it had begun.

Fergusson, too, as we have seen, was a minister in Ayrshire. He was one of Baillie's successors in Kilwinning just as Hutcheson in a way was one of Dickson's in Irvine, where also Alexander Nisbet was settled. Apart from his Commentaries on the Epistles from Galatians to II. Thessalonians, Fergusson was the author of a controversial work which is severely critical of Toleration. In this respect he was one of the conservative opposition to a miscellaneous Toleration that found room for all the extravagances illustrated in Edwards' Gangraena. The Covenanting fathers had no relish for the Radicalism in Church matters for which the Independents stood. They stood out strongly for the maintenance of the unity of the Visible Church and looked upon the system of insulated unrelated gathered Churches as essentially out of keeping with that unity. At the same time as they were against a general and unbounded toleration they were distinctly in favour of showing every consideration to the scruples of godly ministers of a tender conscience. They were opposed to the organising of separate and rival denominations. They favoured comprehension in one national Church with adequate provision for kindly dealing with scrupulous brethren. They did not envisage such a condition of things as we have in the present day. Even in the days of Cromwell the Independents themselves began to circumscribe the limits of the wide toleration for which they had come to plead.

7. James Wood and Robert Blair of St Andrews

When we name Fergusson of Kilwinning in connection with Toleration, it is natural to associate with his opposition to the ideal of the Independents and the Cromwellian *Sectaries,* as they were spoken of in Scotland, the name and the work of James Wood of St Andrews, who was a very definite Resolutioner. His reply to an English champion's plea for Independency is one of the recognised Scots classics in the realm of Presbyterian Church government of his age. In this answer to Lockyer's *Little Stone,* Wood gives the argument which satisfied our Reformers and satisfies their successors still that there is a wider unit of organised Church life than that of the single local Church which is self-elective, self-governing and so far self-sufficing. On this subject Scottish Church literature has had little to say. It has been vocal only when its own system of Presbyterial unity and oversight has been the object of attack. Thus John Glas of Tealing had to be answered about 1730 when John Willison of Dundee led the case against him, and Ayton of Alyth wrote his book on the Government of the Church. Again, when Independency became militant at the beginning of the 19th century, John Brown of Langton—then of Gartmore—wrote with vigour in defence of Presbytery and critically of the rival system. Wood, though he differed from his colleague Rutherford, who was such a strong Protester, was held by him in high esteem. There was in their days at St Andrews another of the great divines of that age. This was Robert Blair. He, like his friend John Livingstone, came in early days under the charm of Robert Bruce of Edinburgh. In the awakening of Northern Ireland his work was richly blessed and his Life in the Wodrow Society volume devoted to him is an authentic account of a remarkable ministry. Blair was a man of great personal majesty, and in the heated wrangles which split the Church from 1652 he took, as we have seen, a leading part with James Durham in the attempt to make peace between the brethren who were estranged. The fate of such peacemakers often is that both the contending sides turn upon them so that they come between two fires. But when heat has cooled down and fury has given way to sobriety the virtue of the peace-maker's efforts comes to be more thought of than when they were rebuffed right and left with little or no thanks. The place that men of such a spiritual calibre held in the Church of the Second Reformation tells of how high the flood-tide of godliness rose in those days. For it was only a spiritual generation that could rightly value such spiritual men.

8. Andrew Gray and Hugh Binning

We have spoken of Gray and Binning as having come under the censure of Baillie. Andrew Gray of Glasgow had hardly passed his majority when his gracious ministry came to an end. The memorials of that ministry had for a long time a wide circulation among the Scottish peasantry. Edition after edition of them was issued in little volumes that are now hard to get, for, with use, they were thumbed out of existence. The last edition appeared in a fair-sized octavo volume about a hundred years ago. Of the writings of Binning there were two rival 19th-century editions, so that they are more easily got than the works of Gray. Hugh Binning was remarkable for his fine gift of expression and for the ripeness of his thought. He, like Andrew Gray, was cut off in his twenties. We have mentioned that he paid some attention to his English style. This, until his time, was unusual among our Scots writers. They had begun since the early years of the 17th century to write in English, though they still preached very often in Scots. The English that they wrote was by no means free from the idiom of their everyday speech. Leighton, however, and Binning took the initiative in giving special attention to the vesture of their thought. A thinker like Binning had thoughts that it was worth a man's while to clothe in worthy words.

9. WILLIAM GUTHRIE OF FENWICK

These two young men—Gray and Binning—excelled both as doctrinal and as practical preachers. But they had among their contemporaries one that excelled even Rutherford himself in the acceptance that his teaching found among the godly of his own and later ages. This was one of Rutherford's own sons in the faith, the fruit of his teaching at St Andrews, William Guthrie of Fenwick, who has lived in the memory of subsequent generations as the author of one book. It is *The Christian's Great Interest,* or *The Trial of a Saving Interest in Christ.* If we except *The Fourfold State* of Thomas Boston, we are safe in saying that no work of divinity in Scotland has had a wider circulation or has exercised a better influence than this one from William Guthrie's pen. He, too, died as a young man, for he was only 45 at his death. As a writer he is remarkable for the soundness of his judgment and the tenderness with which he deals with Christian experience. His book is one of the best-balanced, sober, and considerate of all the treasure of practical divinity that we inherit from the 17th century. It was a favourite in its own day with John Owen. It was edited with an introductory

appreciation by Thomas Chalmers, and about the beginning of
this century Dr Alexander Smellie issued it in a very neat and
handy volume. Wodrow, the historian, was married to a
granddaughter of Guthrie. So we have from his pen such
a full account of the writer as we should look for from
Wodrow, especially from him in his relation to Guthrie's
family. It was in self-defence that Guthrie published. For,
without his consent, so much of the substance of his teaching
was printed professedly from his mouth; and this called for
a corrective which his published work supplied. There also
are in circulation seventeen of his sermons in the volume of
Sermons Preached in Times of Persecution in Scotland.
These, however, though professedly taken down by hearers,
are at a disadvantage as they want the revision and the
imprimatur of the author, and it is only fair to his memory
that he should not be at the mercy of even well-meaning
hearers, but that he should be estimated by what he himself
thought fit to issue from the press.

10. John Livingstone

Among the men of mark of the Second Reformation age
there were few that left such a record as John Livingstone
of Killinchy and Ancrum. He was one that, as we have seen,
felt the spell of Robert Bruce. We have from his own pen
one of the most charming of sketches of his own life. It is
not by any means a studied autobiography. It is a sketch—
a naïve and vivid sketch—drawn from life and to the life;
and it introduces the reader to the goodly circle that might be
spoken of as the spiritual élite of their age and country.
His Characteristics, which the first volume of the Select
Biographies of the Wodrow Society reprints, bring before us
a picture of living godliness as it was illustrated among the
converts of John Welsh of Ayr, such as Hugh Kennedy and
John Stewart, who each of them was Provost of the ancient
burgh. Then Lady Culross and others who were in the circle
of the friends and intimates of Samuel Rutherford pass before
us. There is a little portrait gallery of kindred souls. They
are but sketches given us in miniature, mere thumb-nail

notices; but they show what a leaven of prayer and of power there was at work in those days in Scotland. The country was being prepared, in spite of the appearance of submission to the royal will, for the great upheaval of a renewed National Covenant and then in turn for the successor of that Covenant, the Solemn League and Covenant, which knit the country's destinies to those of Parliamentary and Puritan England.

From Livingstone's own pen we have the story of his experience at the great awakening of the Kirk of Shotts. Here it is : " In that place (Shotts) I used to find more liberty in preaching than elsewhere. Yea, the only day in all my life wherein I found most of the presence of God in preaching was on a Monday after the communion preaching in the Church-yard of Shotts, June 21, 1630. The night before I had been with some Christians who spent the night in prayer and con-ference. When I was alone in the field about eight or nine of the clock in the morning before we were to go to Sermon there came a misgiving of spirit upon me, considering my unworthi-ness and weakness and the multitude and expectation of the people that I was consulting with myself to have stolen away somewhere and declined that day's preaching but that I thought that I durst not so far distrust God and so went to Sermon and got good assistance about an hour and a half upon the points which I had meditated on Ezek. 36 : 25-26, ' Then will I sprinkle clean water upon you and ye shall be clean from all your filthiness and from all your idols will I cleanse you. A new heart also will I give you and a new spirit will I put within you and I will take away the stony heart out of your flesh and I will give you an heart of flesh.' And in the end, offering to close with some words of exhortation I was led on about an hour's time in a strain of exhortation and warning with such liberty and melting of heart, as I never had the like in public all my life time."

Livingstone tells, as Blair also does, the wonderful story of the awakening of Ulster. Much of this is taken over and recorded by Reid in his valuable *History of the Presbyterian Church in Ireland*. We may trace to that awakening as its head-waters the orthodox and Evangelical strain of old

Presbyterianism in the States of America as well as the sturdy Presbyterianism that held its own in Ulster until this degenerate age of compromise and unbelief. We may glance at this again when we take note of the record of the Reformed Faith as it was clothed with power.

Livingstone, after his return to Scotland, was settled at Stranraer and then at Ancrum. It was in this last charge that he was when at the nod of the voluptuary and tyrant Charles II. he was banished overseas and so spent the last ten years of his life in Rotterdam as a banished and silenced minister. In the Scots Kirk of that busy city he had congenial fellowship with companions in tribulation. Among them he might now and then have the chance of opening his mouth as a minister of the Evangel. But his public work was at an end. Among his descendants one of the most noteworthy was Dr John H. Livingston, the Evangelical and saintly ornament in the first years of last century of the Dutch Reformed Seminary of New Brunswick, New Jersey. One of the occupations of the old exile was the work of translating anew the original Scriptures into Latin. He was a well-furnished divine and a good scholar of the old Latin and Reformation type of culture. And so also was Blair and the rest of the eminent men whom we have found to be so many stars in the constellation of the Covenanting Church. Before we have done, there is another yet to mention.

11. James Durham

It would be unpardonable not to give a place among the mighties of his day to one who was among the mightiest of them all. This was James Durham of Glasgow, the judicious Durham. Like Gillespie, he lived for only 36 years. His *Clavis Cantici* was long the key to the Song of Songs for the devout of his countrymen. It belonged to the Commentaries of the Dickson series, and Spurgeon, to quote him again in regard to those valued books, says of it: " Durham is always good, and he is at his best upon the Canticles. He gives us the essence of the good matter. For practical use this work is perhaps more valuable than any other key to the Song."

His exposition of the Ten Commandments is again a treasure of good practical divinity. Take, for example, his discussion of the 4th Commandment and you will see how thorough the sifting process was by which our Reformed teachers came to the conclusions in which they rested in a field that simply bristles with pitfalls. Of his rich exposition of the 53rd of Isaiah, John Duncan said: "Read Durham on the 53rd of Isaiah at my request. He has much repetition and you may be disgusted with that. But it's repetition of a very fine thing, the eating of Christ's flesh and the drinking of His blood. Well, that's what we must be repeating, in fact, all our life long." In the heat of the Commonwealth dispute, when Protesters and Resolutioners were in rival camps, each of the competing Presbyteries in Glasgow did him the honour of choosing him to be its Moderator. From the time that David Dickson heard him as a young captain in the Covenanting army leading the prayers of his company and claimed him for the ministry Durham ran his short course. But though his course was short he left as fragrant a memory as any of the most godly of our saints. In the few years of his ministry he did a work of which the memory is green still for those who feel an interest in the good old cause for which he lived so devoted and studious and strenuous a life and in whose work he abode until eventide told him that the night was at hand in which no man can work. His book on the Scandal of Church divisions has long been looked upon as the Scottish classic on its topic. It had the peculiar honour of being appealed to by the opposing leaders of the Free Church of Scotland 70 years ago, the brave and noble James Begg, the defender of his Church's Constitution, and his young rival, the leader of the party of change, Robert Rainy.

12.   The Faith of the Gospel on Fire

From the days of the Reformation the preaching of Scotland for some generations was an echo or an exhibition of the system of truth set forth in the Reformed Confession. The system was known not only in an intellectual way as it might be learned from the Confession and Catechisms and

Treatises expository and controversial. It was known as a creed, and as such it was held fast from the heart by a Gospel ministry who yearned for the salvation of the souls of their fellows. This meant that the preaching of such a pulpit was not only sound and correct, but that it was also the message of men aflame with zeal for the honour of God and the coming of His Kingdom. It was the happy lot of the Reformed Church of Scotland to have in the ranks of her ministry not a few of whom what was said by David Hume, when he heard John Brown of Haddington preach, might be said: " That man preaches as if Jesus Christ stood at his elbow." Preaching of this kind was to be heard not only in ordinary from week to week; it found a special centre round which it revolved in the services of a communion season.

The type of communion service and season that in after generations became a common feature of national religious life began to show itself in the concourse of hearers and worshippers that gathered round the ministry of men like Robert Bruce when they conducted such services. So it goes back to the early years of the 17th century. The central service of such an occasion was, of course, the administration of the Sacrament of the Supper; the Eucharist or the Thanksgiving. The Latin for this *Actio gratiarum* gave the name by which the Sermon was called—the Action Sermon—as it led up to the Action. This Sermon was devoted to the opening up of the word of the Gospel to which the Sacrament was appended as a seal. That this seal might be understood and appreciated the endeavour was made in the Action Sermon to set forth the truth of our Lord's atoning service crowned by the death on the cross. This brought before the hearer as the broken Bread of Life spread on the Gospel Table the truth that the Gospel proclaims as to who our Lord was, as to what He came to do, as to what He has done and as to how sinners by receiving Him as their own get the good of His service of love. By faith they are to shelter under the covert of His sacrifice in His shed Blood and they eat by faith His broken Body which they find to be the Bread which He gave for the life of the world. So the believer takes his place at the

sacramental table. Such preaching as this was a fitting introduction to the service in which the worshipper as much as
said : " As I take this broken bread so take I the body of
my Lord which He gave to be broken for the life of the world.
As I take this poured out wine so take I the shed blood of
my Lord—the blood that was shed for many for the remission
of their sins. And as I take Him as my own, I give myself
up to Him to wear His yoke, as one of His redeemed ones,
and to do His will." The preaching that led up to engaging
with an understanding heart in this cardinal service of the
Christian confession meant that a solid body of Christian
truth was set before the hearer, and the mysteries of the Faith
were opened up. This served as so much of a guarantee
that the assembled congregation did not engage in the solemn
service of communion in a blind or haphazard way. They
had instruction given to them as to what it all meant. By
degrees the process advanced which met the craving for
serious and suitable preparation for a worthy celebration of
the Gospel Passover until the " preaching days," as they were
called, furnished a regular Evangelistic campaign as the
communion times came round one after another. The
beginnings of this process may be traced, as we have seen,
to the early 17th century. The communion was not often
observed; in some cases in the country it was held once a
year or even once in two years. But when it came round it
rallied to it crowds of hearers and worshippers from neighbouring parishes. And to these parishes in turn there was a
like rally when they held their communion services. Thus
it came about that devout hearers had the opportunity of
observing the sacred service much more frequently than it was
celebrated in their own congregation. And, incidentally, the
Presbyterian unity of the congregations as parts of the one
Church was illustrated. The muster of visitors was often
so great as to allow for the large open-air congregation which
met on the eventful Monday at Kirk of Shotts, when it was
estimated that as the fruit of Livingstone's sermon about 500
were either converted or, having been converted before, were
much helped forward in their spiritual life. This took place

in 1630 and the ripe fruits of that remarkable day were to be found in Upper Clydesdale until near the end of the 17th century.

There is an interesting link between the ministry of Livingstone on that day at the Kirk of Shotts and the Great Awakening that did so much towards building up the Presbyterian Church in the United States of America in its early days to be the mighty Evangelical force that it came to be. There was in the reign of Charles II., during the heat of the persecuting period, an extravagant movement, the followers of which went by the name of the Gibbites or the Sweet Singers. In connection with this movement there was a young man, Walter Ker, who, when the movement was broken up, found it safe to leave his native district and to seek for shelter in the Upper Ward of Lanarkshire or Upper Clydesdale. There he found a home with an aged couple who were survivors, both of them, of the converts at the Kirk of Shotts. They were to their youthful guest what Aquila and Priscilla were to the zealous Apollos. They taught him the way of the Lord more perfectly; and he shed the extravagant or even fanatical notions that he had held when a Sweet Singer. In those troublous times he associated himself with the field-preaching Covenanters and had as a comrade Patrick Walker, the chapman, who wrote the sketches of the suffering worthies of the dark days of the Covenant, which were collected over a century ago and published as the *Biographia Presbyteriana,* and which Dr D. Hay Fleming edited and richly annotated under the title of *Six Saints of the Covenant.* In this work, Walker speaks of his friend Ker and tells us that he was taken prisoner and banished to what was then The Plantation of the Jerseys. The exile made the land of his banishment the land of his abode. He lived to be a very old man and in his later life he was the right-hand helper that William Tennent had as his counsellor and friend. At Freehold he was at the very focus of the southern section of the Great Awakening in 1734 and he exercised a wise and judicious influence in dealing with the young converts and guiding their steps in the way of loyalty and obedience to their Lord. Thus, at the second remove, the spiritual power that wrought in connection with Livingstone was to be seen at work moulding the beginning of the new life of the converts at the heart of the great Evangelical upheaval.

Indeed, on a larger scale the work of Livingstone tells on your American Presbyterian history. We have already taken note in passing of the part he took in the awakening of Ulster in the latter years of the first third of the 17th century. It was the making of the Presbyterian Church in Northern Ireland. There at Killinchy he spent some years of ministry among the Scots planters and among them his work was greatly blessed. The Presbyterian Church in Ireland was thus, through his labours and those of Robert Blair and Robert Cunningham and Josias Welsh and James Hamilton, the daughter of the Mother Church in Scotland. Though Presbyterianism in the States owed something to the Mother Church it owed much more to the daughter. For it was the influx in old Colonial days of the Presbyterians of Ulster who were being crushed out of their ancestral farms that built up in America in pre-Revolution days the Presbyterian Church. This perhaps more than anything else contributed to its strength. Your Alexanders and Hodges were sprung of the Ulster stock. Thus, if we may use such words in regard to what was the working of the sovereign grace of God along a predetermined line, the forces in the spiritual realm that were released in the ministry of Robert Bruce and John Livingstone went far; they lasted long and they may go further still and tell yet in the coming days for the advance of the Gospel.

It was the faith of the Gospel on fire that wrought so mightily in those days of the 17th century. And the Theology of the Reformation with all its plain and undiluted teaching of sovereign grace was the powerful instrument employed in breaking in the spirit of a proud and active race to yield the obedience of faith to Jesus our Lord. The preaching of the godly Evangelical fathers of those days had a solid foundation laid for its earnest application. This was to be found in a rich and full exhibition of the Doctrine of Grace alike as it builds on the humbling revelation of man's sin, and of God's wrath called forth thereby, and, on the other hand, as it sets forth a salvation that is all of God and all of grace in its inception, in its provision, and in its effectual bestowal. This doctrine of salvation they drew from the Scriptures which they took at their own valuation and so looked upon as the very Word of God. The truth of this divine message they laid to heart as it told them their own doom and that of their fellows. The truth, too, of its message they believed when it spoke to them of Jesus our Lord as the Saviour of sinners. They received it as truth when it told of what He has done and won and of how He lives to bestow the life that He died to secure. They would not be content unless they had Him as their own. And as they felt their fellows to be sinners like themselves, under the same curse and needing the same blessing, they yearned over their souls, set forth to them the truth of Law and Gospel and with all earnestness besought them to flee from the wrath to come and betake themselves to Christ the Lord. As they wrestled in prayer with God for power to attend and crown His word they wrestled with their fellows to win them for Him. They bore witness to the truth. They warned of danger. They entreated. They exhorted. They reasoned. They taught. They called. They invited. Nor was their ministry left without the seals that attest the power of the Gospel. For as they were anointed richly with the spirit of their office they preached the Gospel with the Holy Ghost sent down from heaven to crown it with success in His new-creating power.

A message sent forth with such power carried with it its own credentials. The faith that it called into being saw with opened eyes the evidence of the truth that it welcomed. Thus convinced sinners had, like those who heard the Apostles, a witness in themselves which left them satisfied that what they welcomed was no cunningly devised fable, but the very truth of God. A community which got the good of such a message was rooted in the doctrine of the Gospel and tended to become one that was very Theologically minded. And this was none the less the case as the outcome of the Catechetic method of instruction that was current in the Reformed Churches and in the use of which the Reformed Church in Scotland did not lag behind her sisters.

There is a volume edited by Horatius Bonar in which we have gathered together the Catechisms of the Scottish Reformation. These are monuments to the diligence of the Reformers in the task of building up their followers in the systematic knowledge of divine truth. Among them a place is given to the Geneva Catechism. This was much in use, and any one that knows it will acknowledge that a community well grounded in the knowledge of Christian truth as set forth in this handbook had a good foundation laid for the orderly working out of the system of Gospel doctrine. Then we have also another of overseas origin, the Palatine or Heidelberg Catechism in early use in the Church of Scotland. It, along with the Geneva Catechism, is printed in Dunlop's Collection of the Confessions of the Church of Scotland as well as in Dr Bonar's Catechisms. The employment of Calvin's Catechism and that of the Rhineland shows the friendly relation in which the first generation of Reformed Churches stood to one another. This also comes out in the imprimatur that the General Assembly of 1566 virtually put on that most widely accepted of the Reformed Symbols, The Second Helvetic Confession. The general approval that was given to these symbolic documents of the sister Churches of the Reformation shows the extent and the pattern of the doctrinal consciousness that was common to the life of the Reforming movement. The wonderful measure of harmony that was found among the Reformed Churches in various lands was due to the working of a common principle. They had one Rule of Faith and they had one and the same attitude towards it. It was little wonder, then, that when they were content to take and to keep their place at the footstool of their Lord as He speaks by His Spirit in His word they should see eye to eye and be willing to make joint confession of the truth of the Gospel which they had learned in His school.

From the point of view of modern pædagogy as set forth by so many theorists, who aspire to rank as specialists in the subject, exception has been taken to the wisdom of the method taken by the Reformers in conveying instruction. Their critics hold that it was neither wisdom nor sound educational method for them to frame careful statements of Christian truth to be learned by heart by those under their charge. Now we may take it that our fathers never meant to satisfy themselves when a mere rote acquaintance with such statements was attained. They aimed at the opening up of the form of sound words in which they set forth the truth of the Gospel. And when what was committed to memory was opened up by loving teachers at the fireside or in the congregation, the good of having learned the letter of such statements, which were a valuable exhibition of the Faith, came out. And, what was more, those who, in the immature years of childhood, had their minds stored with what at the time when they learned to repeat it might be beyond their reach had, in later years, when their powers came to a measure of ripeness, the chance of working in their mind what they once had learned only by rote. They carried with them from childhood a treasure the good of which they came to know when in after years they asked themselves the meaning of those words with the letter of which they had been long familiar. Often have those who have gone through a course of catechetic training in their early days come to discover how useful this teaching is to them now that in later days they have come to feel the power of the truth. They are like a mill with all its mechanism in order that waited for the turning on of the water that it might work. Once the power is brought to bear upon them they learn to their profit the connections in which the various portions of divine truth stand to one another. And thus they start their new life of discipleship with valuable assets to their credit. When bread is thus cast upon the waters it may be found when most needed—after many days. There is this over and above the blessing that often attends at the time the opening up and explanation of these statements to the mind of the child. For those who teach a Catechism are expected to open up its teaching and explain its meaning.

IV.

THE POST-REVOLUTION CHURCH

THE fiery trial of a long and bitter persecution, to which the
Reformed Church was subjected in the reigns of the two sons
of Charles I., came to an end at the Revolution in 1688-9.
It left the moorlands of Southern and Western Scotland
studded with the graves of humble martyrs who loved not
their life to the death.   It left a memory of honour and of
shame—of shame for the tyrant, of honour for his victims—
that long remained in the heart of the people as a whole. With
the change-over of the Revolution the Presbyterian government of the Church was again recognised by the civil power.
The Westminster Confession, which at the epoch of the Second
Reformation had been adopted as the Church's Confession and
as such had the sanction of the Scottish Parliament, was
again recognised by the State as the Church's avowed
Confession.   This civil recognition had been withdrawn at the
Restoration by the Act Rescissory, but until the Revolution
the Confession which the Church in General Assembly accepted
in 1647 as its Confession, had not this Church recognition
withdrawn from it even by the Conformists during the
Episcopal regime.   There was no question that it was the
Confession of the lawful heirs of the Church which first
adopted it, and now the civil power again recognised it so
that State and Church were at one on the subject.

1. CARSTARES AND HIS BRETHREN

The ministers who had lived through the furnace days
and were the survivors of the old Presbyterian order were
restored to the status from which they had been driven and
to them was entrusted the administration of the government
and discipline of the Church.   If among them there were
comparatively few men of eminence they were not long

restored until they had with them a sprinkling of able men who were of a younger generation. Of these, the most outstanding was William Carstares, who was a consummate man of business. In the polemic department there was quite a school of writers who were ready to do battle on behalf of the Presbyterian model of the Church. Some of them might not stand out conspicuous for the elegance of their style. But they were solid in their reasoning power. Such names, of this class of writers on Church questions, are still remembered as Gilbert Rule and Thomas Forrester and William Jameson and Alexander Lauder and John Park, all of whom wrote with such authority as to be quoted on this subject in after years. It is little enough to say that they were more than a match for their Episcopal antagonists, who were hardly more than an echo of the High Church Caroline Anglicans and who also, in conjunction with the English Non-jurors, soon became higher still. Rule and his brethren, like Shields on the one wing or Vilant on the other or—one who did not live to see the Revolution—Alexander Jameson of Govan, author of an able Apology for the persecuted ministers, were well versed in the Reformed doctrine of the Church as that had been set forth and developed by the earlier Scottish Church writers, and in Holland, France, and Puritan England.

There was one of the ecclesiastical polemics that deserves a word for himself. He was as solid and accurate as his fellows. But he outstripped them in the vigour and raciness and vivaciousness with which he handled his subject. This was John Anderson of Dumbarton and Glasgow, who had been tutor to the Argyll family. There are two of his productions that are fresh and readable still. One of these which has not been reprinted is his series of Letters and Dialogues between a countryman and a curate. The other is a vigorous defence of Presbyterianism which was reprinted in the early part of the 19th century. Anderson College, Glasgow, was founded by one of his descendants, and he was succeeded in his Glasgow charge by the eminent John MacLaurin.

Rule and his fellows knew the home tradition of Melville and Calderwood. It had by no means died out. At the same time as they were firm in their adherence to the Church principles and ideal for which with their brethren they had suffered so cruelly, they were true to the doctrines of Grace. In this they were a contrast to the followers of the hierarchy, among whom Arminianism advanced rapidly as one would expect when a high type of Sacramentarian teaching began to work. To see how decidedly orthodox and Evangelical the restored Presbyterians were one has only to look into their sermons in volume or in pamphlet form, or into such a book as the Memoirs of Elizabeth West, or the correspondence of John Monro. From the former of these books we may see what the type of ministry was that she met with in Edinburgh and the district around it in the last decade of the 17th century. She repeatedly refers to George Meldrum, George Andrew, James Kirkton, John Moncrief and many others. For the notes of the preaching that this diligent and godly servant-maid took down of the many sermons that she heard tell their own tale which shows the quality of the various preachers.

2. THE PREACHING OF THE AGE

The tendency of the preaching was to be experimental as it handled the Evangel in its application, and to be public-spirited in the witness that the pulpit bore to definite Protestant and Presbyterian convictions. The experimental and searching strain of preaching aimed at awakening formalists from their slumbers and establishing believers in watchful diligence and in the assurance of their good state. It wrought, however, hand in hand with a therapeutic method which tended to obscure the openness of the way of return to God and to His favour which the Gospel sets before sinners, and at the same time it made less use than it ought of the freeness of the invitation that shuts them in, as they are, with Divine authority to yield to the Gospel the response of the obedience of Faith. Yet though there was a danger of this teaching developing into a one-sided presentation of the

Evangel which laid more stress in proportion on the side of God's sovereign counsel and the certainty of its fulfilment than it did on the responsibility of the hearer as a sinner to lay hold of the hope that in Christ the Gospel holds out to the chief of sinners, the pulpit on the whole rang true to the Apostolic emphasis on law and grace. Indeed, there was raised up a generation of ministers and of Christian hearers who were worthy of the best days of the Second Reformation age.

3. John Monro

Monro's Letters, which were published by Gabriel Wilson of Maxton in 1722, let one see how a carpenter in Edinburgh could deal with spiritual questionings. The writer died a young man. He belonged to the county of Sutherland, and affords a specimen of the fruits that the Evangel had already brought forth in the Gaelic area of Scotland, and his Letters show the standard of education that even in his day the son of poor and pious parents could have in rural Scotland, far from the seats of higher education.

4. Gospel Power—James Wodrow's Judgment

As to the prevalence of the Gospel with power in post-Revolution days we could hardly bring forward a witness better able from personal contact with things to tell how things were and how they compared with earlier days than James Wodrow, the father of the historian. For about a score of years after the Revolution he was Professor of Theology in Glasgow, and about 700 young men who had been his pupils became ministers. He not only filled a Divinity Chair in the University, he had also acted as tutor in Theology to the Presbyterians before the Revolution in their endeavours to keep up among themselves an educated ministry when the Universities were in the hands of the Conformists with the hierarchy. He had himself taken his Theological course in the days of the Commonwealth, and the early Restoration days before Prelacy was set on foot again. He thus had the chance of knowing well how things were in his youth in the Glasgow area. James Kirkton gives a glowing, if not a too highly coloured, account of what he himself in his later years carried with him as his impression of his early days. He was very much a *laudator temporis acti se puero*. The truth of the account he gave of the pre-Restoration days has been very freely criticised by such a well-informed student as Principal John Lee. Yet if we grant that the picture which Kirkton carried in his memory shows what was the case in only a comparatively restricted area, there may not be so much reason to quarrel with it as a general impression further than that he spread his glowing colours over an unduly extended canvas. In those days one part of the country knew comparatively little of how things might be a score of miles away from home. James Wodrow, however, who was Kirkton's age-fellow and who knew the West of Scotland well, spoke of the spiritual prosperity of his later years as surpassing anything that he knew of the glory of the days of his youth. In Cromwell's days he had seen at close quarters the quarrels of the Protesters and the Resolutioners, and eminent in the Gospel as were the leading ministers of those times, and though they had many worthy godly followers, yet he remembered enough of the seamy side of Church life to keep him from unduly exalting the memories of those early days.

By the way, Professor Wodrow very frankly accounted for the paucity of the Theological books produced by the Scottish divines by the poverty of the country. It had not a reading constituency of any great extent that could afford to buy many books. It was very poor indeed after the failure of the Darien Expedition, and one has only to take note of the poor paper and printing of the books of the end of the 17th century to see the proof of the poverty that prevailed. Were it not for this poverty he was of the mind that Scotland of that age would be no unworthy competitor with the Netherlands in its Theological output. This, of course, was but an estimate of what things might be if there was more wealth.

5. ASSURANCE

We have had occasion to speak of the importance attached in the Reformation age to personal assurance of salvation, and there is a passage in Robert Wodrow's Life of his father that is worth quoting in this connection, although it is somewhat long. Here is what Robert Wodrow has to say : " Some little time after my ordination at Eastwood, coming in to see him as I did ordinarily once a week, I happened to tell him a passage I had lately met with which affected me much. I happened to be in conversation with a worthy and excellent Christian of my charge, under no small depths and distress, and after hearing all the particulars, I reasoned a little upon them, and happened to say that I did not take any of these things to be singular, or temptations not common to man, and I had known Christians, and very worthy ones, under them. Yes, says the other, that was an answer given me a long time ago by worthy Mr John Baird at Paisley, who, after I had told how matters were with me, desired me not to think my case singular, for he himself had gone through many of these things, and some others he hoped I should not be troubled with, and yet he could now say to the commendation of free grace, that for 21 years or thereby (that was some years before his death) he had never gone to his bed without some, he hoped, well-grounded assurance that the sins of the day were pardoned through Christ. When I told this to my father, he said, ' Robin, I knew Mr Baird in part, and he was one of the worthiest men for learning and piety in his time. I can make no judgment on so long a tract of full assurance, unless I knew the man and how he came by it. If there was anything extraordinary he met with that was the ground or occasion of his assurance, I do not so much wonder at it.' " Then the father told what he had heard from Donald Cargill about his own conversion, and went on to say that in the year 1681 he went in and saw Mr Cargill in Edinburgh prison a day or two before his death, and after some conversation asked him how he found matters with him. Mr Cargill answered, " ' as to the main point, my interest in Christ, and the pardon of my sins, I have no doubts there, neither have I been ever shaken since the Lord's condescension to me in my extremity about 25 years ago, which I communicated to you a little after; and no thanks to me, for the evidence was as clear that I could never since once doubt. . . .' 'Now,' added my father, 'if Mr Baird had anything of that extraordinary nature as the spring occasion and ground of his assurance, I do not so much wonder at it; but, Robin, I'll tell you what I can say as to my own case, though I be perfectly a stranger to voices or those extraordinary impressions of Scripture, and I have not been much dealt with in the way of impressions of Scriptures on my soul; the Lord's way of communicating Himself to me was in the road of meditation and prayer . . . and yet,' added he—'this far I can say, that these thirty-nine years I do not remember I was ever two hours, save when asleep, or taken up with other necessary attendance, but I could go, and did go, to God in Christ, as my God and Father.' "

6. ALEXANDER SHIELDS

As regards the rich measure in which the purity of the Gospel was known in the days that followed the Revolution we have the witness of Halyburton, who himself was no stranger to it in St Andrews. But he would not compare what he saw in his own ministry with the glory of the days of Mr Shields or Mr Anderson. Alexander Shields had been the associate of James Renwick in his heroic field ministry and he was afterwards his biographer. He was not long in St Andrews altogether, for he was sent out as a chaplain to serve in the Darien enterprise. With Boyd and Linning, who were his fellow-preachers among the followers of Cargill, Cameron and Renwick, he saw it to be his duty to cast in his lot with the restored Presbyterian Church, and for the short time that he laboured in it his labours were not in vain. Such cases tell of blessings that came down on the Presbyterian Church when it came back to its own house.

Shields was one of the most striking figures of his epoch. In the last dark days of the Stuart tyranny he had been the undaunted field preacher who carried on his work at the risk of his life. When he was satisfied in his judgment that it would be schism on his part to refuse to join the restored Reformed Church he acted on that judgment. This step

many of the rank and file of his former friends among the
hill-folk, as the followers of Cameron were called, refused
to take. He held, however, that the witness which he and
his brethren submitted in writing to the Church of 1690
was of such virtue and value as to exonerate them from
responsibility for the shortcomings and failures of so many
of the Indulged and other Presbyterians in the dark days
and from complicity in the failures and faults of the present
time. In his discussion of the subject of Church Communion
he acted on the old and accepted principles of ecclesiastical
fellowship that were held by Durham and his brethren of an
earlier age. The Cameronian Philosopher, as he has been
called, is best known by his defence of his fellows in the
furnace and of the witness of the Reformed Church of his
country. This work bears the title of *A Hind Let Loose*.
If, as the wise man puts it, oppression made wise men mad
he might be held to justify courses that were at the least
unsafe and irregular, if, indeed, they were not unwarranted,
yet in teaching the limited and delegated authority of kings
and crowned heads he only maintained the principles of
constitutional freedom that had been taught before him by
George Buchanan and Samuel Rutherford and John Knox.
They were Scotland's contribution to the exposition and
defence of liberty.

7. An Uncertain Sound

We have seen to what an extent the teaching of the post-
Revolution Church was true to its avowed Confession, and
the Reformed Faith put forth its renewing energies in the
end of the 17th century and the earlier years of its successor.
There were, however, some of the ministers who had been
Conformists under the hierarchy and now conformed to the
restored Reformed Church in respect to whose loyalty to an
unambiguous Evangel there might be more or less of doubt.
For the Arminianism that early in the 18th century was to
be seen naked and unabashed among the partisans of the old
bishops had even before the Revolution some foothold in
the Conforming ministry of the second Episcopal regime.

Gilbert Burnet, for example, was a decided Arminian, and he stood by no means alone in being so; as Professor of Divinity in Glasgow his teaching would tell on the young men who studied under him. It would be hard to say to what extent, however, this leaven permeated the Episcopal ministry. For among even the Episcopal ministry in the days of James there was such an interest taken in the defence of the common Protestant cause that the militant Protestantism of the London ministers of those days found a sympathetic following in a Scottish reading public which called for the reissue in Edinburgh of some of the anti-Roman sermons printed by the clergy of the English Metropolis. And such an interest in the welfare of the Protestant cause as a rule went hand in hand with loyalty to the Reformed Faith.

The introduction, however, of so many of the Episcopal Conformists to the ministry of the restored Presbyterian Church meant that there was a decided lowering of the average standard of doctrinal preaching. At the same time as there came in along this line a strain of public instruction that was not up to the mark, there was another influence that was at work to modify the type of teaching given forth by the Scottish pulpits. It could be traced to the erratic doctrinal teaching of Richard Baxter in his later years. This was telling on some of the more serious section of the Scottish clergy in their revulsion from excesses that tended toward Antinomianism, and it developed the legal strain which at a later stage showed itself as full-blown Moderatism. The backwash of the English Neonomian controversy affected this school of thought in an unevangelical direction. Yet in regard to the Catholic verities of the Trinity and the Person of Christ there was in this age no uncertain note struck by our Scottish divines apart from the virtual Apollinarianism of the second Robert Fleming in his Christologia. But a score of years later there was less perspicacity and faithfulness shown than there ought to be in dealing with the shifty, tortuous and Arianising teaching of John Simson of Glasgow.

If the younger Robert Fleming ventured to meddle with the accepted doctrine of Christendom as a whole in regard to

the full integrity of the human nature which as a created one
our Lord took into oneness with His own Everlasting Person,
it may be remembered that his field of labour was not in
Scotland but in London. But if he broke away in his teaching
from the Scottish tradition there was a contemporary of his,
also a Scotsman settled in London, who did yeoman service
in the exposition and defence of the teaching of his Church
on the cardinal verities of the Gospel. This was Robert Traill,
who took a manly share in the Neonomian controversy in the
last decade of the 17th century. It was at the time when
the controversy was hot that he wrote his defence of the
Protestant doctrine of free Justification by Faith alone against
the charge of being Antinomian. Traill's other writings, too,
used to be held in high repute as among the choicest and most
judicious Evangelical works produced by sons of the Scottish
Church.

8. SPECIMENS OF THE ORTHODOX PULPIT

For the kind of preaching to be heard from the Scottish
pulpits of this epoch one would have to look into such works
as Alexander Hamilton on Romans VIII., or the volume of
George Andrew's Sermons, or those in fugitive form of
George Meldrum, who was perhaps the most popular of the
Edinburgh ministers. There is also to be found a volume,
entitled *Synaxis Sacra*. It is by John Spalding of Dundee,
who was clerk to the General Assembly in the early years
after the Reformed Church was restored. His work gives a
specimen of the sort of preaching one might look for at a
communion season. It gives also, as well as the Sermons,
the Table Addresses and the Fencing of the Tables. Indeed,
from the place held by the writer it may be taken to be a
representative document of the period. His contemporary,
too, Alexander Wedderburn of Forgan and Kilmarnock, who,
however, did not live to see the Revolution, was the author
of the work, *David's Testament*, in which we see how one
text furnished the starting point of a series of discourses.
From the text the preacher would work out a veritable treatise
in Theology as he opened it up and followed it in its

ramifications. Such a series of Sermons was what went by the name of the minister's "ordinary." We find instances in Boston's Life of the use of the expression "my ordinary." His well-known *Human Nature in its Fourfold State* is a good example of the working out of what is almost a whole body of Theology from a few passages of Scripture. Week by week the succession of these Sermons came round so that often the people versed in Catechetic doctrine could tell beforehand what next subject they might expect to hear handled in the pulpit.

9. Hog of Carnock

In quite a number of cases the Presbyterian ministers of the Revolution age had to fight for their own hand to hold their place in their parishes. For they had to contend with the landed interest, who were often Jacobite in their outlook or, if not, were very lukewarm in their loyalty to the Revolution settlement. The gentry got much more of their own way under the Episcopal order of things. So the lairds and heritors did not take it kindly that they had to accept the Reformed discipline. Difficulties arose also from the machinations of the Episcopal exodus which found that in many instances by their refusal to submit to the civil order they had managed to manoeuvre themselves out of their position and charge as parish ministers. In hundreds of parishes, indeed, the old Episcopal incumbents simply sat tight, as possession is nine points of the law, and when their heritors were like-minded with them, they remained until their death the acting parish ministers. We have seen how some of these incumbents, by conforming to the civil order, were admitted to the ministry of the Church, and introduced and fostered a tendency to favour a kind of preaching that was decidedly legal in its strain. This was preaching which, when it was not positively unsound, was neutral in its character. It steered clear of committing itself to distinctive Reformed doctrine. In connection with the difficulties of the good Presbyterians there is a very illuminating document in the life of James Hog of Carnock. This Autobiography was published towards the end of the 18th century by Archibald Bruce, who, in his country charge of Whitburn, was Professor of Theology to the Anti-burgher Seceders, and was one of the most scholarly and versatile of the divines of his day. Hog's Narrative shows what it meant for himself and his fellows to hold up the banner of the Reformed Church between 1690 and 1707. It was in no way a sinecure to be a Presbyterian parish minister in those times.

Mr Hog, whom we shall see in another connection, was a good Evangelical divine, and from his youth he was a man of war as he contended for the Faith. One of his early works is his reply to Sir Hugh Campbell of Cawdor, in which we may see how a strict Presbyterian, who admired the Westminster documents, was able to reconcile with such admiration his practice in public prayer which failed to give to the Lord's Prayer the place assigned it in the recom- mendation of the Directory for Public Worship. The innovators of the past half-century and more who have managed to destroy the long use and wont of Presbyterian worship in Scotland, tried, as we have seen, to ascribe its plainness and simplicity to the policy of the Protesters in the days of the Cromwellian regime which had a *modus vivendi* with the powers that were, as though by this they favoured Independency and even the old Brownism of England, and borrowed from it their ideas in regard to Public Worship. Such a charge is ill-grounded. For however Wariston and Patrick Gillespie and a few of the Protesters of that day may have been on good terms with their English rulers, the plain worship of the Protesters was but the token of how honestly they fell in with the pattern of worship set forth at Westminster, and so of their good faith in adhering to their Covenant engagements and adopting what, as part of its programme, was meant to be a bond of union between the National Churches of the British Isles. Indeed in this they and their rivals, the Resolutioners, were at one. And it was reckoned no fault in the Revolution Church for a man to have been a Protester 30 years before. For the question at issue between the contending parties was never settled, and it was largely the Protesters and their side of the Church who furnished the martyrs of the Killing Time, and they were well represented in the ranks of the ministry of the restored Presbyterian Church. It was the plain, unadorned Presbyterian worship that had such a baptism of blood which without question came to be recognised as the standard form of worship of the re-established Kirk. And it was this purity of worship that was acknowledged at the Treaty of Union as that which was to be preserved intact in the Church of Scotland after, in 1707, the two kingdoms should become one.

10. CONFORMISTS OF THE LEIGHTON SCHOOL

Now before we turn to look at some of the chief divines of the post-Revolution age there is a little matter that we might first dispose of. There were among the Conformists to Stuart Church policy some men of an Evangelical cast. What of them and the movement, such as it was, to which they belonged? Some of them might find it possible to fall in with the post-Revolution restored Presbyterian Church, but not all. In the 17th century the Evangelical Conformists stood out from their fellows who were loyal to the full and unabated teaching of the Reformed Faith. They were Conformists to the king's pleasure in the control of the Church. It might not be amiss to speak of them as the Evangelical Erastians, for they were Erastian in their subjection to the civil power in the life of the Church. All the contribution that they made to the shaping of the Church's history, so far as they did not strengthen the hands of royal despotism, was in the department of individual influence and personal edification. Their type has been common among the Evangelicals of the Church of England. There they are so far in their place, for they are loyal to the Articles of Religion, and so are prepared to acknowledge the royal supremacy in all causes sacred or civil. Such men in 17th-century Scotland were better versed in the truth in regard to our Lord's Priestly office than in regard to the rights of His kingly crown. At any rate they failed to see in the Visible Church the special kingdom of the Exalted Mediator in which He alone is Lord.

They acknowledged His Headship over each of the members of His Church, but they did not extend that Headship or Lordship to the avowed body of His followers as they make up His professing Church. They owned their earthly king to be subject to the King of kings, but they stretched out the external bishopric that Constantine had claimed as his own to such an extent that they were content to fall in with the sovereign's pleasure not only *circa sacra* but *in sacris*. To this party belonged the amiable Archbishop Leighton, as well as John Forbes of Corse and Henry Scougal. The members of this school tended in their teaching to shade away into mysticism and to exemplify a type of personal devoutness that held itself free from what they felt to be the entangling bond of obligation to observe the Scottish Covenants. The compromise course which they tried to steer was in reality an impossible one. It was, however, their choice. Leighton, the best of them, had to give up in despair of success. He found that he had faced a forlorn hope in trying to conciliate the men of his age to a Church which obviously sacrificed its intrinsic freedom at the call of the king. He had learned also what the quality of the men was with whom he had elected to co-operate. Indeed, his friend and fellow in Conformity, Laurence Charteris, who drew the line at the swearing of the ensnaring Test Oath in 1681 and retired into private life about the same time with Leighton himself, is credited with quoting a remark made by the Archbishop when his eyes were opened to the realities of the situation to which his Conformity had brought him. The words, as given in *The Countryman's Idea of a Gospel Minister*, etc., 1711, are: "It was not without ground that heavenly Archbishop Leighton wished that he with the other twelve (bishops) were cast into the river of Forth with a millstone round their necks, as a no less heavenly soul told me from his mouth." The margin of this Episcopal and Jacobite pamphlet gives the name of Mr Charteris as the informant. Those ministers who, after the Revolution, adhered to Scottish Episcopacy, showed themselves soon as a body to be one of the least Evangelically minded sections of the whole nation, so that the members of the Evangelical Erastian school in the State Church under the Episcopal regime left no permanent mark either on the country at large or on the members of their Church fellowship.

11. An Outstanding Theological Teacher
Thomas Halyburton, 1674-1712

In his *Colloquia Peripatetica*, Professor Knight reports Dr John Duncan as saying : " There are three biographies of which I never tire :—Augustine's, Bunyan's, and Halyburton's. The first is by far the deepest, the second the richest and most genial, and with Halyburton I feel great intellectual congruity. He was naturally a sceptic, but God gave that sceptic great faith. His book against the Deists, in which he deals wisely with Lord Herbert, is a scholastic prosecution of Owenian principle."

In the Life of *Dr Duncan*, by David Brown (p. 411), we have the Rabbi's estimate of Halyburton. These are his words : " I advise every Theologian to acquaint himself with Halyburton. I have great sympathy with his mind. He neither understates nor overstates the value of the law to the Gospel and the necessity of the Gospel to the law. I like his view of a man's acceptance of the Gospel as a cordial approbation of God's way of recovering man. The steps upon which he travelled on the side of the *Gospel* were these, as brought out in his Self-Examination :—(1) ' Have I a cordial approbation of the plan of the Gospel? Am I perfectly satisfied that this scheme both perfectly satisfies God's attributes and is perfectly adequate to my need?' (2) ' In all my darkness and doubt I never wished for another way different from that which is appointed.' (3) ' I am resolved for ever to cling to this, with the expectation—sometimes more and sometimes less vivid—of a good issue.' Then, on the side of the *law* :—(1) ' I do not wish the law altered in any particular.' (2) ' and that even when it runs most counter to my inclinations.' So thoroughly did he go on and into this question of the law, as it were upon himself, that he brought himself to this decision, that he wished no alteration in the divine procedure towards him, but only that he himself should be changed. It may seem a very simple attainment; but if I may judge from my own experience, it is not so easy to consent unto the whole law that it is good, when that means not merely an intellectual assent, but also a moral consent, the ' amen' of the will."

At the foot of the ruined wall of the Cathedral of St Andrews there are two graves side by side, where lie buried two of the brightest ornaments of Scottish Evangelical Christianity, Samuel Rutherford and Thomas Halyburton. Two of the devout matrons of the old-school Presbyterians in the ancient religious capital of Scotland used to have one place that they were wont to visit when they were free from home duties. Those were the days when the tradition held that the housewife was a stay-at-home unless when she went to kirk or to market. The spot that these two went to visit was where in the two graves in the churchyard there rested in their last sleep the dust of worthies that were the glory of their Church and their land. Rutherford and his younger successor were with them names that were not worshipped, but that were more than canonised. So love for the Faith that was theirs and honour for their memory brought the mother and aunt of such a typical old-school man as Dr Hay Fleming to visit and revisit and visit again the spot where lies awaiting a glorious resurrection all that was mortal of two of the outstanding champions for the Faith of Covenanting and Evangelical Scotland. What they were wont to do tells its own tale of the atmosphere in which the defender of the Reformers was brought up.

The name of Halyburton has not such a world-wide fame as that of Rutherford; yet among the great and godly Theologians of his country it holds a place almost higher than that held by the writer of the Letters. In a notice of a reprint of Halyburton on *The Reason of Faith* such an authority as Hugh Martin brackets him with William Cunningham as one of the two greatest Theologians that Scotland has ever produced. Once a day his name was well known among Presbyterians in America when Archibald Alexander of Princeton's choice little work on Religious Experience was widely circulated by the Presbyterian Board. In that book, which one of your greatest masters in experimental religion wrote, Halyburton comes in for the highest and most honourable commendation. Not only is an extended account given of his heavenly exercise on his death-bed, but some pages are given to a quotation from his narrative of his early experience at the time of his conversion. Of this analysis of experience Dr Alexander says: " I have not met with any account which is so full and satisfactory . . . and when it is known to have been written by a man of sound understanding and most exemplary piety . . . when his judgment was matured by much experience it cannot but furnish a decisive proof of the reality of experimental religion which cannot be gainsaid. In these exercises there is not a tincture of enthusiasm. Indeed, holy affections thus produced by the contemplation of truth are the very opposite of enthusiasm which always substitutes human fancies or impulses for the truths of God which it uniformly undervalues. In this case we see how high the exercises of Scriptural piety may rise without degenerating into any extravagance."

The Narrative of which the founder of the Princeton School of Theology had this to say is worthy of being written in letters of gold. If the account that Jonathan Edwards gives of the reality of spiritual light is one of the classic statements of the Reformed Theology on the subject, we have here in brief compass from Thomas Halyburton's pen such an exposition of the reality and character of this light as is worthy of being put side by side with the pages of the writer on *The Religious Affections*. We give it in a very much condensed form. Speaking of his conversion, he says: " I cannot be very positive about the day or the hour. . . . It was towards the end of January . . . 1698. . . . So far as I can remember, I was at secret prayer, in very great extremity, not far from despair, when the Lord seasonably stepped in and gave this merciful turn to affairs. When I said there was none to save, then ' His arm brought salvation.'

God Who commanded the light to shine out of darkness,
' shined into my mind. . . .' He said to me, ' Thou hast
destroyed thyself, but in Me is thy help.' He made all His
goodness pass before me, and proclaimed ' His name. . . .
He revealed Christ in His glory . . .' and I was made, by
this sight, to say, ' Thou art fairer than the sons of men ! . . .'
I saw moreover with wonder and delight how God by this
means might be just even in justifying the ungodly, who
believe in Jesus. . . . And the Lord further opened the Gospel-
call to me and let me see that even to me was ' the word of
this salvation sent. . . .' He, to my great satisfaction, gave
me a pleasing discovery of His design in the whole, that it
was ' that no flesh should glory in His sight . . .' and that He
might manifest the riches of His grace, and be exalted in
showing mercy. . . . The Lord revealed to my soul the full
and suitable provision, made in this way against the power
of sin—that as there is righteousness in Him, so there is
strength . . . to secure us against all enemies. . . . All these
discoveries were conveyed to me by the Scriptures only. It
was not indeed by one particular promise, or testimony of
Scripture, but by the concurring light of a great many,
seasonably set home. . . . But it was not the Bible alone that
conveyed the discovery; for most of those passages whereby
I was relieved, I had formerly in my distress read and thought
upon, without finding any relief in them. But now the Lord
shined into my mind by them. . . . There was light in His
words and a burning, shining light by them shone into my
mind, not merely some doctrinal knowledge, but ' the light
of the knowledge of the glory of God in the face of Jesus
Christ.' The light, that I now had, shone from heaven; it
came by the Word of God. . . . It opened heaven . . . and
it led me up as it were to heaven. . . . It was a true light. . . .
It was a pleasant and a sweet light. . . . It was a distinct
and clear light. . . . It was a satisfying light. . . . It was
a quickening, refreshing and healing light. . . . It was a
great light. . . . It was a powerful light. . . . It was
composing—it composed and quieted my soul, and put all my
questions, as it were, in their due position, and gave me the

exercise of them. It destroyed not but improved my former knowledge. But, as the true idea of light is not conveyed by the ear, so no words can convey the idea of light to the blind. And he who has eyes will need no words to describe it. It is like the new name that none know save he that has it. The first discernible effect of this light was, an approbation of God's way of saving sinners to the glory of His grace. And this I take to be the true Scriptural notion of justifying Faith; for it not only answers the Scripture description of it, by receiving, coming, etc. . . . but it really gives God the glory which He designed by all this contrivance. . . . This discovery of the Lord's name brought me to trust in Him, and glory only in the Lord. . . . And this approbation was not only for a time; but ever after in all temptations it discovered itself by keeping in me a fixed assent and adherence of mind to this truth, and full persuasion of it, that God hath granted unto us eternal life, and this life is in His Son. The next remarkable effect of this discovery was, that it set me right as to my chief end, and made me look to the glory of God, for which formerly I had no real concern. . . . It manifested itself in frequent desires, that the Lord might be honoured and glorified in my life, or by my death. A third discernible effect was, that I was led to look upon His yoke to be easy and His burden light; and to count that His commandments were not grievous, but ' right concerning all things. . . .' I now came to a fixed persuasion that the law was not only just, such as I could make no reasonable exception against, but holy, and such as became God; and good, such as was every way suited to my true interest and peace, and advantage. . . . The duties to which my heart was most averse had now become agreeable and refreshing. A fourth remarkable effect of this discovery was, the exercise of evangelical repentance, which was very different in many things from that sorrow with which I was before acquainted. It differed in its rise. Sorrow before flowed from the discovery of sin as it brings on wrath; now it flowed from a sense of sin as containing wretched unkindness to One Who was astonishingly kind to an unworthy wretch. I looked on Him whom I had pierced, and did mourn. Sorrow formerly wrought death, alienated my heart from God . . . but this sorrow filled my heart with kindness to God and His ways, sweetened my soul, and endeared God to it. It flowed from a sense of His favour to an unworthy wretch that deserved none and was thus a godly sorrow in kindness to God, and a drawing near Him, but with much humble sense of my own unworthiness, like the returning prodigal. . . . A fifth discernible effect was, an humble, but sweet and comfortable hope, and persuasion of my own salvation, answerable to the clearness of the discovery. . . . This discovery manifested that salvation was in the way of self-denial, and trust in the Lord alone; for nothing so soon marred this hope, as the least appearance of self, and stirring of pride. Whenever the glory of the Lord appeared and He spake peace, I was filled with shame, and the deeper this humiliation was, the more the humble confidence of my safety increased. A sixth discernible difference was, with respect to the ordinances of the Lord's appointment. I was drawn to follow them as the Lord's institutions, and His appointed means of our obtaining discoveries of His beauty. I desired ' to behold the beauty of the Lord, and to enquire in His temple. . . .' In a word, I was in some measure sensible of the Lord's hiding or manifesting Himself, according as I performed my duty, and of the necessity of the exercise of grace, particularly faith, in all approaches to God."

It is a pity to have to abridge a document so sane and well balanced. I refer you to its unabridged form.

We learn from the Life of Halyburton how hard pressed he was with doubts and difficulties and unbelief that spoke of the deistic leaven which was so strongly at work in the thinking of men during the years that saw his religious struggles. It was only after a long and sore conflict that he came to be established in the life of faith. In view of such an experience it was not to be wondered at that he took part in the deistic controversy. He had at any rate one precursor among our Scottish writers in essaying the work of Apologetics. This was the first Robert Fleming, who was an exile for the Faith in the Low Countries, and who wrote the work, *The Fulfilment of Scripture,* a book that Halyburton found helpful to himself in affording proof of the reality of serious religion. His own venture in this line bears the title *Natural Religion Insufficient and Revealed Necessary to man's happiness in his present state.*[1] It is of this work that Dr Duncan says that it is a scholastic prosecution of Owenian principle. As one that had felt the brunt of unbelieving speculation on the subject he handled, he discussed the sufficiency of Lord Herbert's Five Principles of Deism. He goes into his subject in the thorough manner that one would look for from a man of his mental calibre and spiritual history. The work is of unequal merit; but he laid out his strength in that region of argument that one would expect him to lay stress upon. He goes carefully into the proof of the Insufficiency of Natural Religion in regard to its discoveries of a deity, its defectiveness as giving direction to the worship of God, and in its discussion of where man's true happiness is to be found. He shows that the light of nature does not give us a sufficient rule of duty, and fails to supply us with motives to enforce obedience. He laid stress, too, on its failure to grapple with the origin of sin and with the means of securing forgiveness if that is to be had. On this last subject he enlarges at some length, and in particular he enters into an elaborate enquiry as to whether repentance is enough to atone for sin, and as to how far one is led to, and enabled to, repent by the teaching of Natural Religion. In this connection he discusses what assurance mere natural light can give as to whether or no pardon is given upon repentance. In dealing with such topics, Halyburton wrote like the solid and able Reformed divine that he was.

The deistic controversy was in its early heat in his youthful days and in his handling of its issues we have a discussion of them from the standpoint of one who accepted with all his heart the Reformed Theology. That Theology was his own, especially as it had been elaborated in the work of

[1] Shedd can hardly have done more than look into this work or he would have formed a higher estimate of its worth. His feeling for literary finish must have swayed his judgment unduly.

British Puritanism, and still more specially in that of John Owen. This connection with Owen's teaching was what Dr Duncan saw when he spoke of Witsius and Halyburton as being of the school of Owen, more approachable, but less than their master. As to what Halyburton might have done had his life been spared one cannot say. He was not quite 38 when he died. Had he lived to see the age of Owen— 66—or Witsius 72, he might have left a more enduring monument by putting his mark, should he do nothing more, on the ministry that he trained and on the Theological teaching of an age that stood in need of the corrective which his teaching was fitted to furnish. His chief practical work is his *Great Concern of Salvation*. It is very valuable, and we can trace the influence of his life in the course of the English Methodist Revival in the 18th century. Sir Richard Hill, in the days of his spiritual struggle, got help from it. And it was given him to read by John Fletcher of Madeley. Let us glance at one or two questions in Theology on which we have Halyburton's judgment.

12.   A QUESTION OF PRECEDENCE

This is a problem in regard to which it may interest you to see the side that Halyburton took in connection with it. It is sometimes asked which precedes the other, the Regeneration or the Justification of a sinner. As a matter of fact there is no precedence in the order of time, though in the order of nature, in a sense, there is. It is through faith as the instrument which lays hold of Christ Jesus as the Lord our Righteousness set forth before us in the Gospel that believers are justified. No sooner does he draw the first breath of a living faith which receives and rests upon the Saviour as He is thus offered to us in the Gospel than the sinner is forgiven and accepted. By his faith he is made one with Christ as his Righteousness and this ensures that his standing is set right as before God. As soon as the knot is tied that unites to the Heavenly Bridegroom, the change of state takes place; and one who was until then a child of wrath is accepted in the Beloved. This change of state is instantaneous, so that there is no interval of time between the first breath of faith and the removal of penal wrath.

Now this faith which unites to Christ and justifies a man who has hitherto been ungodly is itself a fruit of the new birth. It does not by any means precede that birth, nor is it in any degree the cause of it. It is not its cause but its outcome. Yet it is so the fruit of the new birth as that no interval of time elapses between that birth and the breathing of the new life of faith. In the order of time there is not the space that would allow a razor's edge to come in between them. Yet in the order of nature or of cause and effect the one is the cause of the other. The new birth in this sense is the working or the production of faith in the heart and the heart acts that faith as soon as it is wrought. Thus if Regeneration, whose immediate outcome faith is, and Justification which that faith without any interval or delay secures, are each of them synchronous with the first breath of a living faith, they are synchronous the one with the other. Neither is before nor after the other. Yet in the order of nature Regeneration precedes, for it is the logical prius to the faith that receives the Reconciliation.

The soul that thus lives because of the quickening touch of the regenerating Spirit was under the doom of death and deserved nothing else than that the doom should take effect. It is of pure unmerited grace that the quickening Spirit works faith in the heart of a child of wrath. It is for our Lord Who has won life for His clients to bestow that life; and He does as He wills with His own whom He calls from death to life. The called ones had no right to life. They were the heirs of wrath and death, Nay, death might say it had a right to them as its prey. But He Who bore their sin and redeemed them unto God by His blood is entitled righteously to impart His life to them as a thing within His own right. And this He does by His effectual call. It is in His right which He won and wrought out for them that He saves them from the doom under which they lay and so from the death in which they were held which was the expression of that doom. He baptises them with the Holy Ghost. He is then to His ransomed ones their Resurrection, so that their soul, which had hitherto been held in the bands of death, now lives. So the power of His resurrection works upon them to bring them alive. And once He is their Resurrection He is henceforward their Life. When they, through the exercise of their new life, receive Him as the Righteousness of God, they have a title to life in Him and in this title which is theirs in Christ, the Holy Ghost Who wrought on them to bring them from death comes as the pledge of their acceptance to dwell within them and to work out in their lives the fruits of the change of nature that their calling and regeneration has wrought.

In an extended sense Regeneration is a term which includes not only the first infusion of new life in the man who so far has been dead in sin, but the working of the indwelling Spirit, the Holy Ghost, Who is the seal of acceptance. As regards this indwelling and inworking of the Spirit, it is consequent on Justification, for it is the right to life eternal which Justification brings with it that accounts for the indwelling and inworking of the renewing and transforming Spirit of God. By one Spirit the members of the mystical Christ are baptised into the unity of one Body; and in the fellowship of acceptance in that body they receive to drink into one Spirit. Thus the Spirit who quickens in the right of Him Who won the life takes up His abode in these who, as one with Christ by faith, are in Him accepted and have in Him the right not only to life everlasting as the end, but to all that they need to bring them to the enjoyment of that life in its fullness. To bring them to this they need the inward sealing life that will enable them to do to death the deeds of the body and so to live. The Spirit that Christ sends unites the sinner to Himself the Saviour, so that he is born of the Spirit; thus born from above he believes in Christ and in Christ he has the standing of a son of God. Because he is now a son God sends forth the Spirit of His Son to dwell in him. He that hath the Son hath the life. He that hath not the Son hath not the life eternal.

Thus for us everything hinges on our having the Son. In Him the whole salvation of the Gospel is. He took the place of His clients, won life for them, is entitled to bestow it with the blessing of the law, and does indeed bestow it upon them. This He does by calling them to the faith that receives Himself. His call produces the faith that justifies and saves; and so close is the relation between the change of state and the change of nature that as soon as the latter takes place the former takes place too. In the Resurrection of the Lord there was the token of His acceptance in His work; and in the acceptance of Him, the Head, there was virtually embraced the adjudgment of His destined body to life instead of death. This life He lives to see to it that they shall have, so that He is within His own rights when He quickens with His good Spirit those who in themselves are the rightful prey of death. He calls them effectually from death to life.

13. THE OTHER SIDE—Dr A. KUYPER

In connection with this question of priority of Justification or Regeneration, Halyburton has an acute disquisition that goes into the matter with care. He comes out definitely on the side of giving priority in the order of nature to Regeneration, while at the same time he recognised that as to time they are simultaneous. This question of the order of salvation used to be canvassed in the Reformed schools, and we find Dr Abraham Kuyper, in his sketch of Alexander Comrie, coming out with equal definiteness on the other side. Yet though Comrie, as we take it, with his admirer, Dr Kuyper, would give the priority to Justification, the difference between the two answers is largely a thing of definition. When Regeneration is taken in the large sense that embraces the effectual working of the indwelling Spirit of God, it is a fruit of the blessing which Justification brings upon the justified man. It is true that this act of God in grace when He justifies belongs to the category of the relative and not the real; yet it has in it an adjudication to blessing which takes the real form of the indwelling and controlling activity of the Spirit of grace. So the sentence of acquittal and acceptance in the sphere of the relative is operative in the sphere of the real. We may distinguish the two spheres without separating them; and we may rightly lay stress on the strictly forensic character of Justification. ·

We are not free to sunder real and relative grace from one another. The former gets its name not because there is any unreality in the act that justifies the ungodly and that transfers the believer from a state of condemnation to one of acceptance. Such a translation from one state to another is a fact, and in that sense it is real. But when we speak of real grace, we mean the working of the grace of God that affects not our standing but our nature. Thus forgiveness affects the standing of him who was a child of wrath, while inward renewal or the new creation affects the disposition of the soul. The two changes go together; they are inseparable; but the one is not the other.

In Lutheran teaching, which says that Regeneration is through faith, it is an easy thing to maintain the position that this Regeneration is the attendant or consequent of Justification. In the Reformed Theology, faith is the effect and not the cause of Regeneration. In this case the word Regeneration is taken in the narrower and stricter sense that makes use of it to indicate the real change by which the blind come to see, the deaf to hear, the dead to live. In the circles of Reformed teaching where Regeneration is held to follow on Justification, the latter word is used in a sense other than that which it has when we speak of Justification by faith. The latter is Justification in its full sense when the sinful man is actually acquitted and accepted by God in union with the Son of His love whom he receives through faith. The Justification which is held to precede Renegeration in this case is the second of a series of three judicial acts. The first of the series is the Justification which is found in the Resurrection of our Lord, when, having been delivered for our offences, He was raised again for our Justification. As a Public Person Who stood for His constituency, who are destined to be heirs of life, He was given over to death and judgment; and having given satisfaction for them He was acknowledged to be righteous as the Head and Surety of those for whom He acted. So in token of this He was raised from the dead. For death could not hold Him. This was the Justification of the Head for the body and of the body in the Head.· The second of the series is a virtual Justification, which takes place when the Risen Lord pleads within the veil that those whom He has redeemed and who are meritoriously justified in His Person should be loosed from the bonds of spiritual death. As the response to this plea they are called effectually or born again, and thus the second, as the virtual Justification that results from the favourable acceptance of the Advocate's plea, precedes Regeneration and faith. As it precedes faith, it precedes the third of the series or the full-rounded Justification which follows on faith's reception of Christ in His satisfaction. In time the two changes are simultaneous. The question of the priority of one to another is purely one that has respect not to the order of time but to that of nature. Such in kind were the questions that interested and engaged the attention of the scholastic divines of the Reformed Confession. They might at a surface glance seem to be verbal and not substantial. They were not, however, looked at in any such light. Our older divines took very seriously the scholastic side of their work.

When Thomas Halyburton taught that Regeneration in the order of nature goes before Justification, he used the latter term of the full and definite judicial act or sentence which follows on faith's acceptance of the Lord as our Righteousness and of the Righteousness of God in Him. In holding the view that he held on this matter he set forth, as I take it, what was the more common Scottish way of putting the case. For in our Scottish thought Christ as Surety for His own was held to have won the reward of life. And· it is in His title, and not in that of the beneficiary—for at this stage the beneficiary, being yet in his sins, has no title to aught but what sin has earned—it is, we say, in His own title that our Lord sends the Spirit to quicken. Thus, though the man who is to be called by grace is still in himself or

on the score of his personal deservings an heir of righteous
wrath, this does not stand effectively in the way of Him Who
has won life for him to keep Him from bestowing upon His
client the life that He has won.   When by faith they
are made one with Christ, the title to life comes to be the
possession of the called as their own.   Yet still it is in Christ
that they find and hold the title.   To Him they cling after
they have indeed taken Him to be the Lord their Righteousness, and it is in Him that they continue to stand accepted
before God as men who are justified.   He makes over the
title to life to the believer, yet He never loses hold of it as
His own.   It does not cease to be His by being made over
to us.

It may be of interest to put the other answer to the
question of priority in the words of Dr Kuyper, as he discusses
the matter in treating of Comrie's contendings.   Alexander
Comrie was perhaps the most noteworthy of the Scots who
laboured in the Netherlands in the 18th century.   His charge
was not one of the Scots Kirks in Rotterdam or elsewhere,
though he was repeatedly considered for such charges of
which we have a sketch in Steven's History of the Scots
Church in Rotterdam.   Comrie's charge was at Woubrugge, a
village near Leyden, in which he served from 1736 to 1773.
In the National Church he was one of the stoutest defenders
of Reformed orthodoxy against incipient Rationalism; and
along with Hugh Kennedy, an Ulsterman who held the Scots
Church in Rotterdam, he was largely, if not mainly, responsible
for the translation and circulation in Dutch of some of the
best current Scots divinity of his age.   Thus he published
Thomas Boston's *View of the Covenant of Grace* and
encouraged Ross to translate the sermons of the brothers
Erskine, which had a long and extensive vogue among the
peasant folk of the Low Countries.   Indeed, so far as I
know, these old Scots ministers have still a lease of life across
the North Sea when, to the discredit of their own land, it has
almost forgotten their teaching.

But we were to look at Dr Kuyper and his exposition of
the relation in which the two great changes stand to each

other. It will be found in *The Catholic Presbyterian* for 1882, pp. 197-198, 200: " The Lord by a transeunt action first imputes to the sinner the righteousness and satisfaction of Christ which thus becomes not by infusion but by substitution his own, then justifies him on account of this imputed righteousness, and, thirdly, infuses the new life into the justified sinner. This view was always asserted by the Reformers and opposed by their Romish antagonists. According to them in the Act of Justification the sinner is not considered in his own nature, but as he is in Christ. Another question concerned the more direct connection between our faith and Justification. Against the teaching of the Romanists the Protestant Theologians of Reformation times always asserted that first of all the Lord imputes to the sinner the work and sufferings of Christ; that, secondly, this imputation is his real Justification before God; and, thirdly, after this imputation comes the granting and exhibiting to the sinner of what has been imparted already to him, viz., of all the treasures laid up in Christ on account of His infinite merits, and that faith is the first precious gem bestowed on the sinner out of His treasury; which faith, by unfolding its riches, confers upon him in a quite spontaneous way the unquestionable certainty of his deliverance and eternal happiness. The Reformed Theologians held that *in actione Dei transeunte* (the moment in which the thought and will hitherto concealed and shut up in the Divine Being issues from Him and creates an outward reality) first of all comes the imputation of Christ's merits to the sinner being the Justification of the ungodly; then followed the granting of what was imputed originating with the planting in the heart of the *fides potentialis*: and so, finally, the sinner having been made a believer, felt the action in God and leading to the perfect rest of the soul in God's overflowing mercy. The meaning, then, of Justification by faith alone is this :—that by the instrumentality of the faith planted in us by grace, the Holy Ghost induces us to accept and to apply to our own soul the holy benefit granted already to us in the Resurrection of our Saviour; viz., our Justification destined to us from all eternity realised when Christ rose from the dead, and now appropriated, applied, and made true and real for our consciences by the Holy Ghost, but through the instrumentality of our operating faith."

Those who taught that there is a virtual Justification that takes in the order of nature precedence to Regeneration, looked upon it as being in the strict sense a Justification of the ungodly, whereas the Justification of the already regenerate was in their eyes that of the believer who, as regenerate, is no longer ungodly as he once was. To justify a believer may, however, well be called the Justification of an ungodly man, for the salient feature of his exercise as he receives the gift of righteousness in Christ is his deep conviction of his own thorough ungodliness. It is as one who is in himself ungodly that he takes willing shelter under the covert of the Righteousness of God in Christ. He rests in Christ as the end of the law for righteousness to all that believe. In the light of this there is no need to resort to the second preliminary Justification of the systematic series to make out that the gratuitous Justification of the Christian believer is the Justification of the ungodly.

The fact that the change of nature and the change of state are simultaneous so that in the order of time there is no precedence or priority that the one has over the other, makes the discussion of priority one that is scholastic or academic. Regeneration is the production of faith or issues at once in its exercise in the case of the adult. This faith is the first vital breath of the new-born life. No sooner is the man regenerate than he breathes, so that as his faith without any time-lag lays hold of the Righteousness of God his Justification takes place in the very instant in which he passes from death to life. The effectual work of the Holy Ghost in breathing life into the dead soul is the true Regeneration of the sinner who till now is dead in sin. The Spirit comes in quickening might to give effect to the right which belongs to the Redeemer. This is His right, to give life to those for whom He has won it. No sooner does the faith have being that is the issue of His quickening touch than, as accepted in the Beloved, the sinner now justified has as his own the full right to life, and to all that is needed to bring to its enjoyment.   In this is included the indwelling of the Holy Ghost so that because believers are sons, God sends the Spirit of His Son into their hearts, as the pledge of adoption, to cry Abba Father.   He comes to stay in those on whom He has wrought to bring them alive.   It was in their Lord's right that He so wrought.   It is in their Lord that believers have a title to what they need to bring them home. It is in this right that the Spirit takes up His abode in them and seals them.   The Gospel shuts in its hearers to the obedience of faith or to receive Christ as He is offered in its word.

14.   WHAT LED UP TO THE " MARROW " CONTROVERSY?

There were other questions which counted for much in his day in regard to faith on which Halyburton's view of what is its nature and function had a decisive bearing.   We have seen in passing his teaching that the faith which saves is essentially a cordial approbation of God's way of saving sinners through the mediation and righteousness of His Son. And there is no doubt as to the function that one like him of the school of Owen assigned to the faith that justifies. The real Protestant and Puritan teaching on the subject was beyond mistake; but modification of this teaching from two sides created problems for the age in which Halyburton lived and of these we might say a word or two.

In Anglican circles the High Church movement affected what it called Catholic doctrine in the Article of Justification. Without altogether accepting the Roman teaching of Trent it tried to sail as near the wind as it could.   This comes out very markedly in the line that it took in trying to reconcile the language of James on this subject with that of Paul. The clear teaching of the latter had come back to its own in the doctrine of the Reformers.   But this reactionary Catholicising movement sought to make the faith that justifies a kind of *fides formata,* a thing so elastic as to find within its ambit room for repentance and the good works of the penitent. Then this extended faith was made out to be not the mere instrument of effecting union with Christ, but a strict condition, the fulfilment of which is called for that one may win acceptance before God by obedience to the law of faith set forth in the Gospel as a new law. Thus the righteousness of God which is by faith in Christ was set aside as the ground of our acceptance; and our new life as believers and penitents was looked upon as so much of the ground on which our acceptance is built. All this fitted in with the type of Arminianism that we find in such a non-High Church work as Gilbert Burnet's Exposition of the Anglican Articles. William Forbes of Edinburgh, in his *Considerationes Modestae,* in Scotland, like George Bull in England, set the pattern that found a following in this departure from the Confessions of the Reformation.

In meeting the encroachment of a Justifying Righteousness into which, as an essential element, man's own work enters, the Reformed teachers, as they maintained the full and free Justification of sinners by faith in Christ alone, were shut in to lay stress on the position that is held by faith in this important matter. They taught that its place is that of the instrument of apprehension by which a sinner lays hold of Christ and receives and rests upon Him as the end of the law for righteousness. Their teaching on this subject, however, met with opposition from more than the Anglo-Catholics. Men like Richard Baxter, who were swept off their feet by the New Method which became fashionable in the later Huguenot Church, held that to teach that the sinner who believes in Christ is fully accepted before God on the ground of His Son's obedience which He yielded to that law which man's sin had broken, has an Antinomian strain in its bosom. They failed to take in the meaning or the value of the distinction between the law of God in its special Covenant form and in its form of a preceptive index to the will of God bearing upon man's obedience.

The obligation of the law of God as an index to His preceptive will is not made void by the faith that rests on the surety obedience of the Saviour. Nay, the obligation in response to the gracious salvation of the Gospel is one that is more intense than man underlay as a creature. He has been redeemed to serve God with the love and the grateful loyalty of a reconciled and forgiven rebel who is now an obedient child. This obligation of the law as an index to God's will, or as a rule of life, is one that lies upon man as man. It is one from which there is for him no escape. It lay upon man while still unfallen. It lies upon him in his state of sin and misery. It will lie upon man when he is lost forever, and is forever unable to answer the end of his being. It lies upon man redeemed and saved and brought home to heaven. To answer the end of his being will be his unending blessedness. How can it but lie upon man on earth in the Kingdom of God who has been called and born again and justified? He has been redeemed and called that he may serve; and God's will made known is the rule of his service. It is his very privilege that he is under the yoke of his Redeeming Lord, and so is under an obligation to be and to do all that his original creation and the constitution of his nature called for when that nature reflected as a mirror the likeness of God in which he was at first made. By becoming a new creature the believer does not cease to be a creature; and the obligations of creaturehood hold good.

The provision in the Gospel for making the unrighteous righteous was never meant to set aside the elementary and indeed inalienable right which belongs to the Author of our being to claim that His creatures should do His will. Indeed, when our Lord took our nature and became man, this one fact would not of itself bring Him to be under law. To be under law was a distinct step in His humiliation, for law makes its claims on persons and He is Himself in His everlasting Person the lawgiver whose the law is and who is not under law. He took, however, as His own a nature in which He might come under law. He came made of a woman made under the law. This He did, as law is a Covenant of life and of death. He did it on behalf of His clients whose case He undertook as they were under a broken Covenant of law; and in their place He stood. The obedience that

He thus rendered to the law which they had broken was a singular one. It was a thing by itself. The claim of the law in its Covenant form when it was yet unbroken was, "Do," and the promise annexed to this doing was that of life. Its Covenant terms were, "Do and live." This same law when broken did not lower its terms. Nay, as broken, it asked for more as a condition to win life than it did before. Its heightened terms ran thus: "Satisfy and live." This took in all that it had sought before, while over and above its former claim of doing it called for the stroke of judgment to be borne which sin had deserved. If such was the nature of the righteousness wrought out by our Lord, a response in full to the law's claims as a broken Covenant, a thing that He did to redeem His people, it obviously was not meant to set aside the claims of the law which lie upon man in virtue of the very fact that he is a creature. His creaturehood endures as long as his being, and he can come into no state of being in which his Maker is not entitled to claim that the creature shall be all that He, when first He made him, would have him be, and do all that He would have him do.

The concern of Baxter and his fellows on behalf of the claims of law and the secure maintenance of good works and good morals, as though they were imperilled by the free Justification which is in the Lord our Righteousness, was not at all called for. It told, no doubt, of a zeal toward God, but it was a zeal hardly according to knowledge. It was due to their failure to see the profound distinction that lies between the law as a Covenant of life and death, under which our Lord came, and the moral law as an exponent or rule of obedience which furnishes an index to the will of God for the obedience of His creatures. This was a failure that ranged them virtually alongside those very Antinomians whose teaching was such a bogey to them. They both set aside the valid distinction between the law as a Covenant and the law as a rule of life. For it is one of the positions taken up by the Antinomians earlier or later that the law in any shape or form is not a rule of life or obedience to the believer. We find that shunning equally right-hand extremes and left-hand defections from the good old divinity of our Reformers and their school a man like Brown of Wamphray in his *Life of Justification*, and in his Commentary on the Epistle to the Romans, or another like Robert Traill in his *Protestant Doctrine of Justification cleared from the charge of Antinomianism* setting forth the doctrine which from the Reformation onwards was the Evangelical teaching of the Scottish Reformed Church.

The faith that justifies a sinner is that inwrought grace in the exercise of which he receives the Lord Jesus Christ in his obedience unto death as the Lord our Righteousness Who is unto us the Righteousness of God. This is the Righteousness, to use the words of William Cunningham, " which God's Righteousness, required Him to require," as the ground on which the ungodly can stand before Him with acceptance; and it is by receiving the Lord Jesus Christ and resting upon Him as their Righteousness before God that the ungodly, when they believe, build upon this ground. This faith is not to be so packed with various contents as that when we analyse it we find in it love, loyalty, obedience and penitence. It is always attended by all these. They do not, however, enter into it as so many component parts. It is a living faith, the exercise of a regenerate subject. It is a faith that works by love. But in its own proper exercise it assents to the truth of the word that it discerns and consents to the terms on which life everlasting is held out as God's free gift in His Beloved Son. It is a hearty approval of God's way of saving sinful men through the mediation of Christ. In its exercise the heart opens to the appeal and call of the Gospel, and receives Christ as its Bridegroom. In particular, on the one hand it closes in with Him as, in His obedience unto death, the one plea that is put forward to save from death and doom. Thus it receives Him as Priest in His one offering and in His pleading within the veil. On the other hand, there is a giving up of oneself to Him as Prophet, that He may teach, and to the authority of the word that He speaks. It yields also the whole life up to Him as redeeming Lord. Thus it takes on His yoke. So there is in the exercise of the faith that saves what answers to the threefold office of the Mediator. And this fits in with the two sides of the word of promise, " I will be unto them a God and they shall be unto Me a people." The believer takes Him as his own and yields himself up to Him. This is the faith that saves in its full, free and unfettered exercise. It is a faith which has in it both the element of reception and that of surrender. The former of these is the distinctive response of the believing soul to the special grace of the Gospel; and it need not be thrust to one side to give its own place to the element of obedience any more than this fruitful side of faith should have denied to it the importance to which it is entitled.

V.

THE NEONOMIANS AND THE MARROW CONTROVERSY

I.

THE NEONOMIANS

1. THEIR ORIGIN

THE development of discussion in the Reformed Churches consequent on the New Methodism of the leaders of the later Huguenots in the 17th century brought to light a marked tendency to break away from the old Protestant doctrine of Justification. This reached such a height as to obscure the *Articulus stantis et cadentis ecclesiae.* The controversy in England in the sub-Puritan age had secondary results in the Church life of Scotland. The followers of Baxter went by the name of the Neonomians. This name they got from their type of teaching which at this point was of a generally Arminian character. They spoke of a new law of works, compliance with whose demand was held graciously to be a righteousness that won life for the Christian. The Gospel that calls for faith was to them such a new law as called for faith and sincere obedience; and they made the endeavour to pack into the faith that it calls for as much as possible by way of resolution and effort and achievement of a moral character. There was to be seen in this teaching so much of a return to Roman doctrine which ascribes Justification to more than the faith which receives the Atonement. There might be said to be in this line of things a zeal for good works and a jealousy lest Justification by faith alone should make void the law. It looked as if in the last resort Paul must be saved from himself and the leading doctrine of the Reformation would have to be thrown overboard.

The Neonomian type of teaching was a revulsion from

Antinomianism. This reaction was found not only in the High
Church Sacramentarian school of the Anglicans, which was
Arminian in its cast of thought, but also in that wing of
Nonconformity which held itself most aloof from the extreme
of an Antinomian tendency. Thus when in the last decade
of the 17th century the works of Tobias Crisp were published,
and by a kind of trick they seemed to come forth with a
recommendation by John Howe and other Puritans of repute,
there arose a hot controversy that split up the projected, and
so far achieved, union of English Nonconformity, and the
doctrinal consciousness of the orthodox became sensitive and
touchy in regard to any seeming approach to the kind of
teaching that put the claims of law out of action; or it seemed
to betake itself to the other extreme which really put out of
action the Gospel with its revelation of the Righteousness of
God.

2.   HYPER-CALVINISTS

Hermann Witsius was for some time in those years of
King William's reign chaplain to the Netherlands Embassy
in London, and took a share in this controversy by way of
mediating between extremes. It was at this time that he
published his *Animadversiones Irenicae*. In those days, too,
Robert Traill wrote his masterly defence of the Protestant
doctrine of Justification, of which we have already spoken.
The fine discernment of the lines of distinction in Christian
truth that abounded in the era of the Puritans did not, on
an extensive scale, pass down to their successors and the
successors of their successors. The result has been that, to
speak broadly, in English Theology those whose tendency was
Calvinistic inclined to become Hyper in their type of Calvinism,
while the alternative to such Calvinism was Arminianism,
more or less modified in the form that it took. In regard
to the claims of God, each of these extremes worked from a
common principle which they turned to opposite ends. The
Hyper-Calvinistic brethren held that there is no world-wide
call to Christ sent out to all sinners to whom in the letter
the Gospel comes, neither are all bidden to take Him as their

Saviour. On the other hand, they maintained that Christ is
held forth or offered as Saviour to those only whom God
effectually calls. To such positions they came because they
reasoned that man, as a bankrupt in spiritual resources, cannot
be called upon to do what is out of the compass of his power.
He can neither repent nor believe. So it was out of place
to call upon him to do what he cannot do. In this, when
we look into it, we find the common Arminian position that
man's responsibility is limited by his ability. The Arminian
holds to the presence of a certain ability in those that are
called; otherwise sinners could not be called upon to repent
and believe the Gospel. Each side takes up the principle
from its own end. They fail together to recognise that the
sinner is responsible for his spiritual impotence. It is the
fruit of sin; and man's sin does not destroy nor put out of
court God's right to ask for an obedience alike in service
and repentance and faith that His sinful creatures have
disabled themselves from yielding to Him. His title to make
His demand is entirely and absolutely unimpaired. He claims
but His own when He bids man, made in His likeness and
for His glory, serve Him and be the doer of His will as
He makes it known. When He calls upon him to repent He
but asks what He is entitled to. When He bids the sinner
who needs the Saviour receive Him as His own, He is altogether within His rights in doing so. There is a glorious
superiority to man's reasonings shown by Him who bids the
deaf hear and the blind look that they may see. They cannot
do what He bids them do. Yet He claims what is His own
inasmuch as their disability, which is common to the fallen
race, is one that is self-induced. Man, by his sin by which
he fell away from God, has wrecked the spiritual integrity
of his first creation. The mystery—and a mystery it is—of
race unity in the first sin accounts for the present state of
things. Do what we may, we cannot get away from the
obligation that binds us to be all that God would have us
to be, and to do all that He would have us to do. Such is
our sin and not only our misery that we cannot yield the

return of homage that our Maker and King calls for at our hand.

The obligation to do the will of God holds, and this makes it our sin not to honour it. It is our sin that we do not repent when we are called upon so to do. It is equally our sin if we do not believe and obey the Gospel when it tells us of our Lord and bids us take Him as our own. This sin is the crowning sin, and it decisively marks out the unbeliever as the enemy of Christ the Lord. Those who give place in their thinking to the defective and erroneous principle that there is nothing to answer for when there is no power to obey, can find no place in their teaching for commending the Gospel except to those who are already under Divine tuition and have learned to some purpose that they are lost sinners. So the open way that the Gospel sets before the sinner which he may take—and must take—in coming back to God is as good as shut when a therapeutic type of preaching doles out the Gospel to those only who are alive to their ruined plight. Now with this restricted presentation of Christ as a Saviour, the sinner has no end of questionings as to whether or no he is so truly convinced of his sin as to have a warrant to stretch out his hand to take off the Gospel table the Bread of Life as his own. When such a view of things was taken, it tended to make the staple of pulpit work, when it dealt with the hope of salvation, a discussion of case divinity that treated of the stages of effectual calling and new obedience. The prevailing cast of preaching was experimental, and its interest was centred on the work of the Spirit in those who were called by grace more than on the fullness and freeness and suitableness of the Son of God as a Saviour for those that are lost. The note of warning for the unbelieving and the impenitent did not get its own place, and no more did the wooing note that sought to win the sinner to the obedience of faith. The outcome of this kind of preaching was that the eye of the hearer was directed to the hidden man of the heart to the obscuring of the call to look out and away from self to the Saviour. It is not in self in any shape or form that we can find the fullness or the help

or the life that we need. It is in the fullness of the Saviour
that there is a supply for all the sinner's need, and the hearer
of the Gospel has to learn to put forth the faith, that goes
out to Christ, for all that will meet his need, and that looks
away from everyone else as a source of help and hope.
Unbalanced preaching of a closed system thrust to one side
the lesson taught by the looking of the dying Israelite to the
brazen serpent, though such a look was the one way of cure
for him in whose veins the poison of sin was working out
death. In other words, an unduly introspective and one-
sided presentation of the truth that bears on the enjoyment
of God's favour took the place of the free, if also the one-
sided, message of the early Reformers. This earlier message
bore witness to Christ in His fullness and freeness, and bade
the hearers take Him as their own and live in the happy
confidence that He was theirs, and that in Him they had life
and salvation. A kind of preaching that side-tracked the
Evangel and fenced and hedged with elaborate restrictions
and conditions the enjoyment of God's free salvation was one
that, like Hagar, gendered to bondage. Its prevalence invited
a protest and called for a reaction. This reaction, to be
well and wisely managed, must shun the extreme opposite
to that from which it reacted. So when *The Marrow of
Modern Divinity* was found by Thomas Boston in Simprin,
and he tasted it to be as marrow to his soul, there was the
beginning of a reaction. At first this movement was misunderstood and met with much opposition at the hand of those
who clung to the use and wont of a developed Protestant
Scholasticism. Things had come into a state of confusion and
were in sore need of being cleared up.

3. JAMES HADOW

When Boston had devoured the book on which he set such
a value, and from which he felt that he had got so much
good, he let his friends hear about it and it came to be known
in their circle. One of his good friends was James Hog of
Carnock, of whom we have spoken already, and who was
among the best-read and most public-spirited men of his age

in the Scottish ministry. Hog sent *The Marrow* to the press to be reissued, with a preface from his own pen. Carnock, where the editor of this reissue had his charge, was in the Synod of Fife, so that Hog had as his co-Synodals the divines of St Andrews, and among them Principal Hadow, who became the leader in the attack on the teaching of *The Marrow*. Hog was like his friend Boston, one of the exponents of the genuine free principles of the Reformed Church. The old University of St Andrews, soon after the death of Halyburton, came under the influence of a kind of Church life that was more inclined than was right for it to come to terms with the powers that be in civil life as they encroached upon the freedom of the Church. Hadow, while not by any means like the later Moderates, was of the compromising, mediating tendency, which, while it professed a high regard for sound doctrine, was yet not at all prepared to put up a fight for the rights of the Christian people for which the old Reformed divines stood. A man in his position was naturally in touch with the " ecclesiastical machine," or, as it came in after times to be called, " the circumtabular oligarchy," which virtually held the reins of government in the Church's annual Parliament. When Hadow read the little book which his county neighbour republished, he was quick to take alarm in his zeal for orthodoxy. He scented in *The Marrow* the presence of unsound teaching in regard to quite a number of things. For one thing he satisfied himself that the writer of *The Marrow* was a sly Antinomian, and this initial judgment coloured his whole treatment of the book. So he laid his lance in rest and had a bout of tilting at windmills. In particular, he laid stress on the six paradoxes of the writer in regard to the law and sin which might easily, unless carefully guarded, be taken in an offensive Antinomian sense. By the way, three of the six were but echoes of words of Scripture.

Hadow was a systematic divine of the kind that are so wedded to their own technical nomenclature that they take it ill that their terms of art should be used in a sense that diverges from that in which they employ them themselves.

He was, however, by no means alone in his keen opposition to *The Marrow*. In Professor Dunlop's masterly discussion of *The Uses of Creeds and Confessions*, he indicates clearly his opposition, and he might be taken as a specimen of the orthodox men of Glasgow training, and so might be classed as of the same school as Robert Wodrow, who was one of the Committee on Purity of Doctrine. There was another West of Scotland man, Thomas Blackwell of Paisley, who was also active in opposition. There are two works of his that have been published, his *Methodus Evangelica* and his *Schema Sacrum*. In these he shows himself a competent theologian, though it is obvious that he belonged to the Therapeutic school, and that he did not give due prominence to the freeness of the Gospel Invitation, which is extended to all its hearers. He would quite likely insist more on the obligation lying upon them to obey the Law of Faith than on the openness of the access set before them by way of invitation and the free offer of Christ. In later years Blackwell became Professor of Divinity, and Principal in Marischal College, Aberdeen. The opposition of such men to *The Marrow* was not that of unevangelical divines, but of men who were orthodox in the Reformed Faith, and who had got into a groove which led in the direction of Hyper-Calvinism. Dr Cunningham speaks of Hadow and Boston as having, as often happens in theological discussions, " divided the truth between them in the points controverted." In saying so he is at least sufficiently generous to Hadow. But the mention of Thomas Boston in this connection calls for a notice of that remarkable man and good divine who, along with Hog, led the fight against the legal strain of teaching which came in with Neonomianism and which eclipsed the Gospel and abridged its freedom.

4. THOMAS BOSTON AND " THE MARROW "

Boston of Ettrick is one of the brightest lights in the firmament of the Reformed Church in Scotland. He was born in 1676, so that from the experience of his early years he could tell of those dark days when the cloud of wrath

seemed to settle down on his Church and land. He was but
a boy when he had his first taste of the power of the Gospel.
This he got from the preaching of Henry Erskine, the father
of the two brothers, Ebenezer and Ralph, with whom in later
life he was to be so closely associated in making a stand for
a free offer of the Gospel. We have the advantage of looking
at this great and gracious divine, not only in the light of his
other work and the impression that he made upon the men
of his age, but from the frank pages of the *General Account
of my Life,* which he himself wrote. This autobiography is
one of our Scots religious classics in the realm of spiritual
self-portraiture. The work, however, of his pen that has left
its mark deepest on the world is his *Human Nature in its
Fourfold State.* There is no book of practical divinity, not
even William Guthrie's *Trial of a Saving Interest in Christ,*
nor Rutherford's Letters, that was more read in the godly
homes of Scotland than this treatise. It did more to mould
the thought of his countrymen than anything except the
Westminster Shorter Catechism. Such a pre-eminence earned
for it the distinction of being a favourite target for the sharp-
shooters of the Broad Church School. Thus, for example,
George MacDonald made one of his heroes hide his aunt's
copy of it in his fiddle case, where the worthy lady would not
be likely to look for the book of which she was so fond
and which the scapegrace so heartily disliked. Very different
was the estimate of the American Western reader who, as Dr
W. P. Breed tells, a century and a half after Boston was at
his rest, directed a letter to him c/o The Presbyterian
Board of Philadelphia. This appreciative reader was such an
admirer of the book that he wished the author to let him
know of any further works that he might write that they
might find from him such a welcome as he gave to the
Fourfold State.

It is of this work that Jonathan Edwards says that it
" shows Mr Boston to have been a truly great divine."
These words were written in 1747, in a letter to his corre-
spondent in Scotland, Thomas Gillespie, one of Boston's
converts, who was in a few years to become the centre figure

round which militant Moderatism executed its war dance, and at whose head it launched the bolt of deposition from his ministry. He thus became one of the founders of the Synod of Relief. It seems from Edwards' letter to Gillespie, in which he gives such a high estimate of Boston, that he did not agree with how the latter set forth the Covenant of Grace. Indeed, he says that he does not understand his scheme. In saying this he might have in view the fact that Boston did not adopt the old and widely accepted way of distinguishing the Covenant of Redemption between the Father and the Son from the Covenant of Grace which is built upon it. It is by the Covenant of Grace in which Christ is Mediator that the believer comes into possession of the good things promised in and secured by the Covenant of Redemption. The school of Boston were wont to say that the Covenant of Grace was made with Christ as the Head and with His chosen people in Him. It was not unlikely in regard to such a view which set aside the distinction between the Covenant of Redemption and the Covenant of Grace that Edwards expressed this opinion. He does not indicate in particular what he took exception to in the work. If it was not what we have suggested, it may have been what Boston has to say in regard to the nature of faith, for the school of Edwards fell foul of the " Marrow " doctrine of faith and of assurance in Bellamy's review of James Hervey's *Theron and Aspasio*. Now Boston's view on these matters was that of Hervey, or rather it was the other way about, for Hervey was a follower of the " Marrowmen," while Boston was their leading teacher. It is not uncommon in those olden-time disputes to find that the quarrel turned on the particular sense in which words were employed. Men were wedded to the terms of their scheme and system. The system used words in its own sense, so that the difference of a shade in the meaning attached to the key words employed might work out inconsistent or seriously discrepant results in the further stages of inference or exposition or application. It would be well in such cases to come to an early understanding as to the sense which words bear when they are the hinges on which a formulated scheme turns. The quarrels that spring from misunderstanding of crucial terms lend a little colour to Goethe's gibe that Theology as a study deals with words and their uses. In the chief theological discussion of Boston's own career, the "Marrow" controversy, there was a good deal of cross-shooting due to misunderstanding as to the precise scheme of the Covenant in regard to which the dispute raged. For there was a variety of schemes.

Strife in regard to cardinal terms was a legacy from the discussions of the previous century in which the innovations that could be traced back to Cameron affected the substance as well as the form of the teaching of his followers. Brown of Wamphray, who it may be was our greatest divine between Rutherford and Halyburton, in his discussion of Baxter's views in his *Life of Justification Opened,* is valuable as showing the reaction of orthodox Scottish divinity to the innovating scheme which came over from the French schools of Saumur and Sedan. So firmly were divines wont to adhere to their own scheme of Covenanting doctrine as an organon in Theology, that they would fight for it tooth and nail. They were not disposed to adjust their thinking to the setting of a new terminology. So they could fight about the term condition. They did not agree as to when it was a condition strictly so called and when it was only a *sine qua non.* They might agree to say that faith is a condition of a personal interest in the blessings of Redemption. But was that faith only an instrument that effected union with Christ, or was it truly the condition to win life that is proposed by the Law of Faith as though it were a new Law of Works? The opposition to the use of the term condition as applied to faith was very keen on the part of the "Marrowmen." Much of the zeal that they showed in opposing it was due to the place assigned by the followers of Baxter to faith and obedience, as though these were the proximate ground of the justification of the sinner and not merely the one of them the condition of application which ties the knot between the sinner and the Saviour, and the other the outcome of the union thus brought about. What ties the knot is faith, while obedience or works are the outcome of the living faith, which alone is faith indeed.

Boston brought a fresh and vigorous mind to bear on a variety of problems in Theology which he handled in his Miscellany Questions. Here we see how the men of his school were moving away from some of the positions that were taken up and held by Rutherford and the divines of his age. These were in the realm of Ecclesiology and related to the nature of the Visible Church and its constituent membership. One might almost say that the leaven of something like the old Independent views of Church fellowship was modifying the older Presbyterian ideas of the Covenanting age. Indeed, when the case of John Glas was dealt with by the Church, there was what looked very like a rift in the ranks of the brethren who had come to be looked upon as a party by themselves owing to their common stand on behalf of *The Marrow*. Those of them who lived to the north of the Forth concurred in the discipline meted out to Glas, while those of them who lived south of the Forth were thought to be in favour of less drastic action. Two of Boston's most intimate friends went as far indeed as to graft a Congregational Church on to the Presbyterian polity of their charges. And yet they were allowed to hold their regular Presbyterian standing in spite of this. Their action was winked at. These were Henry Davidson of Galashiels and Gabriel Wilson of Maxton. What they did seems to have gone further than the mere grouping of serious people into fellowship societies. There were in the 18th century many private Prayer and Fellowship Societies, admission to the membership of which was strictly guarded. These bore a certain likeness to Independent Churches. They did not, however, take upon them to meddle with the Sacraments. They were thus rather Conferences and Societies than Fellowships or Communions. They exercised a watchful kind of discipline in regard to admission, recognition and exclusion of their membership. They were found in many parts of Scotland. Co-option was not always the door that admitted to membership of such societies. Wodrow, who could not be said to have much sympathy with

the " Marrow " way of putting things, was almost gleeful
when the appearance of a division could be seen in the ranks
of those who had as one band stood so stoutly side by side
in defence of what they looked upon as the very pith and
core of Gospel truth. He looked upon their action as more
or less of a factious kind.

When we link the names of the two contemporaries
together, Wodrow and Boston, it is of interest to note how
provincial a man's reputation might be in his own day whose
name is as closely associated as any with the history of his
own age in the judgment of posterity. When Wodrow had
occasion to write one of his yearly bulletins to his wife, in
which he gave her an account of the General Assembly, it
was obvious that when Boston first came within his ken the
historian of Eastwood had little, if any, idea of the outstanding qualities of the pastor of Ettrick. He was to him
but a country brother from another Synod. Those were the
days when the Synod played a part in the Presbyterian polity
of Scotland that belongs to a fast-receding past. The means
of communication have knit the country into one, so that it
is now no longer the formidable thing it once was to go on
a journey to the General Assembly in the Capital.

In his secluded upland parish, Boston was a model of
studious diligence, and in his Autobiography we have the
record of memory and of his conscientious review of his inner
life and experience. Dr John Duncan speaks somewhere of
Boston's conscience as having been, in the Scots phrase, a
" pernickety " one; that is, one that paid heed to details, even
petty details, and did so with undue rigour of self-scrutiny
and self-censure—scrupulous in fact. In his manse in Ettrick
he kept in touch with the big public questions of his day,
and at the same time fought his pastoral battles as he sought
to break in his people to godly order and discipline. Thus
he had his troubles, not only with ungodliness untamed,
unabashed and unbroken, but also with the right-hand
extremes of the Cameronians, the Hill-men, who stood aloof
from his ministry. Of this latter problem there is an extant
monument in his sermon on the sin of Schism, in which he

taught the self-same doctrine of Church unity that found favour with the divines of a century before his time. They recognised but one " face " of the Church in Scotland and had not learned to stretch their doctrine of Church unity so as to find room in the one Church for a number of distinct, and even rival or at least separate, denominations. We are familiar with a different state of things.

The libraries of country pastors were not too richly furnished with books. This meant that diligent students made the most of what they had and were all the more willing to welcome and value accessions to their stores and to master what they had in hand. There were, however, valuable theological works to be had for use in the several Presbyterial libraries. In his study Boston came to be perhaps the most thorough student of his Hebrew Old Testament that Scotland had in his day, or, indeed, at almost any time. He made a special study of the Hebrew accents. In his early days the discussion raised by Louis Capel as to their value and authority was still a burning question and the matter was a live issue. Boston would go at least as far as Francis Turrettine or Heidegger in the importance that he attached to the power and value of the Massoretic points—that they bore witness to an authentic and trustworthy tradition. His pet study was to find out the precise meaning and substance of each of these points and of the whole accentual system as a unit. His *Tractatus Stigmologicus Hebraicus* was the outcome of these studies. It was published a few years after his death, in the Netherlands, in 1738; and in 1752 it saw a second edition. This small quarto in Latin is a lasting monument to the painful thoroughness with which he wrought in his chosen field. It is likely that it is the most elaborate treatment that any Hebrew question has met with at the hands of the Scottish ministry.

In the handling of the case of Professor Simson, Boston at one stage stood alone in dissociating himself from what he thought an inadequate censure of serious error. He regarded the finding of the Assembly as the unduly lenient treatment of a man whom he looked upon as deeply implicated in deadly heresy; and this man as a Professor of Divinity was in a position to do untold harm to the rising ministry of the Church. As a matter of fact, Simson was the means of disseminating unsound teaching and was untrue to the cardinal verities of his Church's Confession, to the maintenance of which he was pledged. Not only was he tainted with the Neonomianism of England, but he could not be trusted to set forth or defend the mystery of the Trinity in unity. His teaching wrought havoc among the ministers of the Synod of Ulster, the most of whom studied at Glasgow. The result was a long and widespread prevalence of Arianism in Northern Ireland. It is to this instance of solitary witness that his friend, Ralph Erskine, refers in his elegy to Boston's memory. " The great, the grave, judicious Boston's gone, who once, like Athanasius, stood firm alone."

The hard work that was done in the study of Ettrick manse found an outlet in the press, and not the least important piece of service that Boston did was to be seen in the Notes with which he enriched the 1726 edition of *The Marrow*. This edition he issued anonymously. The name of the publishing editor was given as Philalethes Irenaeus. In that connection, too, he took his full share in preparing the elaborate answers which the " Marrowmen " gave in to the Assembly's Commission on Purity of Doctrine. It is a matter of interest, as casting light on the state of theological erudition, to take note of the divines, home and foreign, from whose writings the " Marrowmen " quoted or to whom they appealed as men of acknowledged standing and weight. These were— *English* : Pemble, Burgess, Perkins, Owen, Manton, Gouge, Cross, Dod and Cleaver, Parr, Troughton, Robert, Willet, Jeanes, Amesius; *Scots* : Knox, Boyd of Trochrig, Brown of Wamphray, Adamson, Craig, Bruce, Davidson, Dickson, Durham, Forbes, Gillespie, J. Melville, Rollock, Rutherford, Scharpius, Traill; *Foreign* : Luther, Melanchthon, Calvin, Beza, Chamier, Rivet, Maresius, Witsius, Mastricht, Wollebius, Zanchius, Paraeus, Danaeus, Junius, Piscator, Alting (H. and J.), Gomarus, Bucanus, Polanus, Walaeus, Wendelinus,

Essenius, N. Arnold, Riissenius, Heidegger, Turrettine, the Leiden Professors.

Appeal was also made to documents of Church authority, such as The Articles and Homilies of the Church of England, The Lambeth and The Irish Articles, The Helvetic Confession and The Palatine Catechisms, The Belgic Confession and The Belgic and French Catechisms.

The Commission on Purity of Doctrine had submitted to his brethren and himself a formidable questionnaire by way of doctrinal inquisition. In this whole business the minister of Ettrick had a leading part to play. It is so much of the irony of history that the man whose name came to be popularly associated with the high-water mark of Scottish orthodoxy had to run the gauntlet of such a suspicious inquisition as sought to trip up and condemn himself and his friends. It looked as if they did not come up to the standard of the orthodox faith which the inquisitors held to be that of the Church.

The Committee on Purity of Doctrine was not an *ad hoc* body set up to deal only with *The Marrow*. It was in existence for some time before the famous case came under its notice. The Assembly in those years was on edge with suspicion in regard to any doctrine that could be at all plausibly construed as making in the direction of Antinomianism. On this subject the Baxterians were ready to make an outcry. At the same time the Church had, in the hands of its managers, shown itself culpably lax when the very citadel of the Christian faith was in danger owing to the teaching of John Simson. It used to be said, with what measure of truth we do not venture to affirm, that in Scottish courts the saying held good, " Show me your kin, and I will show you your law." In Church circles such partiality in judgment was not unknown. The first Simson case dragged over three years, from 1714 to 1717; the second lasted even longer, from 1721 to 1727, and in the end the heretic was merely suspended from his functions, but left in the enjoyment of his emoluments. Such a record did not compare at all well with the sharpness and haste of the Assembly's

Committee in its dealing with the alleged unsoundness of *The Marrow*. The Committee was to make up for left-hand defections by right-hand extremes.

II.
THE MARROW CONTROVERSY

1. Its Course

The Marrow controversy brought to a head the conflict of two strains of teaching that could not be reconciled. There was that way of putting things which dealt in a very grudging and gingerly fashion with the grace of the Gospel, and fenced its freedom with such restrictions and conditions as turned it into a New Law and abridged the comfort and assurance of salvation that believers are warranted to cherish. There was, on the other hand, the type of doctrine that made Christ the all-in-all of salvation and that secured the interests of law and morals, not only in the way of setting forth the just claims of law as such, but also in that of stressing the absolute need of having the law written in the heart and heeded in the life, if a man is to be free to conclude that he is indeed in Christ and that Christ is in him as his true life. This mould of teaching did not make our obedience, less or more, the condition that satisfies the Covenant claim of the law. New obedience is the way that leads to the Kingdom, but not the procuring cause of the title to the blessedness of its children. The one strain was the teaching of the Legal, the other of the Evangelical school. The one dealt in merit which lives from man to man and which even aspires to lay his Maker under obligation. The other rested for acceptance before God in the merit of Another, who took our nature and place that he might save from everlasting death. The one in its ethos looked back to the refinements of the schoolmen on which an imprimatur was stamped at Trent; the other is reminiscent of the Wartburg and Geneva.

In the course of the English Neonomian passage-at-arms in the decade 1690-1700, the Baxterian school was disposed in a wild and indiscriminating way to charge the orthodox with making void the law when they taught that as a Covenant of life and of death its preceptive claim, as well as its punitive sanction, had been met in the work of the Lord our Righteousness. They treated it as a mere figment of the theological schools that the distinction should be drawn between the law as a Covenant of life or of death and the law as a Rule of obedience which, as the law of Christ, opens up the will of God to regulate the homage to be paid to Him by His redeemed people. Thus the Antinomians and they came to be almost at one; and in common they rejected the well-considered and balanced teaching of the Reformed Churches, as currently accepted by sound divines and embodied in the statements of the Westminster Confession, in regard to the law as a Covenant and as a Rule.

Now some of the men of this legal or unevangelical strain held a high place in the councils of the Church of Scotland and they posed as the champions of law and good morals. This they did at the price of setting aside the teaching of their own avowed Confession. They were the advance guard of a retreating host that was giving up the high ground which had been won and held in the doctrinal advance of Reformation and post-Reformation days. They were the pioneers of the school which, under the regime of Moderatism, had no place in their teaching for the special, gracious provisions of the Evangel and nicknamed those who preached it as " Highflyers." This epithet was applied to the Evangelicals in this connection because, forsooth, they took to do with the high theme of a supernatural order of Grace which set forth and stressed the mysteries of the Gospel, that of Godliness, that of Reconciliation, and that of the New Birth.

The suggestion that a doctrine was unfriendly to the interests of good morals was enough to bring it under suspicion, although it might be that there was not a scintilla of evidence to give ground for the imputation. There are timid souls who are easily carried by a cry. They hear a slogan; they take it to be as good as it sounds; they answer its call; they stampede. It was largely on the fears and prejudices of such a constituency that in an unscrupulous

way the promoters of the unevangelical tendency played. The
men who were outspoken in their attachment to an unabated
and unmutilated Evangel were with them suspect. So when
one of these, so prominent among the Evangelicals as Hog
of Carnock, prefaced and recommended an English work of
the Cromwellian days, even though it had met with the
approbation of some of the Westminster divines, this gave
a chance to the shortsighted guardians of the Faith to distinguish themselves by their zeal for purity of doctrine. The
very men who were disposed to be lax and lenient in dealing
with a scion of the old Levitical Church families in the
person of John Simson—Hadow, however, opposed Simson
on his second trial—were at once up in arms against an exotic
production which came from an age when England was known
to be overrun with the vagaries and fantastic dreams that
marked the era of the Long Parliament. It was easy to
generate prejudice. There was a Presbyterian prejudice that
could be played upon as against a book by an Independent.
Indeed Independency is still a favourite bogey with a certain
school of High Presbyterians.

It is but fair, however, to bear in mind that the
Evangelicals sometimes gave a handle to their opponents by
the incautious way in which they expressed themselves. For
example, a few years before the "Marrow" came upon the
carpet, the Assembly had condemned the "Auchterarder
Creed," as it was called. This was an attempt on the part
of a Presbytery to checkmate legal doctrine by getting an
avowal from would-be licentiates that sinners as such are
called upon to come to the Son of God if they would forsake
sin and flee from wrath. The schools disputed in regard
to the relative priority of faith and repentance. The form
in which the Presbytery of Auchterarder put its test was,
to say the least of it, unfortunate and lent itself to mis-
construction. The proposition offered for subscription said :
"It is unsound to teach that men must forsake sin in order
to come to Christ." What was aimed or struck at was the
teaching that one has to qualify for coming by faith to Christ
by first forsaking sin, as though the coming to Him was not

itself a forsaking of sin, and saving faith and true repentance were not inseparable. This proposition was now under the ban of the Assembly and any teaching that leaned in the same direction as this proscribed test was looked upon with suspicion. In connection, too, with *The Marrow* itself, there were a good many unguarded expressions that, taken by themselves, had an Antinomian sound. These had to be explained and glossed when Boston came to edit the work in detail. This was the case in regard to what were called the "Antinomian Paradoxes"; and some of the more incautious expressions of Martin Luther had to be taken not exactly in a literal sense. The atmosphere of suspicion and jealousy that had been generated for years in the realm of purity of doctrine was that in which Hog's edition of *The Marrow* saw the light. It soon caught the eye of Principal Hadow.

The Principal of St Mary's College, St Andrews, entered the lists against *The Marrow* with hearty goodwill and there was soon on foot a war of pamphlets. The offending book was brought under the notice of the Committee on Purity of Doctrine. It was by them reported on to the General Assembly. And the Assembly, accepting its Committee's report, lost little time in launching its anathema of condemnation. The book was condemned on several counts. The first of these was its Doctrine of Faith and of the element of Assurance which it held to enter into that grace. Due note was not taken of the fact that the word Assurance might be used with more meanings than one. Then it was condemned on the alleged ground that it taught universal Atonement and Pardon. It was further condemned as teaching that holiness is not necessary to salvation. Another ground of condemnation was found in its teaching that Fear of Punishment and Hope of Reward are not allowed to be motives of a believer's obedience. The finding also charged the book with teaching that the believer is not under the law as a rule of life. Then the six "Antinomian Paradoxes" are condemned; for the distinction of the Law of Works from the Law of Christ, made use of to give them a good sense, was held to be inadequate to warrant them. Lastly, special expressions culled from the book were set forth in order only to be condemned. In a word, the Committee on Doctrine produced a partisan document and not a judicial report. It was one which virtually took Principal Hadow's criticism as a fair account of how things stood. Such was the action taken by the Assembly of 1720. The matter was not to end here.

Against this finding, Boston and eleven of his brethren took action by submitting a representation on the subject to next General Assembly. This elaborate document in criticism of an Assembly finding brought them before the Committee on Purity of Doctrine; and a series of twelve queries was submitted to the twelve representers to be answered. These queries they looked upon as meant to be ensnaring, and they held that they were put to them without good or sufficient reason. The defenders of the Gospel were put on their defence as if they were impugners of the Faith. Yet they answered the queries. The answers given in were prepared with great care, and though they were submitted to the Committee, that body saw to it that they were not submitted to the General Assembly of 1722, which again accepted the Committee's report. This second report was not yet a satisfactory one; but it was more guarded than that of 1720. In the pamphlet warfare, the edition of *The Marrow* of 1726, with Boston's notes and two pamphlets from the pen of an unordained licentiate, Robert Riccaltoun, are perhaps the most valuable documents. Riccaltoun's *Politick Disputant* exposes Hadow's method of attack in a thorough and scathing and sarcastic fashion, such as Witherspoon at his best might employ. His *Sober Enquiry* is looked upon as perhaps as able a piece of writing as was called forth in the whole course of the controversy. It was the work of a man who showed himself to be at home in handling questions of Christian doctrine.

2. M'CRIE AND BROWN OF WHITBURN

The volume whose reissue in 1718 raised such a commotion was last issued from the press about the beginning of this century, under the editorship of Dr C. G. M'Crie of Ayr. The editor lost a great chance of making his edition a final one. He failed to reprint with the book the very valuable account of the *The Marrow* controversy given by his eminent grandfather in the pages of the *Edinburgh Christian Instructor* for 1831-32. When these articles appeared, the Church and the public very much needed to be instructed in regard to the real issues that were at stake in the old controversy of a century before; and no man was more capable than Dr Thomas M'Crie to supply the needed instruction. The call for it came about on this wise.

In dealing with the doctrine of Universal Pardon which was taught by John Macleod Campbell of The Row, the General Assembly of 1831 leaned in its sentence on the condemnation in *The Marrow* case of the teaching of Universal Atonement and Pardon. This might be taken as a reassertion that such a doctrine was really taught in *The Marrow*. M'Crie, with his interest in the subject as a Seceder who was pledged to uphold the Evangelical truth that was condemned in the condemnation of *The Marrow*, and with his masterly acquaintance with the relevant history and literature, set forth the story of the whole business so as to make clear that the findings of the Assembly in 1720 and 1722 were not well grounded. The edition of his Miscellaneous Writings and his Life by his son, the second Thomas M'Crie, held out the hope that these four articles would be republished, and along with them a further one which traced the subsequent course of the " Marrow " teaching in England. This hope has not been fulfilled. Had Charles M'Crie seen to the reissue of his grandfather's work he would have done a thing of much more value than anything that he achieved by his editorial care, as it is easy enough to come across copies of *The Marrow*, while it is by no means easy to come across Dr M'Crie's articles. So far as I know, the article dealing with the later disputes in England on the subject of *The Marrow* teaching has never yet seen the light.

We should be without excuse as we speak of these things if we did not mention another valuable work dealing with the teaching of *The Marrow* which is of Secession authorship, a work that a man should look up who wants to have in handy form a " Marrow " exposition of the merits of *The Marrow* controversy. It is from the pen of John Brown of Whitburn, the son of John Brown of Haddington, and the father of John Brown of Broughton Place, Edinburgh. It is his volume, *Gospel Truth Accurately Stated*. This is an exposition of the subject that will be of interest to anyone who desires to learn what the teaching of Boston and his fellows was which told so much upon the thinking of Evangelical Scotland. Brown of Whitburn wrote also a Life of James Hervey, who alone of the Fathers of the Methodist revival in England was a definite " Marrowman." Toplady, however, was also almost another, for he was a great admirer of Ralph Erskine's Sermons, and in them we have the essence of " Marrow " teaching. The special interest of Whitburn's life, apart from the promotion of the Gospel cause, and mainly subsidiary to that end, was the exhibition and maintenance of the Evangelical truth set forth in *The Marrow,* and of that truth set forth in the same proportion and with the same emphasis. He was a lover of good men. In the family succession of John Browns he was less conservative than his father, more steadfast than his son.

It is a thing of curious interest that the two rival Secession congregations of an upland parish in West Lothian had at the same time and for years as their ministers two of the best-equipped Evangelical teachers that were in their respective denominations. For if John Brown was the minister of the Burghers, he had as his Anti-burgher neighbour Archibald Bruce, who was Theological Professor to the Synod to which he belonged. Bruce was M'Crie's mentor; and so diligent was he with his pen that he attained the rare distinction of keeping single-handed a printer going steadily printing off his work; for the volumes, original or translated, and the pamphlets that his prolific mind and pen produced, seemed to run in an unending succession. He was a model for diligence.[1]

In the Life of Dr Thomas M'Crie there is given some correspondence that he had with Dr Charles Watson of Burntisland, in which there is a statement in brief compass of " Marrow " teaching which is worth quoting. He is speaking of Adam Gib, and says: " He was acute, but was sometimes like a man who cuts his own finger by the fine edge which he has given to his instrument. I never could receive, nor, indeed, well apprehend, his doctrine about the two interests, both of them objects of faith as taught in the passages extracted (Gib's *Display of the Secession Testimony*, Vol. 2, pp. 169-174) and in a recommendatory preface which he wrote to an edition of Dr Owen on Redemption (*The Death of Death*); nor can I reconcile it with the ' Marrow ' doctrine of which he was a warm friend, but according to which the believer regards Christ as his, not in possession, but in the free offer of the Gospel." This seems to be the true " Marrow " view of the assurance of faith that the hearer of the Gospel is warranted to cherish in view of God's free grant of Christ as a Saviour to sinners of mankind. He is warranted to feel assured that Christ as a Saviour is held out to him in the Gospel to be taken as his own. Of this gift thus held out the believer says: " I take Him as my own." Here is faith's fiducial act. In the passage quoted we may see with what candour M'Crie could criticise the former leader of his own denomination for whose memory he cherished due veneration.

The view that Charles Simeon took of the Assurance of Faith taught by James Hervey—who was, as we have seen

[1] The most recent treatment we have seen in matters of " Marrow " interest was one of the very last articles from the pen of Dr David M. Macintyre, Principal of the Bible Training Institute of Glasgow, which he contributed to the *Evangelical Quarterly*. A few years earlier, quite a competent account of this passage of doctrinal history appeared in the proceedings of the Scottish Church History Society. This was from the hand of Mr Donald Beaton, then of Wick, and now of Oban, who has been for years a Theological Tutor in the Free Presbyterian Synod in Scotland.

in his doctrine of the Gospel, only a "Marrowman" over the Border—shows how easy it is to trip and stumble in understanding what the initial assurance is of having Christ and salvation in Him that Hervey, in common with the "Marrow" school, taught. It was a persuasion or assurance that in the overtures of the Gospel the Saviour is held out to all to be by them taken as their own. The reflex assurance that He is ours indeed as our Saviour could be reached only as the outcome of the faith that takes Him home to our heart as our own and does not leave Him on the Gospel table for others when we will not have Him for ourselves. One could be sure of having Him in this sense only when he was sure that with his heart he consented to be saved on the terms proposed in the overtures of the Gospel. To have caught the precise meaning of *The Marrow* on this point would have saved Hadow and his friends a world of trouble, and not only his friends, but the friends of *The Marrow* too. Simeon was not alone in his misunderstanding of the assurance of faith taught by Hervey.

The "Marrow" doctrine of faith did not find favour with Sandeman and his followers, nor with the New Englanders as represented by Joseph Bellamy, the former quarrelling with the assurance of an actual reception of Christ, the latter finding such an assurance to be the only one worth speaking of as it is confirmed and justified to the believer by his finding in himself the inward marks of regeneration. The analysis of faith favoured in the school of Edwards found a vigorous exponent in Andrew Fuller in his *Gospel Worthy of all Acceptation*, in which he joins issue with the "Marrow" teaching.

3. The "Marrow" Teaching Vulnerable

Perhaps the most vulnerable side to the teaching of the "Marrow" school in regard to the assurance which enters into Saving Faith is the fact that when Faith is spoken of as calling upon the name of the Lord, the proposition, that Christ is mine in the offer and in Him salvation, can have only a seminal measure of justice done to it, and that especially when faith is weak. Yet it may be said to underlie, however germinally, the warrant that we have to call upon God through Christ with the hope of being heard. Weak faith hardly rises at times above a sigh of aspiration or a cry of distress which brings the Christian as a suitor to the Throne of Grace. Here, however, the doctrine of the warrant is of use in encouraging a boldness and confidence that minister to the present comfort of the suppliant.

Now the exercise of saving and justifying faith may vary widely in its range. It may be the response of a full assurance that takes Christ as one's own and is so clear and definite in its acting as that the believer is left free from doubt as to what he does. Or it may rise no higher than the cry of distress that goes out for help to the Almighty Saviour. It yields, however, weak though it is, obedience to the law of faith, and finds its fullness in the Mediator, and it asks at His hand. There was a vast difference between the boldness and confidence of the disciple who left the boat and walked on the waters to go to His Lord, and the cry that told of his felt distress and his need when finding himself sinking he cried, " Lord, save me : I perish." The faith that is well warranted is not always free from fetters nor does it always reach its full height. Yet it is real and true as far as it goes. For to betake oneself to the Lord as the Hearer of prayer is faith in action. He who prays owns and confesses need and desire on his own side, and on the Lord's side a fullness of power and a willingness to hear and to save. Such an exercise of faith does not bring with it the same measure of comfort and of confidence as when with assurance it says, " I will trust and not be afraid." Yet in its own way it puts glory on God's truth and power and grace, and it is an exercise that is not in vain, for the Lord does not turn a deaf ear to the cry of the poor or the distressed.

In this connection the full confidence to which the old Reformation doctrine of faith was meant to lead, though it is an eminently desirable attainment when it is in exercise, is by no means exclusively the faith that gives glory to the faithfulness of God. Thus to insist upon it as the only shape that true faith takes is to mistake and give an inadequate or a cramped view of the subject; for the faith that is in grips with unbelief is faith as truly at work, though not so consciously triumphant in exercise as is the free and unshackled working of the faith that can boldly utter its challenge, " O death, where is thy sting? O grave, where is thy victory?" It creeps in under the covert of the worthy Name that it pleads and holds out against unbelieving fears. So while it is wise and right to aim at and encourage the direct acting of faith as it lays hold of its object and says " Amen " to the word of promise, it is also wise and right to deal tenderly with the bruised reed and the smoking flax. And such tender dealing calls for the recognition of faith, as faith, even when the beat of its heart is feeble and the believer himself is sorely tried with the whisperings of unbelief. At the same time as tender consideration is called for the weakness of the weak they are not to be encouraged to rest satisfied with a meagre or poverty-stricken measure of attainment in the faith that glorifies the word and the heart of God.

To insist on getting the believer to say, " I believe that Christ is mine and life is mine in Him," is to lay stress on the clearest direct actings of faith on the promises of God as essential to its very being. It may, of course, be held that logically underlying the suit of the suppliant there is the equivalent of such a proposition of direct faith. Yet while it is good that faith should come to its free and unfettered warranted exercise, and this gives Gospel comfort, it is not a wise or a kind or a good thing to overlook or set aside, as of little or no account, its weaker workings in which its principle may be found only in the germ. For faith is faith even should it be weak. And our Lord will not refuse to own what He Himself has wrought in even the weakest of His people.

It was to cut through a tangled undergrowth of questionings and doubts and challenging difficulties that the men of the " Marrow " school laid the stress that they did on the full warrant that each hearer of the Gospel has to take to himself the Saviour as his own. But when they insisted on the free right that we all have to take the Bread of Life off the table of the Gospel for our own food, they were, in their practical teaching, far from overlooking the need for self-scrutiny on the part of the child of God that he may satisfy himself as a rational, responsible agent that in his life he brings forth the fruits of the new birth. Nor did they fail to recognise the source of habitual assurance of salvation that is found in the joint witness borne by the regenerating with the regenerated spirit that those, who have been born from above and who live a life of faith and obedient loyalty, are the sons of God. They did not hold that an assurance that Christ is held out to us to be taken as our own is the same thing as an assurance that we have indeed received Him and have found in Him acceptance with the Father and the adoption of sons. They drew a distinction between the assurance of faith and the assurance of feeling. The method that these men followed of presenting the Gospel, with its privileges, its fullness, its freeness, and its appeal, was fitted with the Divine blessing upon it to further the assurance of salvation as it encouraged a direct resort on the part of the hearer to the Saviour for himself. The grace of assurance had been thrown too much into the background under the therapeutic method which measured out the comfort of the Gospel to those only who already knew that they had reached the stage of ripeness which fitted them for the due appreciation of its all-round, suitable provision. In keeping with this kind of preaching they dared not to stretch forth their hand to take Christ as their own unless they found that they were qualified as convinced sinners to lay hold of Him as suited to their recognised need. This method tended to weave a web of questions and to produce a labyrinthine maze which involved certainty of one's good state in a mist of difficulties, and it ministered to the doubts and hesitancies of a legal spirit that was bent on winning God's favourable notice by its own endeavours to prepare itself for Him.

It is true that it is only the convinced sinner that will prize the Gospel. But to be convinced that one is a lost and ruined sinner to whom Christ is held out, one does not need to be convinced that he is a truly convinced sinner. It is enough that he be convinced that he is a sinner. The Spirit convinces of sin, and the convinced sinner, as the result of his conviction, is sure that he is a sinner. He may not be equally sure that he is a truly convinced sinner. As a sinner —and this he knows himself to be—he is bidden come to Christ so that when he is sure that he is a sinner he should know that he is welcome to receive the Saviour. As a sinner it is for him to welcome the message that welcomes sinners to the great salvation. This "Marrow" way of putting things was well fitted to bring in the unbelieving hearer of the Gospel as guilty in his own conscience and before God of unbelief as a sin, for it taught him that as he was welcome to come to Christ he lay under an obligation as a sinner to give a hearty welcome to the Gospel. In doing what he did to clear this matter, Thomas Boston deserved well of the men of his own and subsequent generations.

As regards the offer of Christ in the Gospel, though there have been differences among our divines as to its destination, there has been no serious difference as to the fact that in the Gospel Christ is held forth to the hearer, and that the hearer is thus bound, as he is called upon, to accept Him as his own. Those among Scottish Calvinists who have restricted the offer of the Saviour and of salvation in Him to the elect have been an almost negligible minority. Though the opponents of the "Marrow" teaching were to a large extent in the habit of offering Christ and His salvation to convinced, or qualified, or prepared, or penitent sinners only, they held to an obligation to believe in Him by the command of God laid upon all men to whom the Word comes. This they held even when they acted in their fencing and restrictive way, as though Christ were not offered to all. They would not deny that the impenitent who did not believe the Gospel would have to answer for their unbelief as well as for their impenitence. They needed to have their understanding of things cleared up, and this was what the teaching of Boston and his brethren was fitted to do. That teaching has left a permanent mark on the method of the Scottish Evangelical school.

VI.
THEOLOGY IN THE EARLY DAYS OF THE SECESSION

1. Outlook of Early Seceders

THE attitude of the Secession in its early days to the Confession and Constitution of the Church of their native land was a thoroughly conservative one. They had no quarrel with either. Their quarrel was with a prevailing faction who, they believed, were more or less false to the Confession and who perverted the machinery of the Constitution of the Church to tyrannous ends that it was never meant to serve. In regard to the doctrine of the Gospel they were in sympathy with the witness borne by the " Marrow " brethren. Indeed, Ebenezer Erskine, one of the first four Seceding leaders, who was in fact himself the storm-centre of the movement, had been one of the " Marrow-men "; and of the twelve Representers, as they were called, he was far from being the least active. For in drawing up the answers that were given in to the queries of the doctrinal inquisition that dealt with the business he took a leading part. In attachment to the " Marrow " teaching, all his fellows in the step that they took in declaring their Secession from a prevailing party in the Church Courts were at one. They, in seceding, took their appeal to the first free, faithful and reforming General Assembly. It might well then, be said that they were militant members of the Evangelical and orthodox wing of the Church's ministry. So the action that they had in contemplation in organising the Secession was to be on conservative and Old School lines. It was not as innovating radicals but as wakeful and orthodox guardians of the Faith that they took the line they did. Indeed, when their Secession was an accomplished fact, they did not lose much time in taking steps to pledge themselves to the Covenanted position of their fathers of the previous century.

167

This they did to safeguard the attainments in Reformation of earlier days. They drew up a bond in keeping with the situation in which they were as Churchmen and in it they pledged themselves to carry into effect the ends that their forefathers aimed at in the days of Charles I. With this as their attitude it was to be looked for that they would show great care in respect to the doctrine that they preached, confessed and countenanced. And such was the case.

The Seceders were critical of the grudging and ungracious way in which the truth of our Lord's essential Godhead had been vindicated in the case of Professor Simson. He had, indeed, at long last been silenced, but instead of being deposed he was merely put under suspension. And those who had been so culpably lax in regard to the foundation truth of the Gospel itself in their leniency toward a teacher who was obviously a stubborn heretic had been in hot pursuit of the men who avowed their attachment to the Evangelical teaching of the "Marrow." Then also, after the Secession was declared, the mantle of the Church's charity had been thrown over the heterodoxy with which Professor Campbell of St Andrews was charged. The easy way, too, in which the irregularities of Glas of Tealing had been dealt with was in striking contrast with the harshness with which the rod was laid on such a free and faithful criticism of backsliding as was the ground of high censure in regard to Ebenezer Erskine's Synod sermon. They might well lay emphasis on the partiality with which discipline was administered. So they stressed also the tyranny that encroached on the right to dissociate oneself from the findings of the supreme and subordinate courts which the dissenter felt to be a burden on his conscience as being out of keeping with the claims of truth or with the Constitution of the Church. The Testimony emitted by the Seceders made clear enough the grounds on which they acted. And in the early years of their history they drew up and adopted an important and valuable theological document called the "Act of Grace" which was meant to vindicate the Doctrine of Grace as it had met with injury at the hands of the unfaithful leaders of the Church.

This document was the work mainly of Ebenezer Erskine and Alexander Moncrieff, both of whom were good theologians, as indeed their brethren, who with them were the first four Seceders, all were. This Act of 1742 stands on record to show what the views were that they held in regard to the cardinal doctrines which they felt themselves called upon to vindicate from injury that had been done to them.

2. The Evangelical Message

It is of interest to observe that the former brethren of the Seceders, who saw with them on doctrinal matters yet did not see it to be their duty to secede, were quite alive to the working of a legal and unevangelical leaven in the pulpit teaching of many of the ministry. So in the endeavours that were made to rally and organise the orthodox side of the Church by Willison of Dundee and his friends, who showed their strength in the Assemblies from 1734 to 1736 in which they sought to win back their separated brethren, there was passed an important Act of Assembly which was meant to deal effectively with the situation. It is, though somewhat long, worthy of being quoted, as it gives an idea of what an old Scottish Evangelical would look upon as the kind of preaching for which the Gospel pulpit was set apart. It runs thus :—

" The General Assembly being moved with zeal for the honour of God and our Lord Jesus Christ; especially at a time when the Christian revelation is openly impugned, and infidelity, deism, and other errors do so much prevail; they do hereby recommend to all ministers, and preachers, seriously to consider and observe the directory of this Church concerning the preaching of the word, which is approven by the General Assembly, 1645, and in particular, that they be careful to warn their hearers against anything tending to Atheism, Deism, Arianism, Socinianism, Arminianism, Bourignianism, Popery, Superstition, Anti-nomianism, or any other errors; and that in their sermons they insist frequently upon the truth, necessity, and excellency of supernatural revelation the supreme Deity of the Son and Holy Ghost, as well as of the Father, together with the oneness of the Godhead, our sinful and lost estate by nature, the necessity of supernatural grace, and of faith in the righteousness of Christ, without which the best works cannot please God; and that they make it the great scope of their sermons to lead sinners from a covenant of works to a covenant of grace for life and salvation, and from sin and self to precious Christ : and the General Assembly recommends to all who preach the Gospel, when they handle the doctrines of God's redeeming love, and of His free grace in the justification and salvation of sinners, the blessings of the Redeemer's purchase, and privileges of the new and better covenant, to study to manage these subjects, so as to lead their hearers unto an abhorrence of sin, the love of God and our neighbours, and the practice of universal holiness, seeing it is one great end of the Gospel to destroy the works of the devil, and to teach men to live soberly, righteously, and godly in this present world. Upon which account it is incumbent upon all who preach the Gospel, to insist not only upon the necessity and excellency of faith in Jesus Christ for salvation, but also upon the necessity of repentance for sin and reformation from it, and to press the practice of all moral duties both with respect to the first and second tables of the law, as indispensably necessary in obedience to God's command, to testify our gratitude to Him, to evidence the sincerity of our faith for the benefit of human society, the adorning the profession of religion, and making us meet for eternal life, seeing without holiness no man can see the Lord.

"And the Assembly do seriously recommend to all ministers and preachers of the Gospel, that in pressing moral duties, or obedience to the law, they show the nature and excellency of Gospel holiness, and enforce conformity to the moral law, both in heart and life, not from principles of reason only, but also, and more especially of revelation : and in order to attain thereto, it is necessary to show men the corruption and depravity of human nature by their fall in Adam, their natural impotence for, and aversion to, what is spiritually good, and to lead them to the true and only source of all grace and holiness, namely, union with Christ, by the Holy Spirit's working faith in us, and renewing us more and more after the image of God; and to let their hearers know, that they must first be grafted into Christ as their root, before their fruit can be savoury unto God; that they must have a new principle to animate, and a new end to direct them, before their actions become gracious and acceptable in the sight of God; and that they teach them the necessity of living by faith on the Son of God, in a constant looking to and dependence upon Him, as the great Author of all gracious influences, for the performance of every duty; and, withal, that after their best performances and attainments, they must count them but loss and dung, in point of justification before God; and to make it their great desire only to be found in Christ and His righteousness. And that ministers, in application of their sermons, do endeavour rightly to divide the word of truth, speaking distinctly to such various cases of the converted and unconverted, as rise natively from the subjects they have been handling; and that in the whole of their discourses, they take care to suit themselves to the capacity of their hearers, as to matter, method, and expression, and to the prevailing sins of the time and place, with all prudent and zealous freedom and plainness; as also, that they make gospel subjects their main theme and study, and press with all earnestness the practice of moral duties in a gospel manner; and that they forbear delivering anything in public, that may tend more to amusement than edification, and beware of bringing into their sermons and public discourses, matters of doubtful disputation, which tend to gender strife, rather then to promote the edification of Christians. And the Assembly exhorts all to study to maintain the unity of the spirit in the bond of peace.

" And, finally, the General Assembly recommends to all Professors of Divinity, to use their best endeavours to have the students under their care well acquainted with the true method of preaching the gospel as above directed; and that Presbyteries at their privy censure, inquire concerning the observation of this Act."

This piece of Church legislation was passed after long and repeated consideration in the years preceding the Assembly of 1736 which adopted it. In those years serious efforts were put forth by the Evangelicals to obviate what they looked upon as the final disaster of a definite Secession. Though they were a majority in the ministry, the friends of the Gospel were more or less of a mob for lack of organised unity. They lacked coherence of policy. Thus, in spite of all the goodwill that would have staved off the final breach with the Seceders, the men that had control of the machine, or, as they were called, the " Managers," succeeded, even in those reforming Assemblies, in getting a good deal of their own way. Of this,

the Seceding brethren took full note. It was the weakness
of the devout Evangelicals that they lacked concerted counsel
and action. They were men taken up, it is true, more with
the spiritual functions of the ministry of the Word than
with the manipulating of the courts and the management of
Church business. They were not adepts in the arts of the
wirepuller. There were others, however, who were wide
awake in regard to the outward concerns of the Church and
what could be got out of them. They knew the ropes and
they could get their own way. The desiccated ecclesiastic
who is a past-master in jobbery and gerrymandering is not
of to-day or yesterday only. Secular Churchmen of this
unevangelical kind were a minority of the ministers for years
after the Secession had become a recognised feature of the
Church life of the country. They were, however, drilled
and compact as an organised force and this told on Assembly
decisions. It was only in the latter half of the 18th century
that this party came to be a definite majority in the ministry.
Before that came about, as the story goes, there was a
vote in the Assembly in which John Witherspoon led
the Orthodox and beat his rival, Principal Robertson.
Witherspoon had taken the precaution of organising his forces
and could tell Dr Robertson that he had beaten him by the
use of his own weapons. Robertson, as the successor of
Patrick Cuming in leading the Moderates, was in command of
the disciplined forces that could be counted upon to answer the
party whip. They indeed brought Assembly business into
some such order as was to be seen in the British Parliament.
And to this may be traced the use of the expression of the
" House " for the Assembly in current Assembly usage.

3. "THE BREACH" AND AFTER

All this, however, has taken us away from the Theology
of the early Secession. Though the body was very much
of one mind to start with, yet the Secession was broken in
two in 1747 by a dispute as to whether or no Seceders could
consistently swear a certain clause in the oath taken by the
free burgesses of a few Scottish towns. The leaders knew

their own mind. But they had the defects of their qualities. They wanted their own way. Those who held the negative in regard to the warrantableness of swearing the Burgess Oath called themselves the General Associate Synod and were popularly spoken of as the Anti-burghers. The other party who would not make the matter one of discipline were the Associate Synod or popularly they were called the Burghers. The former, which was distinctly the more militant of the two Synods, was, for his lifetime, dominated by the forceful personality of Adam Gib.

It is curious that the settlement of such an ecclesiastical warrior in Edinburgh as its first Secession minister called forth a protesting pamphlet from the Cameronian side which spoke of the new minister as an intruder or usurper. They did not mince matters in these days. And Adam Gib could give as good as he got. He was a man of war from his youth and he was a candid critic of the position taken up by the Cameronians. He may have been known to have been of this mind before he became a minister. So it was not so strange that a protest against his ministry came from their side. In a year or two he had a great part in drafting the Synod's Answers to Nairn's Reasons. Mr Nairn, who had been a Seceder, thought it his duty to join the remnant of the Hillmen and when he took action he gave in his reasons. The Synod's answer to these reasons sets forth the orthodox reply to what was looked upon as the right-hand extreme of the Anti-Government Party, as the Cameronians or the Old Dissenters were called.

In the decade that followed the Breach of 1747 there was a fight among the Anti-burghers which brought to light the presence among the champions of orthodoxy of a doctrine of Universal Redemption. The culprit was none other than Gib's right-hand man in his militancy against the Burgess Oath. This was Thomas Mair of Orwell, the son of Mr George Mair of Culross, Boston's friend. George Mair was the friend of Fraser of Brea of a former generation and of Thomas Boston of the Secession generation. It was under the auspices of his son, Thomas Mair, that in 1747 Fraser's

work on *Justifying Faith* was published, in which he asserted
a redemption of all mankind. This redemption was of a
peculiar kind. All were held to be redeemed, the vessels
of mercy to be vessels of mercy, and the vessels of wrath
to have in their cup the special ingredient of what was called
Gospel Wrath or Gospel Vengeance. This we may see from
these words of his, pp. 223-224: " . . .Therefore the Lord
Jesus reaping the Manifestation of His Grace on the Elect
and Gospel Wrath and Vengeance on Reprobates, and getting
a Name above all Names, which was it the Lord ultimately
designed; He indeed reaps the travel of His soul, and the
fruit of His Labours, as they extend to both the Elect and
Reprobates in a different Way : for look on the Salvation of
the Elect in itself, it is not a Fruit worthy of Christ's Death,
excepting so far as it manifests the glorious, marvellous and
infinite Grace of God; and so the Damnation of Reprobates
for their Contempt of a crucified Saviour, as it manifests
God's glorious Justice and Gospel Vengeance is some Way
the Travel and Fruit of Christ's Death, to purchase both
which by such Means, and in such a Way, the infinite Wisdom
of God did not think the sending of His Son to die, a vain
and profuse Waste, and this being thereby attained it cannot
be said inefficacious; if it be said the Reprobates were
inexcusable, however, and Christ might have manifested His
Wrath on them and glorified His Justice though He had
never died for them; grants all, and so might reap the Glory
of His Grace on the Elect in saving them though Christ
had never died for them, if He had so pleased, and so much
both Rutherford and Twiss maintained; was therefore the
Death of Christ needless or in vain." [1]

[1] Here are some references to the teaching of this book of Fraser's
pen :—

1. There is a universal Redemption though not in the Arminian
sense, pp. 216, 219, 269.

2. The difference between the general and special Redemption
consists only in the different destination and end, pp. 221-2.

3. Christ died absolutely for the sins of those He died for, viz.,
every individual of mankind, pp. 169-173.

4. Remission really purchased to all men, pp. 176-183.

5. Christ obeyed and died in the room of all as Head and Representative of Fallen men, pp. 246-7.

4. BREA'S TEACHING

This bizarre doctrine of a Redemption that issues and was meant to issue in nothing else than greater wrath for the lost may have been treated by the writer as a speculation which he did not mean to publish; for Fraser lived for many years after he was released from the Bass, where he was a prisoner when he wrote his work on *Justifying Faith,* and to all appearance took no very definite steps for fully more than a score of years before his death to let the world or the Church know those special views that he had put on paper. And it was well-nigh half a century after his death before the treatise was published. Gib questions the good faith of the publisher or the editor who saw to the publication. This challenge may have been made because the name and repute of Fraser, as one of the old field preachers in the days of persecution and a sufferer on the Bass Rock for the good cause, were fitted to give a good introduction to the teaching of a volume which purported to be his work. It is not easy, however, to make good a charge of bad faith against the editor even to the extent of being guilty of interpolation. Yet the fact that the author himself did not publish the rudely executed treatise might point to its being only a roughly worked-out theological problem that was set aside or held up by the writer as not a satisfactory solution to the question that he had set out to answer. It was not from the author's MS. but from a copy that the work was printed.

It was to counteract the teaching ascribed to Fraser that Gib edited in 1755 *Owen on Redemption,* with the introduction to which Dr M'Crie referred in his letter to Dr Watson of Burntisland in which he dealt with Gib's attitude to "Marrow" teaching. Mair's teaching, though put under the ban of the Synod, proved to be contagious. He had some sympathisers, not only among the Seceders, but in the ranks of the ministry of the Reformed Presbytery, as the Cameronians were now called. Covenanting zeal was running to seed when it had a better grip of its doctrine of the Kingship of Christ, and laid corresponding stress upon it, than it had of the true nature of His sacrificial work as a

Priest. Among them the adherents to Brea's scheme broke off and formed the New Light Reformed Presbytery. And such is the irony of history that the only avowedly Socinian or Free-Thought Congregation in Edinburgh is the present-day successor of what started as a Reformed Presbyterian Church.[1]

Among the Seceders there was one minister at least who, after a fashion, dared to hint that there was something to be said in favour of a universal Redemption, either Fraser's scheme or perhaps rather the teaching of the Amyraldian French school. Or he might perhaps have had an eye to the type of universal Redemption associated with the name of Davenant. The hint was thrown out that there is an aspect of Redemption that is universal. This Seceder was George Thomson of Rathillet in Fife, who ministered among the Burghers. He had been a schoolmaster with Mr Mair at Orwell and imbibed his teaching. When Mr Mair was condemned by the Anti-burghers his schoolmaster became a Burgher and in 1782 he published a tract in which he aired his views on Redemption. He did this in a somewhat cautious manner. It was a hint rather than an assertion. These are his words :—" The question then is, Though there be a speciality in the death of Christ respecting an elect world; whether there is a universality in it respecting the whole world, etc." (pp. 24-26 of *A Compendious View*, etc., 1782). Unless I mistake, this George Thomson became a preacher among the New Light Reformed Presbyterians who held to a double reference of the Lord's redemptive work on Fraser's scheme. He joined this body in 1783. But Thomson's course was altogether a very erratic one[2] and the fact that he held

[1] The case for the New Light section at the Breach of the Reformed Presbytery is set forth in a pamphlet of 64 pages with the title, *The True State*, published in 1753. It was answered in 1754 in an able pamphlet of 212 pages, entitled *A Serious Examination.* This reply is ascribed to the second John Macmillan, who was then a young man of 25 or so. It is an elaborate argument on behalf of the definite saving efficacy of our Lord's atoning work.

[2] After years spent among the New Light Reformed Presbyterians Thomson returned to the Associate body and took part in the New Light Burgher Controversy as a pamphleteer in defence of the Old Light side.

a position did not affect the general state of things among the Seceders. They continued through the 18th century to be Old School Evangelical Calvinists.

There is a suggestion that one might make in regard to the Assembly's condemnation of *The Marrow* on the ground alleged that it taught universal Redemption. Culross, where James Fraser laboured in his latter years, is on the very border of the county and within the bounds of the Synod of Fife, and it came to be known by Principal Hadow, who, of course, lived in that county and Synod, that Fraser had taught a doctrine of Universal Redemption[1] so that he might conclude that those who were of his circle, as some of the " Marrowmen " were, shared in the taint of the same error. This conclusion could be no more than a surmise; for neither Boston nor the Erskines gave any reason for suspecting that they were off the orthodox lines on this subject. Indeed, the " Marrowmen " expressly disclaimed the teaching of Universal Redemption. The condemnation, however, of *The Marrow* because of its alleged teaching on this head may be due entirely to an inference from the words it employs when it says to the Gospel hearer as such, " Christ *is dead* for you." The " Marrowmen," as a class, were as clear in regard to a definite and efficacious Atonement as any Scottish divines of their age could well be. To say anything to the contrary would be to misunderstand or misstate their teaching altogether.

5. A GLANCE AT LARGE

The contendings of the Secession on behalf of the Faith, especially in that branch of it to which Gib belonged, are set forth in his *Display of the Secession Testimony* which appeared in 1774. This work called forth by way of a counter-blast *The Testimony Displayed*, which the Burghers issued in 1779. In both branches of the body the " Marrow " teaching as to Faith and its warrant in the offer of the Gospel

[1] He learned of this from Allan Logan of Culross, who was a keen Anti-Marrowman. He might have known of it, too, from John Carstares' criticism of Fraser on this score as far back as 1677. For, even so early, his peculiar views were known.

held its ground. As years, however, passed some of the Old
School Evangelicals who were not of the Secession were
disposed to criticise the preaching of the Seceders for the
alleged reason, not that it did not give the offer of Christ
and of life everlasting in Him to sinners, but on the score
of its being one-sided in that it did not lay on the need for
the new birth as the work of grace such a stress as was
proportionate to the emphasis that it put on the need of a
change of the sinner's state in his free justification. But
this criticism may have been of a carping and merely fault-
finding character, as the literature of the early Secession
sounds no uncertain note in regard to the necessity there is
that a sinner to be saved should experience a change of
nature as surely as a change of state. Yet it is quite possible
that the proportion of the Faith might have been better kept
and that less justice was being done to the realm of real
than to that of relative grace. In other words, the Lutheran
element in their preaching may have outrun what we may
call the Augustinian. Or with their doctrine of faith and
its warrant they may have laid less stress than they should
on the serious self-examination of the Puritan school.

The published work of the first days of the Secession was
in the main of a doctrinal nature. This was so to a large
extent even when it was of a polemic character, and in this
region we find that metaphysical questions were quite within
their orbit when they discussed the merits and the relations
of Faith and Fancy.[1]

The works of the two brothers Erskine had a wide
circulation far beyond the constituency of the denomination
which they adorned. Ralph Erskine in particular was very
popular and his Gospel Sonnets, which are full of " Marrow "
doctrine, were circulated at least nearly as widely as his
Sermons. These latter were almost as well known and as

---

[1] *Faith no Fancy* is something more than merely a long pamphlet.
It is quite an elaborate controversial essay in which Ralph Erskine
discusses the psychological character of the believing exercise of the
Christian soul. This Treatise on mental images runs to about 150,000
words.

much valued among the Reformed folk in the Netherlands as they used to be in the Home Country.

Ebenezer Erskine and his son-in-law, James Fisher, were partners in producing what was at first spoken of as *The Synod's Catechism*, but came to be known better as Fisher's, for it was the younger man that finished it and perhaps had the main hand in most of it, though the greater share of the earlier part has been attributed to Ebenezer Erskine. This exposition of the Shorter Catechism attained a greater vogue than any other in Scotland, even than Willison's, though his was very much in use. Fisher's Catechism thus exercised more of a formative influence in moulding the thoughts of religious homes and in making so many of the people of Scotland skilled in theological matters than did any other single catechetical work expository of the Shorter Catechism. It continued to be issued down until the middle of the 19th century; and it found acceptance far beyond the ranks of the Secession. The Presbyterian Board at Philadelphia, in its first forty years, sold almost 20,000 copies. Moncrieff, like the Erskines and Fisher, was also a capable theologian, but Wilson of Perth seems from the texture of his thought to have been at least not a whit behind the ablest of his brethren. His *Defence of Reformation Principles* set fortn the case that the Fathers of the Secession could make for themselves in defending their line of action. He seems to a reader to be inclined to lay more stress on a pure Church than on a true one in the matter of visible unity of fellowship. And though he was the abler man of the two he does not make out his plea on the older Scottish doctrine of the duty of preserving the unity of a true Church, against his antagonist, John Currie of Kinglassie. Currie was well read in the older Scottish divinity and argues along the line that Rutherford and Durham would take a century before.

The outcome of the virtual schism of 1652 between Resolutioners and Protesters was to be seen in the laxer attitude as to Church unity that was shown by the Cameronian party and now by the Seceders. Men's minds had come to be accustomed to see altar set up against altar in rival denomina-

tions that held separate communion. Thus it came to pass
that, instead of the one Church for which the older
Presbyterians strove, a modified ideal of Church unity and
fellowship found a welcome from what claimed to be the
right wing of Reformed orthodoxy. Currie, as we have
named him, was one that pleaded on behalf of the older
Reformed Church system against Erastianism as surely as
did the Seceders. In this, his contemporary, John Willison,
was of one mind with him. The Testimony issued by the
latter is one of the characteristic works of the Evangelicals.
In another department of Church theology their friend, John
Warden of Gargunnock, did a careful bit of work. He wrote
an extensive essay on the Sacrament of Baptism. This was
issued as early as 1724. Warden was one of the same set
as the men who took an active part in the Awakenings of
Kilsyth and Cambuslang and who kept in touch with transatlantic Evangelicals in the Monthly Letter which tells of the
fruits of the Gospel in days of revival on both sides of the
ocean. His son, also John Warden, left behind him a carefully
wrought-out system of Theology presented almost entirely in
a catena of Scripture quotations relevant to the various heads
or topics into which a system of Theology is divided. The
minister of Gargunnock was not a special favourite among
the friends of the " Marrow," for he was a man who went
so far with them, but failed to go the whole way. But no
more did most of the Evangelical ministry in Scotland of
their day go all the way with the " Marrowmen." As to
the merits of the controversy they were to a great extent at
sixes and sevens. There was, however, much real sympathy
among them with the fight made for a free Gospel and for
an open way for sinners to Christ, such as the " Marrowmen "
laid stress upon. This sympathy was cherished on the part
of men who might put things in another way than the
" Marrow " brethren did. Some of them were loyal, for
example, to the teaching and method of Guthrie of Fenwick,
who was in the front rank of Gospel preachers of his time,
and they did not forget that when he laid stress upon the
truth that though no words will take effect till God pour

out His Spirit, yet ministers must still press men's duty upon them and charge them that they give the Lord no rest till He send out that Spirit which He will give to them that ask for Him. Guthrie taught, "that though none cordially close with God in Christ Jesus, and acquiesce in that ransom found out by God, except only such as are elected, and whose heart the Lord doth sovereignly determine to that blessed choice, yet the Lord has left it as a duty upon people who hear His Gospel to close with His offer of salvation, as if it were in their power to do it." Warden's descendants held an honourable place in the Church's ministry after him, and one of them had the honour of resigning at the Disruption of 1843 what was held to be the richest benefice in the Church of Scotland. This was Dr Patrick Macfarlan of the West Kirk of Greenock.

6. Secession Writers

But we were speaking of Secession literature. It was solid rather than showy, as one may see by looking into the Sermons of Arnot of Kennoway, or Swanston of Kinross, or the works of Adam Gib, or John Brown of Haddington. MacEwen of Dundee we name by himself. He was one of the brightest ornaments of the Secession movement. He died at the early age of 28. But he left a book that embalms his memory. It is called *Grace and Truth*. This work deals with the types of Scripture in a vein of fine Evangelical teaching and it is expressed in what was regarded as the classical English of the middle of the 18th century, in the florid and ornate style of James Hervey. In matter of style he was a marked contrast to many of his fellows, though some in both wings of the Secession aimed at good expression. We find Dr John Erskine of the Greyfriars passing a high encomium on MacEwen's work. And such a high and dry Anglican Churchman as Dean Burgon makes the rather grudging admission that the best book he knew in English on the types was by a Scotsman and a Presbyterian.

Of the solid type of Secession production are the Sermons of David Wilson of London and John Muckarsie of Kinkell

and John Hunter, their first ordained minister, whose work
was cut short almost at its outset, and James Scot of
Gateshaw, who, like James Fisher, was a son-in-law to
Ebenezer Erskine. It illustrates the firmness with which the
old Seceders held to their Church distinctions that Scot, as
an Anti-burgher, took part in the deposition, if not the
excommunication, of three such revered relatives as his wife's
father and uncle and brother-in-law. This he did seeing that
they did not accept the Anti-burgher reading of what the
times called for. When James Scot came home from the
militant Synod he had his wife to face. He told her what
had been done. When she heard the facts she was ready to
act. " You," said she, " are my husband, but you are no
longer my minister," and as long as she was lady of the
manse she went off each Sabbath about ten or a dozen miles
to join in the worship of a Burgher Church. Her husband's
Sermons are extant, but they are rare and hard to get, as
indeed is most of the comparatively fugitive devout reading
of those days. It may be that Alison Erskine read the
Sermons that she would not go to hear. Those worthy people
might be called angular and narrow; but there is no denying
that they had grit. Some of them might even be gritty. When
each respected the convictions of the other it was possible
for couples to live in harmony even in such cases. There is
a valuable devotional work called *Solitude Sweetened*, by
James Meikle, surgeon in Carnwath. This worthy Seceder
was a strong Burgher and his wife was an equally convinced
Anti-burgher. But each of them let the other take the way
that to each of them seemed best. So in regard to Church
connection they agreed to differ. Meikle in early life had
been a student looking forward to the ministry of the Gospel
in the Secession, but he came to be satisfied that, owing to
a defect in voice from which he suffered, he was not called
upon to be a preacher. So he became a surgeon in the Royal
Navy, and in the surgeon's bay or his quarters aboard an
18th-century ship of war he penned his meditations. These
show what a good practical divine he was, and, with the
voice given, what an effective preacher he might have been.

His works are a very fine specimen at once of the sound theology and of the devoutly meditative life that prevailed in the 18th-century Seceder circles.

The Secession kept alive the witness for the Reformed Faith in many parts of Scotland when the State Church came under the blight of a ministry that had no place in its message for the good news of a gracious salvation. And it told not only in Scotland. It spread over the Channel to Northern Ireland, where it took deep root and rivalled in strength the Synod of Ulster, and reached out beyond the Borders in the south to many parts of England and even made its way overseas to America. America, indeed, is in its debt for the training of that bright particular star of the pulpit of the Western Hemisphere, John Mitchell Mason of New York, who wedded the purest Evangel to the richest and most manly eloquence. Though in the process of the years the Secession body broke away to a large extent from the outlook of its fathers and founders, yet it long remained a bulwark of the faith and an unambiguous witness to a gratuitous supernatural salvation. It produced many men of decided character; and even when it was slipping away from the moorings of its first days there still were to be found a remnant, some of whom were the greatest men that the whole movement could show. The work of these men will call for special mention when we come to deal with New Light and its development.

7. JOHN BROWN OF HADDINGTON

Before we part with the Secession and its teaching we should say a word or two about Brown of Haddington and his work. As for many years Professor of Theology to the Burgher Synod he did much to transmit the pure Gospel strain of teaching for which the Seceding fathers stood and he did what he could to keep his scholars on the old lines all along the battle front. His System of Theology is a monument to his diligence in his calling. His Dictionary of the Bible and his Self-Interpreting Bible had both of them a wide circulation. He was also the author of expositions of the Shorter Catechism, the simpler of which, as a child's Catechism, was as much used in Northern Ireland, where, as we have seen, the Secession had a strong hold, as Willison's Mother's Catechism was in Scotland. Until at least last generation in Ulster farmhouses when the young folk were not old enough to be taught the Shorter Catechism it used to be said they were still on the " Brown." It was Scots-Irish Presbyterians with such an early training that helped so much to build up and recruit the ranks of American Presbyterianism.

In one of the posthumous pieces from his pen John Brown deals with the measure or the extent to which the Righteousness of Christ is imputed to His people with a view to their justification. In this article he takes up the position that each believer has not the whole of that righteousness set to his account, but only as much as is required to meet his own need. It was the kind of scholastic question that invited controversy, and it is of interest to find that among the Antiburghers the other side of the question was taken. The teaching that prevailed among them was that nothing less than the full sacrifice of the Lord is set to the credit of each of His clients. The matter in dispute is like the question, " Has each man the whole of the sun for himself or only what he needs of it? " He has all that he needs directly and indirectly. His fellows, too, have their share and all the good that he gets of fellowship with them is the measure in which he benefits by the sun's light and heat that those others get. It has often been said that there is such merit in the blood of the Cross that one drop is enough to redeem a sinner. This hyperbolical mode of speech leaves out of account that the one drop which in that case will save must be the last drop that the Lord shed in giving His life as a ransom for many. To be a ransom for any His life must be laid down; and what was done for all was done for each. He who was Surety for all was Substitute for each. When we are dealing with what was infinite, what was needed for one was enough for all. Every man who has the light and warmth of the sun has the whole sun shining upon him, yet he has not the whole light as his own that the sun gives forth.

We have taken a look at the Theology of the Scottish Reformed school in the early days of the Secession. These were days when the mordant acid of deistic critical unbelief or 18th-century illuminism was eating into the substance of religious thought and life in wide circles of the nation. The thinking of the unevangelical school fell under this blight. The Evangelicals, both in the State Church and in the Secession, felt the impact of the newest fashionable modes in the realm of faith and thought. But instead of welcoming or yielding to them they swept them aside as so many mere flimsy or cobweb speculations and pursued the even tenor of their believing way in the conviction of the trustworthiness of the historic Christian tradition. So little did they regard the presence of the enemy at the gates as a menace to the stability of the Christian Confession that their theological interest found its centre of gravity in dogmatic questions which belonged rather to the wranglings of Polemics than to the problems of Apologetics.

8. JOHN GLAS AND HIS WORK

We have spoken of the contrast that was between the sharp and harsh discipline dealt out to Erskine and his brethren and the measure of patience and forbearance that was extended to Glas of Tealing. We might for a little look at him and his place in the life of the Church of Scotland in the 18th century. Tealing is a parish not far from Dundee in the county of Angus; and Angus was a county which, in the first half of that century, was a hotbed of Jacobite intrigue and of Episcopal recusancy. Its territorial influence was one of the chief assets of the exiled Stuart house. In such an area the Presbyterian cause had a hard battle to fight to hold its own. It was thus a very awkward kind of thing for the ministers to find that one of their number had come to espouse those views in regard to the Church which the Sectaries of the previous century had held and which had succeeded in wrecking the programme of the Solemn League and Covenant. For until the third decade of the 18th century, and even later, orthodox Presbyterians still attached great importance to that instrument and to what it stood for in the life of Britain; and when they were face to face with Episcopacy entrenched in the baronial circles of their bounds they were apt to be all the more insistent on standing for the programme of their Covenanting fathers. They could not but feel keenly that an esteemed brother, for such in their eyes John Glas was, had taken up with notions which cut under the ground of Presbytery and made such a thing as a national Church, or a national Reformation, or a national Religion or a national Religious Covenant a sheer impossibility.

Glas became also the founder at the second remove through his writings of the old Scots Independents, who, however, never became a great body. His followers adopted, with what they held to be Apostolic Independency, old Apostolic customs which they looked upon as obligatory, such as the observance of the decrees of the Council of Jerusalem, the washing of the saints' feet, the common meal, or love feast, and the holy kiss. In his work, *The Testimony of the King of Martyrs,* their leader was the first in Scotland who was a native advocate of the doctrine of Church and State that refuses to acknowledge that the State, which is a divine institution, owes certain helpful duties to the Church, which is also a divine institution, that these institutions should work in harmonious co-operation, and that in fulfilling the duties that lie upon it towards the Church the State is called upon to throw over it the shield of its defence, and, without usurping a lordship over its faith and practice, is bound to countenance and further, as far as that lies in the region of its competence, the profession of the truth of the Gospel and the purity of the Church's profession of faith. In other words, he became a Voluntary about a century before Voluntaryism, as a solution to the problem of the right adjustment of the relation of Church and State, came to be in Scotland the pivotal occasion of angry controversy for some hectic years after 1829. In this connection he was the pioneer of the contendings of a later day.

9. SANDEMANIAN FAITH

Apart from his teaching in regard to the Church, Glas taught a doctrine as to the nature of faith that did more than lay stress on rooting this grace in the intellectual nature of man. His teaching was to the effect that faith is an intellectual assent. This view of things was set forth with greater vigour and emphasis by his son-in-law, Robert Sandeman, after whom the Glassite Churches came to be spoken of as Sandemanian. Sandeman was a propagandist. There was a somewhat similar doctrine of faith that was taught by John Erskine of Edinburgh, who was the younger contemporary of Glas, but who sought to lay stress not on the likeness but the unlikeness of their views. The tendency to stress the essentially intellectual character of faith often goes by the name of Sandemanianism. Dr Erskine laid such a stress on the rooting of faith in the, intellectual side of man's being, but he was emphatic on the point that his view of the matter was not that of the Glassites. He held that faith is radically belief of the truth and this is an exercise of the understanding by way of assent. He went on, however, to teach that what is rooted in our exercise of the understanding goes on to function as an exercise of the emotional powers and of the will so that as the result of the initial assent there springs up a consent of the heart. This is more or less a psychological analysis and may, according to the emphasis that is laid on the initial assent and the final consent, be either a modification of the Reformed doctrine which lays stress on the trust which is the working of the will as the essential element of saving faith or its logical differentia; or it may be only an attempt to illustrate the position that in the exercise of trust the believer does not act blindly. Erskine's doctrine on this matter was that of Dr Alexander Stewart of the Canongate, Edinburgh, and of Dr Thomas Chalmers. It was usually regarded by Scottish Evangelicals as an approximation, to say the least, to the Sandemanian doctrine of faith. This kind of doctrine was current also among the old Scots Baptists as well as the old Independents. Their chief writer was Archibald Maclean. The influence in

the direction of fostering such a doctrine of faith was
mediately or immediately one that radiated out from the
movement which had its origin in the teaching of John Glas.
In his case it may have gone back to the teaching of John
Cameron in the previous century. It is pretty obvious that
such a type of teaching is fitted to put a premium upon what
is held to be orthodox doctrine, and to lay less stress than
is called for on the reaction of the emotional nature to the
truth of the Gospel and on the activity of the will as that
goes out in the trust of the heart and its attendant obedience
in the life. It has its affiliation along the line of descent
from scholastic discussion which has hardened itself into
concrete form in the Roman teaching as to what the faith of
the Gospel is. With its view of faith Sandemanianism tended
to be very orthodox in regard to the certainty with which
the purpose of God in grace will work itself out in the
salvation of His chosen people, while it held itself coldly
aloof from any display of feeling in the exercises of a religious
life. It was the beginning of the movement that created this
problem which the Presbytery of Dundee had to tackle; and
their process ended in the deposition of Glas. This sentence
was afterwards mitigated so that the door of return was
opened for him, but he did not avail himself of the overture
which such a gesture involved. In the conduct of the case
against him it fell to John Willison, one of the most amiable
and affectionate of Evangelical men, to take a leading part.

VII.
THE 18TH-CENTURY CONTRAST—
EVANGELICALS AND MODERATES

1. John Maclaurin

WE have looked at representative divines of the beginning
of the 18th century and of its first third in speaking of
Thomas Halyburton and Thomas Boston. They had a younger
contemporary who lived into the second half of the century,
whose name calls for special notice. The third of the
succession of the John Browns among the Seceders did not
stand quite side by side with his conservative forebears on
the old ground that they held. He parted company with the
definite doctrinal tradition for which his grandfather of
Haddington had stood. It was not, then, so significant as
it would be if he had held to the theology of his family that
in his edition of Maclaurin's Essays he recognises the author,
John Maclaurin of Glasgow, to have been the leading
theologian of Scotland in the 18th century. In forming such
an estimate he was not far out. And yet Maclaurin was
not the founder of a school nor has he left extensive literary
remains to tell of his activity with the pen. But what he did
was eminently well done, and there is one piece of his work
in particular that, as a classic in the homiletic department,
shows the application of Scottish Theology at its best. It
is his Sermon on *Glorying in the Cross of Christ*. Of
this discourse, Dr Robert S. Candlish is reported to have said
that it was the greatest sermon ever preached. Such words
are a hyperbole : the praise is exaggerated. The sermon,
however, is a noble monument of rich doctrinal and Evangelical
teaching such as the Scottish pulpit has never surpassed.
Though it is the best known of Maclaurin's works, it can
hardly be said to excel his Sermon on *The Sins of Men
not chargeable to God*. This masterly discourse was preached

by its author when he was still a young man of under 30,
ministering in the quiet country parish of Luss on the side
of the lovely Loch Lomond.   The parish of Luss in
Maclaurin's time, that is, over 200 years ago, was still one
in which the minister's main work would be done in the
Gaelic language. His hearers were plain country folk. Yet
for such an audience he prepared a sermon which, for
profundity and compression of thought, will bear comparison
with the best compacted work of his contemporary, Bishop
Joseph Butler.   In contrast, however, with Butler's works, it
shows, as everything that Maclaurin did showed, how
permeated with the salt of the Evangel all his teaching was.
He ranked amongst the most highly cultivated men of his
generation.   Born in the manse of Glendaruel in Cowal in
the county of Argyll, he took his University course at
Glasgow and finished his theological studies in Holland.   In
his ministry he carried out the traditions of the pure Theology
that still prevailed in the schools of the Netherlands, a
Theology which was, as a scheme of Christian teaching, his
own hereditary treasure.   For the first generation of post-
Revolution ministers of the Synod of Argyll in the circles
in which his father and uncle moved were worthy specimens
of the Evangelical and Covenanting ministry of Scotland who
found a shelter under the kindly Protestant shield of the
great family of Argyll.   To this class belonged his father,
whom he lost when young, and his father's brother, the
minister of Kilfinan, on the shores of Loch Fyne, in whose
manse and under whose care he and his brother Colin were
brought up. This brother, the friend and interpreter of Sir
Isaac Newton, was as much distinguished in the field of pure
science as the minister was in his own walk of life.   For
Colin Maclaurin was the outstanding mathematician of his
native country in the 18th century. The intellectual gifts of
the brothers were of the highest order.

There are two strains that were intertwined in the
teaching of the young minister of Luss, who afterwards was
better known as the minister of the Ramshorn Kirk in
Glasgow, a Church that is now called St David's.   These

strains were the Evangelical and the Apologetic. The men who are conspicuous for the place that they give to the Apologetic side of Christian truth do not often excel in the richness of their vein of Gospel preaching. In Maclaurin, however, both veins are found. He sensed what an unbelieving age needed and he laid himself out in delivering his message to commend it, not only to the heart but to the head. And in doing so he shunned that rusticity of speech and pronunciation that was still a common thing among the Scottish ministry and that served to repel the more educated classes and to prejudice them against the plain message of the pulpit. This profound thinker, with his firmly knit and compact thought, was one of the best-known preachers of the Gospel of his time, one of the leaders in religious revival, and one of the correspondents of Jonathan Edwards, whom in many respects he resembled. In both of them massive intellect went hand in hand with heart godliness of the most pervasive, controlling and winsome character. On the two sides of the Atlantic they were leaders and brethren in the work of the great awakening which broke in on the slumberous Church life of 200 years ago. This work raised up a crop of witnesses who were called to hold aloft the banner of the Reformed Faith in the days of declension and apostasy in the Churches of New England and Scotland both—days that were at hand and that were destined to last until the end of the 18th century.

Edwards died in 1758. Four years earlier Maclaurin predeceased him. The year of his death was that in which his elder contemporary, Ebenezer Erskine, was also taken away. Erskine, among the Seceders, was distinguished in his preaching for the exhibition that he gave of the freeness of the Gospel of Christ and of the majesty with which that Gospel sets before us the God of all grace. The two worthy men did not by any means see eye to eye in regard to some of the public questions that divided the Church of their day. Yet as surely as Erskine was the sworn foe of Erastianism, there was no mistake as to Maclaurin's opposition to it. The tyranny of a drilled and disciplined faction, which by

organised and preconcerted joint action captured the management of the courts of the Church and worked it in the interest
of their own less than worthy ends, and their high-handed
policy found few men more disposed to stand up against them
than the author of the elaborate pamphlet which came from
Maclaurin's hand in criticism of the despotic line of action
that brought about, through the deposition of Thomas
Gillespie of Carnock, the formation of a new Presbyterian
denomination.

This new Church, when it was fully organised and
gathered strength, came to be known as the Synod of Relief.
It grew to be a Synod with more than 100 Churches and
represented an Evangelical and for many years an Orthodox
tendency which sought to keep in touch with that wing of
Methodism to which George Whitefield belonged, and which,
in taking this line, tried to avoid any undue entanglement
with the doubtful questions that had come to be bones of
contention among the successors of the Covenanters. Such
questions had split the Secession and stirred up controversy,
not only with the National Church, but with the Cameronian
Remnant. These debated things bore on the precise relation
in which the Covenanting witness of the previous century
stood to the faith and duty of the Church and nation in the
environment of another age.

In Maclaurin's later days, when he wrote anonymously
on this subject, the success of Robertson's rigorous Moderate
policy was not yet by any means the assured thing that it
came to be in a score of years after his time. If the
Orthodox were but to adopt the tactics of their opponents
and combine in following a considered policy they could still
outvote the Broad Church Erastians. If only they had always
men like Maclaurin and Witherspoon to lead and organise
them, things would have been different. Their forte, however,
was not the sphere of the ecclesiastical schemer and manager.
Had they given better heed to what could be done in the
region of the Church's public business the vogue of fashionable Moderatism might never have come to have the place
which it got in the life of the Church. We have seen already

that in the years that followed the Secession of 1733 the Orthodox bestirred themselves to undo the mischief that their opponents had done, and for a few years they kept up their effort and controlled the General Assembly. This showed the advantage that there was in working in concert. The region, however, of Church politics was one in which they felt themselves less at home than in that of preaching the Gospel to their fellows. So their effort as militant ecclesiastics was short-lived.

The Apologetic strain that was in Maclaurin bears witness to the call of his time. His lot was cast in a city; and Glasgow already had cliques and coteries that were prepared to welcome the fashionable Deism of the age. Men like Boston and the Erskines and Willison were rooted in the Evangelical tradition of Reformation and Covenanting times and their followers and hearers were of the same general outlook with themselves. They felt but little of the impact of deistic unbelief on the life of the community. It was otherwise with Maclaurin and his predecessor, Halyburton. They were in touch with the type of unbelieving thought which from the middle of the 17th century onwards had been telling on the academic and fashionable circles of the country. They took their share in the work of Christian defence. The times called for it. And they answered this call.

One has only to note how, in the course of his own spiritual struggles, Halyburton had to grapple with the problems that were raised by the objections of the Deists. These struggles belonged to the last decade of the 17th century and Deism was the fashionable New Light of the age. It was quite fitting when he came to have a firm foothold for himself that he should be the leader in his Church in the opposition to Deism. His *Reason of Faith* is of the same type of believing Protestant defences as the work in the same department of his master, John Owen. It is an exposition of the reasonable character of the autopistia which historical Reformed Theology taught to be inherent in the Scriptures and which it held to be the ultimate and everyday reason on which working Christian faith proceeds as it accepts the witness, and bows to the authority, of Holy Writ. Such belief is rooted in, and it is owing to, the witness that is borne by the Spirit by and with the Word in the heart. This work was over and above his *magnum opus*.

In the case of Maclaurin we have one who was not only in contact with the currents of thought that were working in his own Church and land, he was a man, too, that carried with him from his early days the knowledge of the influences that were telling in an unfavourable direction on educated people in other lands. He had the more comprehensive view of things of one that had the advantage of pursuing his theological studies in the divinity schools overseas. In these, he had an ample opportunity of learning how the Cartesian doubting and questioning in philosophy was affecting the theological thinking of the younger generation. So he brought home with him a wider outlook than that of his home-bred contemporaries apart from Halyburton. In his work on the Prophecies and as a seasoning element in his other writings the Apologetic strain comes out, not perhaps so much explicitly and directly as in the guarded and careful way in which he makes his positive affirmations. He spoke as he wrote in this vein like a man who was cognisant of the objections that hearers, who might be opponents, would be likely to take to the substance of his statements. So he put them in the best defensive form that he could find and an open-eyed reader or hearer would appreciate the positive truth of his teaching. This he firmly held, none the less firmly indeed that he took a cautious and irenic method to state his case. Irenic the method might be said to be, though it was adapted to disarm unfriendly criticism and to guard his clients from the quibbles and objections that were rife in circles to which they might have ready access. In his piece which deals with prejudices against particular aspects of Gospel truth, writing for an age whose great bugbear in religion was Enthusiasm to which all serious thought on spiritual things was apt to be set down, he handles such unfavourable judgments as preoccupied the mind of his hearers in regard to the more mystical side of definitely

revealed truth, as, for instance, the teaching of the Scriptures
on the subject of our Union with Christ; and we may quote
the closing paragraph of the section in which he handles this
topic as a specimen of his style in dealing with the matters
that he has in hand :—

" Man naturally loves honour and dignity; and, indeed,
ambition to be great, if it were directed to right objects, would,
instead of being a vice, be a cardinal virtue. Man is naturally
a sociable as well as an aspiring creature. These joint
inclinations make men love to be incorporated in societies
that have dignity annexed to them. The subject we are
treating contains all the attractives that can reasonably affect
one that loves society; it is made up of the choice of all
other societies; contains all the true heroes that ever were,
and comprehends the flower of the universe. The meanest
member is promoted at the same time to a near relation to
the infinite Creator, and to all the best of His creatures;
allied to the Spirits made perfect in heaven and to the
excellent ones of the earth : he can claim kindred to the
patriarchs and prophets, and martyrs, and apostles, and all
the other excellent persons who adorned this world and of
whom it was not worthy. Though they be in heaven and
we on earth, one Spirit animates them both. Surely it is
industrious stupidity, if one contemplates such a society, without being enamoured with it; and all other society, or solitude,
is only so far valuable as it is subservient to it. A society
headed by infinite perfection, cemented by eternal love,
adorned with undecaying grace, supplied out of all-sufficient
bliss, entitled to the inheritance of all things, and guarded by
Omnipotence : a society as ancient as the world, but more
durable; and to whose interest the world and all that is in
it are subservient : a society joined together by the strictest
bands, where there is no interfering of interests but one
common interest, and where at last there will be no opposition
of tempers or sentiments; when its members, now many of
them scattered far and near, but still united to their Head,
shall one day have a glad universal meeting in an eternal
temple never to part, and where they shall celebrate a jubilee

of inconceivable ecstasy and transport without mixture, without interruption, and which crowns all, without end."

There is a paragraph picked almost at random from Maclaurin's pages; and one can taste in it the quality of his thinking and work.

The Apologetic strain, as distinct from the Dogmatic or the Polemic, was to be found in only a modified degree in the preaching of the Evangelical school as a whole. They adhered in the main to the method of witness which proceeds without preliminary argument on Scripture and on its teaching as authoritative, a method that called for instant surrender and submission to their message. They aimed at bringing home the truth that they preached to the heart of their hearers so that by the inward teaching of the Spirit the body and system of Bible truth might evince itself to the conscience to be indeed of God. Thus they sought to set it forth that it might shine in its own light of self-evidence and constrain the conscience of the hearers to own it as being of God and as such stamped in its every fibre of warp and woof with the mark that tells of its heavenly character and origin. On the polemic side they would freely argue, with Scripture authority to back them, in defence of the doctrine that they taught. There were men of the Orthodox school in whose work a more undiluted strain of Apologetic showed itself. Such, for example, was Sir Henry Moncreiff Wellwood, who was, by the end of the 18th century, one of the most outstanding of the Evangelical clergy. His friend, Andrew Thomson, in his Sermons on Infidelity, illustrates the presence of the same strain; and Thomas Chalmers, in his Astronomical Discourses, is the outstanding or representative man of such a tendency among the Orthodox. As a rule, it was among the Moderates that this side of things was specially cultivated.

The Moderates, in their Apologetic work, found themselves more at home in the defence of the outworks of the Faith than in the exposition of the citadel truth that the outworks only flank and guard, being to it but as the husk is to the kernel; and their work gives less place than was due to it to the internal evidence that special revelation carries with

it in its own bosom.[1]   However much this defence of the
possibility and the truth of the miraculous might be needed
in academic circles or in fashionable society, it was very
much at a discount among the rank and file of the Church.

2. John Inglis and Missions

Perhaps the best specimen of the work of this ecclesiastical
school in the department of the clearing away of difficulties
in matters of Christian teaching was Dr John Inglis, to whom
the credit belongs of securing, over a century ago, a place
for Foreign Missions as a definite scheme in the programme
of the Church of Scotland.

When the Church embarked on its overseas enterprise
it was the first National Reformed Church that, as a body,
set on foot a corporate missionary undertaking of its own
and recognised the organised Church to be in one of its proper
functions a Foreign Missionary institute.   This was something distinct from the Colonial evangelising policy of the
Dutch Oriental Empire, as, for example, in Ceylon.   It was
only in 1829, however, that Alexander Duff was sent out as
the first agent of the Church as such in the Foreign Field.
In taking this step, the Church in effect avowed that it was
as surely its function to be aggressive in sending forth the
Word of Life to the ends of the earth as it was undeniably
its calling to be conservative of the truth of the Word by
confessing and standing for it at home and seeing to its
transmission to the succeeding age.   Under Dr Inglis'
leadership the step was taken which, thirty years before, Dr
Hill had refused to take in the General Assembly of 1796.
Inglis, in view of his soundness of doctrine, might be spoken
of not as a Moderate, but as an Evangelical Erastian.   His
clear views of Divine truth, and the care and caution with
which he expressed them, put him on his Apologetic side in
the line of succession from Maclaurin.   That succession is
to be traced in other lines as well.

[1] This held good on the whole, though we find Duncan Mearns of
Aberdeen criticising with vigour Thomas Chalmers' early work on
The Evidences for its exclusively objective character.

It was a succession not of direct influence so much as of spiritual affinity and likeness of natural endowment that was seen in the work of men like those two great divines, Marcus Dods of Belford and James Maclagan of Kinfauns. Of these men we shall have something to say later on. They were intimate friends in the ministry, and when Dods published his remarkable work on the Incarnation of the Eternal Word, in which he set forth the true Catholic faith on the cardinal mystery of godliness and put the crudities and heresy of Edward Irving in their true setting, he embodied as a chapter of that work one of Maclagan's discourses which dealt with the sympathy of Christ and which shows the high standard of preaching that might be heard from the pulpits of quiet country parishes. This sermon, which was not prepared for publication, was as masterly as the other chapters of the work in which it finds a place. These two comrades in the Faith were distinctly of the same specific type of thought, outlook and mental outfit with Maclaurin.

3. THE MODERATES

There was a contrast between Evangelicals, of whom Maclaurin was such an outstanding specimen, and the men who arrogated as their own the designation of the Moderates. This name which they took to themselves came to be one of evil odour with the serious Christian people of the country. If it really meant what it said, there would be not only no harm in such a description; there would be the very opposite. It was a name that was at first not given but taken. When, however, it took on a special meaning it was given by others, but by that time it had become more or less a byword or a name of reproach. When it was first taken by the men themselves it smacked of a fine conceit that its donors had of themselves when they thought they could afford to class those that were not of their party as the Immoderates, or the Extremists. They themselves, of course, were strangers to the wild views of such extreme men. When the name is rightly understood it is seen to have been but a party badge and it was an implicit libel on those from whom it was withheld. Those who chose such a flattering designation as their own called their rivals the High-flyers.

At an early stage after the Revolution Settlement those who believed in the freedom of the Church, and showed this by standing up against the encroachments of the civil government on that freedom, came to be spoken of as the High Presbyterians or the High Churchmen. Now in England the High Churchmen went by the nickname of the High-flyers, and as the Anglican High Churchmen made some show of standing for the freedom of the Church in Convocation, from the pulpit, and in pamphlet warfare, their nickname seems to have been borrowed to be bestowed on the Scottish Evangelicals who not only laid stress on the high mysteries of the Faith, but also held to the Church's freedom. The men who in Scotland did this bit of borrowing aspired to be regarded as central-minded. As we have seen, they came to have the control of the headquarters and the organisation of the Church. They were in touch with the public authorities, to whom they deferred, and each became a convenience to answer the ends of the other. Each of them found the unbending and uncomplying Evangelicals to be obstacles in their way, blocking their centralising and unifying policy, which was not unlike a Totalitarianism before its time, and so they lost no love in relation to such impracticable and unyielding elements. Those Evangelicals were the men who held and preached the mysteries of the Faith; the tendency among the Moderates was to give a minimum of the characteristic truths of the Gospel. Their claim, forsooth, was that they were too modest to aspire to such high doctrine as the mysteries of the Faith called for and thus their nickname for their opponents of High-flyers came to be one that reflected on the high character of the doctrine that was characteristic of the Evangelical pulpit.

The " Machine," to use a modern phrase, got into the hands of the men of a Broad tendency. And their leaders, without having the name of bishops, tended to exercise the governing and managing functions that were, as a rule, associated with the diocesan prelate. This is one of the weaknesses of the practical working of the Presbyterian system when its leading and most pushing men develop the lust for power that is so natural to the ecclesiastic, and the rank and file are disposed with meek, if unwise, docility to allow their aggressive fellows to exploit at the same time themselves and the Church. The typical ecclesiastic is apt to be an authority on the virtues of the minimum so that he puts forward the least possible claim in regard to a high tone of spiritual life or to faithfulness to the claims of that godliness which should be the badge, and have its home in the bosom, of the Church of God.

The worthy representatives of the Reformed Tradition were men who adhered strictly to the Faith as confessed in the Church's symbols and who stood out stoutly in defence of the *jus divinum* of Presbytery and the inherent freedom of the Church to do the will of the Lord, its one Head and King. This they did without yielding to the civil magistrate if he sought to impose his will on the Church in its Confession or in its practical obedience. They had no quarrel with the freedom of the king to obey the word of the King of kings; but under cover of the plea that he was doing so, the supreme ruler might at times pursue a policy of aggrandising himself at the expense of the freedom of the Church of God; and the Evangelicals held that in obedience to their Head and Lord they were bound to carry out His will even when it cut across the programme and policy of the great men at court. If the will of Christ was other than what the civil authority claimed it to be, they felt themselves bound by Apostolic example to obey God rather than men.

It is easy to see how there might come to be a clash of judgment between two such mutually independent authorities; and the quality of the stout champions of the intrinsic freedom of the Church would possibly make it hard to make up the peace between them once it was broken. They, however, were at least no more likely to break the peace than were the secular powers; for these looked with a jaundiced eye at the claim of the Church to be free. The holders of civil office have often regarded this claim as though

it were a demand for an *imperium in imperio* which made
for a divided allegiance.   Men of a supple and yielding
nature whose convictions were fluid and whose conscience
was elastic, and so could stretch a point, were cut out for
the office of finding a *modus vivendi* in days of stress and
strife such as came when a clash between the powers took
place.   They did not by any means make a point of holding
the crown of the causeway as they took the line of least
resistance.   They might claim to be middle-of-the-road men
while this was far from being the case.   Their special
equipment went along with a politic zeal for holding the
reins in their hand and shaping in their wisdom the course
that the Church should take.   The managers of Church
business came at an early date in the 18th century to be
men more or less of this type.   And such men, while
obsequiously truckling to their earthly superiors, were the
very men who found a compensation for eating so much
humble pie when they rode roughshod over their brethren.
They did this to secure that their compromising counsels
should have effect given to them.   When such men came to
be the rowers of the ship of the Church they brought it into
great waters, and the policy that they initiated and pursued
issued, before all was done, in breaking the Church Reformed
in the midst of the seas.   As they carried out their policy
they brought it about that the fair name by which they called
themselves became a byword.   Indeed, by the end of the 18th
century, they exposed themselves to the stinging sarcasm of
Rowland Hill, who saw their work on his visits to Scotland.
Their profession of moderation had worked its way to such
a pitch that they satisfied themselves with being moderate
not only in their faith but in their love to God and moderate
in their obedience to His will, while they inclined to be
immoderate in the licence they allowed themselves and their
allies.   For it was notorious that as they indulged their
liberties they went beyond bounds in disregard to the law of
God.   Those liberties showed themselves in the excesses of
intemperance at which they winked or in which they indulged,
and in the easy way in which they turned a blind eye to

what they excused as the amiable or good-humoured vices
or peccadilloes of their boon companions. And these were the
men that spoke of their Evangelical neighbours as being
Antinomian because they held and taught the doctrine of free
justification by faith alone. In their own conduct they showed
how little regard they had for the claims of that law for
which they professed to be so zealous. Indeed, they claimed
to be so zealous for it that they set it up in opposition to
the teaching of the Gospel. When men of such lives manned
the pulpits it was little wonder that the ministry came under
reproach, the Church was forsaken, formalism was at a
premium, godliness was under a cloud, and practical infidelity
came to prevail. All this was so in various districts of the
land and in different classes of the community when the
shadow of such a upas tree fell upon them. This was the
outcome of an attempt to improve on the Gospel. For this
unbelieving school sprang from a revolt against the teaching
of a free gracious justification for sinners. The legal strain
of preaching that they introduced called for the stress that
the friends of the Evangel felt bound to lay on the doctrine
which the Moderates set at naught. This legal strain came
down from the Baxterianism of their first leaders. It soon
became work salvation run to seed. The doctrine, if doctrine
it was, that prevailed among those Moderates was that of
salvation by works, and it was decidedly Pelagian in its
character. It might make the boast of being a doctrine of
salvation by character or conduct so that creed and conduct
were set up as though they were rivals or sundered alterna-
tives that fell out with one another, whereas there was no
reason why they should not be the best of friends. The
meagre Pelagianism of this unevangelical school was a thinly
veiled Universalism, if, indeed, it had any veil at all to
hide the nakedness of its rejection of the whole Gospel
scheme of salvation through Christ as the Mediator.

Such was the outcome in the realm of doctrine of the
disclaimer made by the Moderates. They deprecated, as we
have seen, the idea that they should be so presumptuous as
to meddle with the high things of Christian doctrine such

as the Covenant of Grace with its train of attendant mysteries, the mystery of godliness in the incarnation of the Lord, the mystery of reconciliation by the blood of His atoning Cross, and that of the New Creation or the New Birth. Their bald naturalism found no very appropriate place for the incarnation, nor could it fit in with its scheme the mystery of the Triune Godhead. This was in keeping with the negative character of so much of the religious thought of the century. It was not that these mysteries must be denied. It was enough that they should be set aside and left severely alone and that little weight should be attached to a denial of them on the part of others. It compromised with unbelief. The Moderate movement was thus part of 18th-century Illuminism and shared with the rest of that tendency in its exaltation of reason and common sense. These were made the arbiters of truth; and Revelation was subjected to their measuring rod. The seat of infallible authority was found in man's own bosom. So Moderatism in doctrine came to be very much a synonym for the unbelief that treated the special truths of the Gospel salvation as little better than the theological lumber that had come down from a bygone and unenlightened age. With such an outlook on the Faith as a whole the Moderates, of course, found it easy to adopt an indifferent or even a hostile attitude to the *jus divinum* of Presbytery and the liberties of the Church. So far as anythink like doctrine was found among them, it was a loose type of Arminianism or even Pelagianism which verged on Socinianism. For the blight that overtook the descendants of the Puritans in England and later in New England told upon them. It was the cold blast of the unevangelical *Zeitgeist* of the 18th century. Such a type of thinking had no quarrel with the Deism which was rampant in fashionable circles. Indeed, some of the leaders did not take it ill to be spoken of as Christian Deists. This kind of thing allowed the Church to walk arm in arm with the world in its own ways. It was a convenience for worldly Churchmen.

It was not at one bound that the unevangelical school came down to such a depth of estrangement from historical

Christianity. The descent was a thing of stages. The earlier working of the unbelieving leaven was to be found among those who, as Conformists under the Episcopal regime, had imbibed the Broad Churchism that was at work in Anglican circles, and who found it easy to conform with the order of things that came to be uppermost. It was not so bigoted as to make High Church claims for Prelacy or Presbytery or anything else. If it did not believe in principle it did believe in interest. Men of this indifferent persuasion found it a convenient thing to conform to the restored Presbyterian Church and their influence told upon it in the next generation. Hand in hand with a fondness for latitude of creed there was at work the earnest but legal strain that marked the first Neonomians, the followers of Baxter's line of teaching. This latter strain was the more respectable of the two, but it soon gave way to the Broad Church tendency which professed to be eminently practical. Its concern was with what is outward and visible and palpable. In more modern speech it would be described as realist or as ethical or as a species of social regeneration teaching whose supreme concern was in a pragmatic fashion with tangible results in the region of the conventions of neighbourly life. In those days, Tillotson was its ideal preacher and he found many imitators who, indeed, only too often made his works a quarry from which they borrowed entire discourses. They believed in and practised the imperial policy of annexing what belonged to their neighbours. Plagiarism was with them a sincere form of unacknowledged flattery. Tillotson continued to be the idol of this school until the star of Hugh Blair came to be in the ascendant. The reign of the Whig Revolution Moralists thus continued for a long time. It was the extent to which this type of thought and of preaching had succeeded in ousting the Evangel from its place that called, as early as 1736, for the Act of Assembly which dealt with the matter of preaching. As this alien tendency wrought, it need hardly be said that the preaching of catechetic doctrine was at a heavy discount. And the parishes that had as their pastors men of this school came to be estranged increasingly from the faith and traditions of the Scottish Reformation. The freezing wind of such an age brought blight in its train. And even when another Gospel had not displaced that of the Apostles there was a suspicious willingness to screen such an alien message from being matter for discipline when it was proclaimed by others.

4. WITHERSPOON ON MODERATISM

It came to be looked upon, indeed, as the correct thing, that is, for those who would be up to date and abreast of the advancing age, to affect a dash of heresy. It was easy to earn the name of a scholar or of a fresh or independent or original thinker by taking this line. In Witherspoon's *Ecclesiastical Characteristics* this feature of the Moderate movement, as it was to be recognised by the middle of the 18th century, is hit off to the life. The sting of his satire was in its truth. And the picture that he draws of a modish Moderate formed on these maxims of moderation which he gives in detail will stand as typical for the reproduction of the like tendency in later days. These are some of the prescriptions that he gives :—

" I. All ecclesiastical persons of whatever rank, whether Principals of Colleges, Professors of Divinity, Ministers, or even Probationers, that are suspected of heresy, are to be esteemed men of great genius, vast learning and uncommon worth; and are by all means to be supported and protected.

" II. When any man is charged with loose practices or tendencies to immorality he is to be screened and protected as much as possible; especially if the faults laid to his charge be ' good-humoured vices.'

" III. It is a necessary part of the character of a Moderate man never to speak of the Confession of Faith but with a sneer; to give sly hints that he does not thoroughly believe it; and to make the word orthodoxy a term of contempt and reproach.

" IV. A good preacher must not only have all the above and subsequent principles of moderation in him, as the source of everything that is good, but must, over and above, have

the following special marks and signs of a talent for preaching.
1. His subjects must be confined to social duties. 2. He
must recommend them only from rational considerations,
viz.:—the beauty and comely proportions of virtue and its
advantages in the present life without any regard to a future
state of more extended self-interest. 3. His authorities must
be drawn from heathen writers, *none*, or as few as possible,
from Scripture. 4. He must be very unacceptable to the
common people.

" V. A minister must endeavour to catch as much of the
air and manner of a fine gentleman as possibly he can.

" VI. It is not only unnecessary for a Moderate man to
have much learning, but he ought to be filled with a contempt
of all kinds of learning but one; which is to understand
Leibnitz's scheme well; the chief parts of which are so
beautifully painted and so harmoniously sung by Lord
Shaftesbury, and which has been so well licked into form and
method by the late immortal Mr Hyndman.

" VII. A Moderate man must endeavour, as much as he
handsomely can, to put off any appearance of devotion, and
avoid all unnecessary exercises of religious worship, whether
public or private. . . .

" XII. As to the world in general a Moderate man is to
have great charity for Atheists and Deists in principle, and
for persons that are loose and vicious in their practice; but
none at all for those that have a high profession of
religion and a great pretence to strictness in their walk and
conversation."

We are not unacquainted with the fashion of adapting
such measures, *mutatis mutandis,* to the present day.

5. 18TH-CENTURY CULTURE

The movement in the direction of a less provincial outlook
affected both the thought and the speech of Scotland. We
have seen how Robert Leighton and Hugh Binning strove to
express themselves in good and standard English by the middle
of the previous century. The movement to follow in their

steps could hardly be spoken of as a precipitate one. Though Maclaurin has been noticed as putting his thoughts in an English dress, yet his contemporaries, Boston and the Erskines and Willison, still showed a marked home influence on their English expression. Boston is remarkable for the lucidity of his style, yet though he was a Border man he belonged definitely to the Scots side of the Border. But the culture and polish of the London Augustan age of Queen Anne began to tell on the literary expression of Scots educated circles before the first half of the century was over. It has been claimed on behalf of Moderatism that to it is due the credit of promoting this cultural levelling up of speech. It had its share in the work. But it had no monopoly. John Erskine and John Witherspoon and William Crawford of Wilton and Robert Walker were, in the matter of general culture, the age-fellows and the compeers of the Blairs and Homes and Robertsons and Carlyles of the Moderate school. They were content, however, to lay out their strength in the work of their own calling. And though at a later stage the Evangelicals fell in with the fashion of writing in northern Johnsonese they retained the benefits of a more cultured speech as a class without being swept off their feet by attempts to float on the bladders of windy bombast. MacEwen of Dundee, among the Seceders, modelled himself, as we have seen, on the flowery style of James Hervey, for it was the mode; and Hervey was a great favourite with the Seceders, as he so definitely adopted the " Marrow " doctrine of faith and the method of presenting the Evangel that was current among themselves.

Among the sermons of the period during which Moderatism prevailed there are few that read better than those of Robert Walker of Edinburgh. He was an Evangelical of the Evangelicals, being one of the inner circle of that godly set in which Lady Glenorchy found herself at home. His sermons on the score of simplicity and freedom from what is tinsel and artificial in style would appeal to the plainer taste of subsequent generations more than do the polished

periods of his colleague, Dr Hugh Blair; and in this respect
Walker was far from being alone.

The monopoly claims put forward on behalf of the
Moderates as the party of culture are subject to heavy
deductions.   They had their ornamental figureheads, but they
had also in their ranks a long train of uncultured boors who,
to quote Burns, confused " their brains in college classes ";
they went " in stirks and came out asses."   In one thing,
however, they excelled.   That was in the use to which they
put their consolidated influence as the dominant party.   They
made the most of this asset for securing to their own men
the preponderance in the seats of learning and from University
chairs they leavened the thought of the rising ministry.   In
Glasgow there was felt the impact of the teaching of Francis
Hutcheson and William Leechman, an unapostolic succession
to that of John Simson.   Edinburgh had Robertson as
Principal with Hugh Blair in the Chair of Rhetoric.   Aberdeen
had Gerard and George Campbell.   St Andrews became a
nest of Moderates, so that the tradition of Halyburton died
out in its Divinity School.   By the end of the century George
Hill was Principal of St Mary's there, and he was the
acknowledged leader of the dominant party in the Church
courts.   As Professor of Divinity he delivered a course of
systematic lectures that were definitely and ably Calvinistic.
Dr Hill was satisfied that on its merits the Confessional
Theology is entitled to be recognised as the teaching of Holy
Scripture.   Yet in his Church policy he was a supple Moderate
who could show himself firm enough in standing up against
anything that could, with a show of plausibility, be accused
of being affected with the taint of Enthusiasm.   The age had
not yet passed when any thought or life that gave place to
the working of the Spirit of God was quickly dismissed as
so much Methodism or Enthusiasm.   For what it called
Enthusiasm was the pet aversion of the cold 18th-century
culture.   It made the most of the prejudice awakened by the
excesses of the French prophets, the Quakers and other
extremists.

6. Moderatism Timid and Subservient

In the panic of reaction which followed on the upheaval of the French Revolution, Hill was the leader of the Assembly in its refusal to take steps to promote the cause of Foreign Missions, and thus, as we have seen, he sacrificed for a generation the credit that his Church would have had of being the first National Church in Christendom to take up aggressive work in "The Regions Beyond" as part of its normal and acknowledged activities.   He was in favour of letting the "Happy Establishment in Church and in State" function normally or, in other words, go on in the humdrum fashion which it followed ever since his Party had got hold of the reins of office.   That Party wrought hand in hand with the civil government of the day, and its unwritten concordat worked out to the Erastian result of making the Church little more than a pendicle of the life of the State, a department which in its courts was allowed to have the shadow of self-government so long as it took no step to which the civil rulers might take exception as out of keeping with their line of State policy.   It was a convenience for the politicians to have so many trusty confidential agents in the parish manses of the country.   These men were the creatures, and so quite naturally the defenders, of the system of lay patronage.

Tory Jacobitism had in the days of Queen Anne restored the system of Church patronage with a view to the wrecking of the Presbyterian Establishment.   It wrought havoc in the Church.   To a large extent the lay patrons who had their power given back to them were of the Jacobite faction, and in the latter years of Anne's reign, with their power as patrons restored to them, they made the attempt in some cases to settle as the incumbents in vacant parishes their own Episcopal and Jacobite nominees.   Once the landed gentry or the patrons got into the saddle they kept their seat and it was the policy of the managers in the Church to keep on good terms with them.   Each buttressed and bolstered up the other, so that in the course of years the abuses of the system of Church patronage almost put an end to the old

Reformed teaching that recognised the right of a Christian congregation to make choice of its own pastor. By degrees the Orthodox or the Popular Party, as the Evangelicals were called, fell in with the order that prevailed or at least weakened in their protest against it. Yet the voice of witness for a better order was not altogether put to silence.

The Church policy of William Robertson was one that fitted in with the State policy of the earlier part of the reign of George III. But Robertson, though he was what would now be called a Liberal in Theology, could draw the line when his Party took a course that he deemed to be ill-advised. A few years before his death he gave up the Party leadership, for the hotheads among them, who might be said to be fierce for moderation, chafed under the obligation that was laid upon them to own the Church's Confession as the Confession of their own Faith. This they looked upon as laying a restraint upon their liberty. They sought to have the bonds relaxed that laid this obligation upon them. Now Robertson could hardly be said to be one whit more orthodox than the agitators. Yet he was not prepared to tinker with the old legislation under which the National Church held its place. He might fear that his unruly followers would bring the old house down about their ears; and his line of policy was *quieta non movere*. He thought it the part of prudence to let well alone and to let sleeping dogs lie.

7. MODERATISM AND THEOLOGY

But what was Moderatism so far as the orderly study of Divine Truth was concerned? It had very little use for such a thing at all. Theology was not one of the elegant things of life in which secular culture delights; and such were the things by which this Church tendency in its higher circles set store. They were the very breath of its nostrils. Its thinking was a nebulous philosophy of life that yawned over divinity of any other kind than a little Apologetic reading. It found a place for George Campbell's answer to David Hume on *Miracles* or for James Beattie in his Essay on Truth. The author of this essay was one of the literary men of his day.

His *Minstrel* is not quite forgotten yet, or, at least, it is remembered that he wrote such a poem. Campbell's Lectures on *Sacred Rhetoric* and *Criticism* and his work on the Gospels may still be met with, as well as his treatise on Ecclesiastical History. He wrote with marked ability on professional subjects that covered a wide range. In his criticism he set up as the candid critic who was specially candid in dealing with what he thought the faults of the old Reformed ideal in Church and doctrine. Then Blair's Sermons created a sensation. He was meticulously careful in matters of style and taste. In keeping with the traditions of his school he dealt largely with the virtues and the vices. When he took up a Gospel theme his treatment of it was note-worthy, not for what he had to say but for what he left unsaid. The success of his Sermons furnished the rank and file of his Party with a new quarry from which to hew out their pulpit message, if they did not annex them altogether. They had been long enough borrowing from Tillotson. The change over to Blair supplied a little variety for hearers that did not sleep.

We have spoken of the almost Deistic strain of teaching that was to be found among men of the Moderate Party. It was in the company and fellowship of men of such a tendency that the gifted Robert Burns moved. He became their spokesman in his caricatures of the Old School Evangelicals of his native Ayrshire. Russel and his predecessor, Oliphant of Kilmarnock, became the targets for his shafts. It is said that some of these were pointed and sharpened by one of the Moderate leaders. Oliphant and Russel, who were afterwards ministers respectively in Dumbarton and Stirling, were two of the outspoken Orthodox men who were felt to be awkward neighbours by the Bard's clerical friends. The latter of the two was a Boanerges; and we may see the stark, if rough-and-ready, vigour of his style in his published sermons, a few of which are given in the memorial volume to his son—who was one of Dr Chalmers' highly esteemed friends—Mr Russel of Muthill. Such an outspoken preacher of law and Gospel could easily come into conflict with the circle of Burns'

friends. Oliphant again was like Russel in his Orthodox and
Evangelical preaching. He took part of his training for the
ministry among the Burgher Seceders and so sat at the feet
of James Fisher. When he joined the National Church he
brought with him the Gospel soundness of the early Secession.
He was the author of a Catechism which gives a taste of his
quality. This little book supplied a mean handle to the
Moderates of Dumbarton when he was settled there. They
felt galled that such a man had become their minister and
they took their own way to show the dislike that they had
for him. They sent the bellman through the town with the
public notice, "the whole works of the Rev. James Oliphant
for twopence." Mr Oliphant was in later years one of the
senior intimates of Dr John Love of Anderston.

The shuffling unbelief of the Ayrshire Moderates came out
of cover when M'Gill of Ayr ventured to give to the world
his *Essay on the Death of Christ,* in which he showed himself
to be a Socinian. He was brought to book, and had to with-
draw this publication; but though so far it came under censure
its writer was let off lightly, for the case was huddled up.
The Moderates were very easy in their dealing with errorists.
At the same time they did not like to be faced with a charge
of heresy. Of one of them it is told that when a statement
he made in a Church court was challenged as heresy his
answer was: "Moderator, if that is heresy, I recant it."
Men who were themselves vulnerable could not afford to be
too hard or strict on others. So those were days of doctrinal
laxity.

The period of the ascendancy of this Moderate school was
roughly from 1760 to 1810. If that was the duration of the
umbra it was preceded and followed by a considerable
penumbra. Yet, even when the eclipse was on, the Moderates
did not have things all their own way. For there were
districts of the country that enjoyed their brightest Gospel
day when a darkness that might be felt brooded over others.
And though the outstanding Evangelical teachers might be
few they were tried and true. We may look at some of them.

8. John Witherspoon and Scottish Theology Overseas

In the days of his Scottish ministry John Witherspoon came to be looked upon as the foremost of the younger Evangelical writers, preachers and Churchmen. It was his eminence in these respects that won for him the two invitations extended to him to become the President of the College of New Jersey. His practical writings speak for themselves. The concise work that he wrote on Justification and its companion volume on Regeneration show him to have been a well-equipped Reformed theologian. His going to the New World linked Presbytery at an early stage in the States of America, or, as they were when he went, the American Colonies, with Presbyterianism in its old home in the English-speaking world. His influence on and connection with the Orthodox Westminster teaching that came afterwards in the early days of the Princeton Seminary to be called Princeton Theology show the importance of the part that he played in the exposition and defence of the Reformed Faith. In his days before the Seminary was set up, Theology was taught in Princeton College. Witherspoon also introduced to the American public the Scottish Apologetic Philosophy of Common Sense. Though so much of his mature work or that of his later years was done in the land of his adoption to which he rendered such conspicuous service, yet Scotland will not give up her hold on one of the best gifts she bestowed on the New World.

9. Lady Glenorchy's Circle

Mention has already been made of Robert Walker and the quality of his work. His name brings before us the set that was attracted by the godly and gracious Lady Glenorchy, who filled a like place in Scotland in furthering the cause of the Evangel to that held by her excellent, if more masterful, contemporary in England, Selina, the Countess of Huntingdon. Eminent among this set was Robert Balfour, who died minister of Glasgow Cathedral. We have not so much from his pen as from that of Walker, but what we have is of

high quality, albeit that it is set forth in the style of which
Samuel Johnson set the fashion. It is only the curious that
now come across his fugitive sermons. He did not print
much, but he impressed his generation. As one of the Lady
Glenorchy circle he is linked with the memory of his friend,
John Erskine, and as one of the Glasgow ministers with that
of John Love. Of these two, John Erskine is looked upon,
after Witherspoon left for America, as the most prominent
leader of the Evangelical school during the Moderate ascendancy. The other was in many respects the most striking and
outstanding figure of later days among the Evangelicals in
the West of Scotland.

10. DR JOHN ERSKINE AND HIS FRIENDS

Dr Erskine, in his early years in the ministry, was settled
at Kirkintilloch, which is about a dozen miles out of Glasgow.
He had been, in his student days in Edinburgh, one of the
young men who took a lively interest in the work of George
Whitefield on his first visit to Scotland. And in his Western
charge he was within easy reach of Cambuslang and Kilsyth
which were the most noted centres of the great awakening
of 1742. He was from the very outset of his public work
a thorough Evangelical, and the students who were of his
fellowship in Edinburgh were of one mind with him in this.
His biographer, the friend of his old age, Sir Henry Moncreiff
Wellwood, gives some notice of these young men. Witherspoon was his contemporary, as was also William Crawford
of Wilton, who died a comparatively young man, and whose
Dying Thoughts were long a popular work in devout
Scottish circles. Another of the set was James Hall of
Dunglass, who was cut off before his college course was done.
Of him John Erskine wrote a Memoir, one of the first things
that he sent to the press. This is now a very rare little
book. The outlook of the subject and the writer was
one. And what was the writer's outlook from the first was
his outlook to the end of his long ministry. He was not
ashamed of the Gospel of Christ. The social circles in which
he and his young friend Hall moved were those of the landed

and legal aristocracy and these were by no means in the
18th century noted for their Christian thinking or their devout
living. Yet among them there was a remnant who must have
been all the more conspicuous by the contrast that they
afforded to their class. In a former generation there had been
more of them. But in Erskine's day, which was the hey-
day of the Moderate regime, they were comparatively few.
Even then, however, Whitefield found quite a number of his
friends in the upper classes. Of those upper classes there
were devout and honourable women whose memory was long
fragrant, such as the Countess of Leven and Lady Glenorchy
of whom we have already spoken. As a link with an earlier
Covenanting strain there was Mrs Jean Trotter, whose godly
meditations are extant to tell of her exercise of mind in
Scripture truth. She was the daughter of a Lord Provost
of Edinburgh and a granddaughter of the Lord President of
the Supreme Court in Scotland. On her father's side she
was one of the Stewarts of Coltness. Her paternal grandfather was one of the closest friends that George Gillespie
had. Then there were the sets in which Colonel Blackader
and Colonel Gardiner moved, so that though there were not
many noble that were called it was not the case that there
was not any. Of these, some were less firmly grounded in
the knowledge of the Reformed Faith than others, and were
in danger of being swept off their feet by the zealous and
earnest teaching of John Wesley, who at one stage looked as
though he would find a great welcome in Edinburgh for his
wing of the Methodist Revival. John Erskine saw the
danger in which so many of his friends were of being taken
aside by Arminian teaching. He sounded an alarm. This
was sufficient. The eyes of his friends were opened to the
difference between Wesley's teaching and the old Reformed
way of setting forth the Gospel, so that whatever sympathy
they might have for the awakening note of Wesley's teaching
as it spoke of man's sin and responsibility, they would have
none of his Arminianism. Thus the Evangelicals of the
Scottish capital were kept on the Old School Reformed lines.
A hundred years later revival movements brought into vogue

a type of teaching in some respects not unlike that of Wesley; but when in the 'seventies of last century John Kennedy of Dingwall sounded a note of warning he was looked upon as a Cassandra whose warnings fell on deaf ears and whose message was out of date.

Dr Erskine's charge in Edinburgh was that of a collegiate minister in the Greyfriars' Church and there he had as one of his elders the father of Sir Walter Scott. In his *Guy Mannering* Scott makes his English visitor attend a service at Greyfriars' and hear a sermon from the minister of his youth. We have in his description of the scene a pen-picture of the Evangelical patriarch. In Greyfriars' he had a difficult position to fill, as he had for his colleague in the charge his old college contemporary, William Robertson, the leader of the Moderates. The story used to be told of how on one occasion Robertson, on the Sabbath morning, expatiated on the beauty of virtue and ventured to say that if Virtue in all its beauty were only to be seen on earth all men would fall down and worship it. To meet teaching of this kind Erskine may have had to change his afternoon sermon. But whether he had to change or no he managed to get in his answer. Virtue, he said, had come to this earth incarnate in the Person of the Son of God, yet men were so far from falling down to worship Him that with wicked hands they took and crucified and slew Him. Human nature was not the same to the two men.

In connection with Dr Erskine's relation to Dr Robertson as his colleague, John Aikman, who became in after years an Independent minister in Edinburgh, used to tell the tale of a visit he made to London where he hoped to see John Newton. Before setting out he called on Dr Erskine. The doctor asked him to convey his Christian regards to Mr Newton whom he commended as a man of God. The one thing that he was surprised about in regard to him was that he could stay in a Church which taught Baptismal Regeneration. Mr Aikman saw Mr Newton and conveyed to him the Christian regards of his good friend in Edinburgh. These, Mr Newton said, were very acceptable, for he looked on Dr Erskine as a man of God; the one thing about him that he could not explain to himself was that he should find it possible to have Dr Robertson as his colleague.

While Dr Erskine was still a young man he became one of the correspondents of Jonathan Edwards, who had quite a circle of Scottish friends to whom he wrote and who wrote to him. In the course of this correspondence Edwards expressed himself as dissatisfied with the loose way in which Church government was managed among his fellow-Independents and expressed himself as willing to fall in with Presbytery as that Church government was practised in Scotland. His Scottish friend wished to find a home in Scotland for his brother in New England after his Church had cast him out; and it was as President of a College which was under Presbyterian auspices, the College of Princeton, New Jersey, that Edwards ended his career.

It was not to be wondered at that one who was so keenly interested in the cause of his Lord and the maintenance of the Faith as Erskine was should take a lively interest in the spread of the Kingdom of God. It was in the last decade of his life, a life which lasted until he was a few years over 80, that the scene took place when he felt called upon to speak out in the Assembly of 1796. Hamilton of Gladsmuir, on the Moderate side, was arguing against receiving the Overture which prayed that the Assembly should take action to advance the cause of the Gospel in other lands. In his argument the young man pleaded that education and civilisation must come first and then the Gospel might follow. The aged Erskine, when the speaker sat down, rose and said: " Moderator, rax me that Bible." He got the Bible and read from it the account of how the Apostle Paul laboured as the door opened among the barbarous people of Melita who showed him and his company no small kindness. He did not wait until they were first educated and civilised.

A man of the doctor's public spirit could preach when he saw cause on public questions, and among his discourses is one that he preached and printed when tension was growing between the court policy of George III. and the American

Colonies. It is entitled, *Shall I go to War with my American Brethren?* Among the old Evangelical Presbyterians the love of constitutional government and freedom that characterised the Whig policy which brought about the Revolution of 1689 was still alive and strong, and those who cherished sentiments of this kind were in sympathy with the defence of popular rights.

Erskine was looked upon by Dr William Cunningham as the most important theologian in Scotland in the latter part of the 18th century. We have already seen that in his analysis of faith he took a line that laid special stress on the working of our intellectual nature as the root exercise of the faith that saves. So long as it is held that the faith which has its origin in the exercise of the understanding as it deals with the propositions in which the Gospel is set forth has its necessary and invariable complement in the exercise of the will as it receives and rests upon Christ who is freely held out in the Gospel, it is no serious divergence from the common Reformed teaching which lays stress on the trust of the heart as the cardinal exercise of the faith that saves. It is in such a case no more than an endeavour to trace as a psychological phenomenon the roots of the faith that the Christian exercises as he receives Christ the Lord. This is much the same as what Dr Owen says: " Faith is in the understanding in respect of its being and subsistence, in the will and heart in respect of its effectual working." Dr Erskine says in his *Dissertation on Faith*, p. 191 (Edinburgh, 1808) : " Nor will I peremptorily deny, that in some scriptures receiving Christ may signify, the heart choosing, and the affections embracing and cleaving to Christ, as our Prophet, Priest and King, and the whole soul consenting to, approving of, and delighting in the Saviour and in the Gospel-scheme of salvation through Him. But then, in these scriptures, it denotes something different from faith, though I readily allow it intimately connected with, inseparately attending or necessarily flowing from faith, and therefore essential to the Christian character."

The friends of Dr Erskine's old age were the men who welcomed Charles Simeon and other English Evangelicals when they visited Scotland. They were such men as Walter Buchanan of the Canongate Church, Edinburgh, Thomas Davidson of the Tolbooth, Edinburgh, whose grandson, Randall Davidson, was the late Archbishop of Canterbury, and a younger man who died in early life, David Black of Lady Yester's. There were also Thomas Jones of Lady Glenorchy's and John Colquhoun of Leith. This last was the leading divine in the State Church who, in his teaching, was a thoroughgoing "Marrowman." The worthy man got round the awkward corner that Findings of Assembly should be honoured even when one did not agree with them. He did this in his own way. Students of divinity used to consult him as to what they should read. One of his advices we give in its original Scots form : " Noo, I daurna advise ye to read *The Marrow o' Modern Deeveenity,* for ye ken the Assembly condemned it. But they didna condemn Tammas Bowston's notes on *The Marrow.*" Dr Colquhoun's preaching was very much prized by the older school of Evangelicals who were less under the influence of Orthodox Methodism and who held to what was a definitely Scottish Gospel tradition. His works dealing with such themes as the Covenant of Works, the Covenant of Grace, Law and Gospel, Evangelical Repentance, Spiritual Comfort, the Promises and so on are quite a small library in which his Theology, which was that of Boston, is set forth in a clear and solid way. He was a special adept at bringing his message to bear on the conscience or the spiritual case of his hearer. The Covenant Theology was still the popular form with the Evangelical ministry for presenting Gospel truth until well after his days. Over and above Scottish works expository of the Covenant such as those of Rutherford, Patrick Gillespie, Boston and other " Marrow " divines, there were few books dealing with the subject that had more value put upon them than Hermann Witsius on the *Economy of the Covenants* as that work circulated in Crookshanks' translation.

Before we pass from the age of John Erskine there is one of his own generation that we ought not to overlook as a representative man for the West of Scotland. This was John Gillies of Glasgow, the son-in-law of John Maclaurin. He wrote the *Life of Whitefield* and gathered a Collection of all the authentic narratives that he could lay hands on which told the story of spiritual awakening in the Church of God. It is perhaps the finest thing of its kind that one can look to for information in regard to this aspect of the history of the Reformed Churches. It appeared in two volumes and they are hard to get, but there is an edition issued in one volume about 100 years ago under the oversight of Dr Horatius Bonar. This edition is more orderly in the distribution of its material, and, on a less scale, it gives information in regard to awakenings from 1780 on till about 1840. These were later than the previous issue of the Collections. This work of Dr Gillies is of special value, naturally, in regard to the fruit of the Gospel in the British Isles, but it deals also with America and the Continent of Europe. It goes by the title of *Gillies' Historical Collections*. Dr Bonar's edition is a close-printed work of nearly 600 pages.

Other names might be given of worthy men who did good work in the dark days of the Moderate ascendancy in holding the Faith and furthering the cause of the Gospel such as George Muir of Cumnock, John Snodgrass of Paisley, James Kidd of Aberdeen, John Robertson of Kingussie and Alexander Stewart of Moulin. Of these, the last was years in the ministry before he felt the power of the Gospel for himself. A visit from Simeon of Cambridge was the occasion of his enlightenment; and soon after the change took place there was a time of refreshing in his parish. To this inland parish of Perthshire belonged a young couple who felt the power of the Revival. They were the parents of Alexander Duff of Calcutta, who was honoured to do so much for the cause of the Gospel overseas. Dr Stewart was a fine scholar and a highly cultured man. As we have noted in passing, he agreed with Dr Erskine and Dr Chalmers in their analysis of faith and in the stress that they laid upon the primary activity of the understanding in apprehending the truth of, and assenting to, the propositions that set forth the object of faith on which its exercise terminates. They did not shut out the element of trust.

11. JOHN LOVE

There was one name that we coupled with that of Erskine as an Evangelical of special note, and before we leave the age of the Moderates we must give some account of him. It is the name of Dr John Love of Anderston, Glasgow. He was one of the most massive men of his generation. John Love was born in Paisley in 1756. The influences that were about him in his early years were of a neutral, if not of a negative, character. He, however, came under the power of Divine grace while still in his teens, and we have in the two volumes of his Memorials a detailed account of his early spiritual history. He came in touch with the circle of serious godliness in Ayrshire which became the butt of the satire of Robert Burns, and, if John Love is to be taken as a specimen of the men who belonged to that school, it must have had within it some of the best and noblest characters produced by Evangelical Christianity in Scotland. It was in London, at Hoxton, in a small Presbyterian congregation that he was ordained to the ministry, and here in his small sphere he laboured for a number of years. The fewness of his flock did not take away from the thoroughness and conscientiousness with which he prepared for the pulpit. At the same time his very freedom from pastoral labours made it possible for him to do the work that he did as one of the founders of the London Missionary Society, of which he was one of the first Secretaries. This was work that he could not have taken on if he had the exacting claims of a large city charge to meet. His zeal in the cause of Foreign Missions made him, on his return to Scotland, one of the moving spirits of the Glasgow Missionary Society. At Anderston he had a great congregation that rallied about his ministry, and there he became the recognised centre of the Old School Gospel folk of the West of Scotland. He was a

man of a great mind with a majestic type of thought. His
thinking was of a searching and penetrative quality as well
as of a comprehensive range. In his early spiritual experience
he was very thoroughly searched by the teaching of Jonathan
Edwards and the men of the older New England introspective
school. This left its mark on his teaching in turn. And he
was remarkable for how he opened up not only the truth in
regard to God's glorious Being and Name, but also in
particular the truth in regard to the sovereign effectual work
of the Holy Ghost in the New Creation. He believed in
thoroughness of self-examination and he practised it. There
was with all this a serene aloofness about John Love so that
men might say of him that his soul was like a star and dwelt
apart. Yet for all his majesty and aloofness he was as much
loved as he was revered by a wide circle. In those days
there was no man who was more looked up to or in whose
judgment his friends more implicitly rested. His charge at
Anderston was what was called a Chapel of Ease, so that in
his time there was no seat for him in the Church courts.
This helped to concentrate his attention on the special work
of the preacher and the pastor. After the lapse of more than
a century since his death his memory is still green, and the
volumes of sermons or discourses or letters or memorials
which he left are enquired after to this day. When we come
to speak of John Duncan we may see the special place held
by Love's searching ministry in the life of the West of
Scotland. It was once said in criticism of his works that
his discourses were only skeletons. This called forth the
reply that the bones then must be the bones of a mammoth.

12. THE BROTHERS HALDANE

When the General Assembly of 1796 declined to take
action to promote the aggressive evangelisation of the world,
one of the arguments put forward to justify such a policy
of inaction was that there was quite enough for the Church
to do about its own doors. It was indeed quite true that
there was already a problem of Home Heathenism. The
lapsing of the masses had begun. Those, however, who

pleaded this as a reason for doing nothing to spread the Gospel to the regions beyond hardly thought that they would be so soon taken at their word and that inroads were to be made on the outfield of lapsed Christianity in Scotland. Such, however, was the case. It was due to a great extent to the remissness of the dominant party in the ministry of the Church that things were as they were. For by the end of the 18th century Moderatism, as a system of easygoing semi-Deism, had time to bring forth fruit in keeping with its principle, and over large areas of the land the Gospel was conspicuous in the pulpits by its absence unless among the Seceders and the old Dissenters. When the great truths of the Faith were not the staple of the public preaching there went along with an unevangelical pulpit a neglect of the oversight of home instruction and so of congregational catechising. This issued in the production of a constituency that were grossly ignorant of Christian truth. So there was a field for missionary activity to be found without any need of going overseas to India or elsewhere to seek it. We must, however, in fairness bear in mind that the Industrial Revolution had begun and this produced the congested population of the seats of industry. To meet the needs of this situation the Church was remiss in making adequate provision. Now among those who were zealous for Foreign Mission work, but whose zeal was repressed, there were two brothers who came to be prominent in the work of Christian Evangelism and Philanthropy. These were the brothers Haldane, Robert and James Alexander.

The Haldanes belonged to one of the oldest families of the landed gentry. Robert was the owner of the fine estate of Airthrey near Stirling; and James, as the captain of an East Indiaman, held a lucrative post that was looked upon as one of the plums of the nautical profession. They were the nephews of Admiral Duncan, Lord Camperdown, with whom Robert served for a time at sea as a midshipman. They both were converted in early life and were in close touch with the Evangelical circle that moved about John Erskine in Edinburgh and the similar group that were the friends of

John Newton in London. With the ardour of youth they
devoted themselves to the cause of the Gospel. Robert sold
his estate that he might finance, and engage in, Missionary
work in India. But the heartless and heathen policy of the
East India Company laid an embargo on his scheme. When
the Assembly's finding in 1796 shut the door on Foreign
Mission work to be carried on under the auspices of the
State Church as a body, James Haldane, in company with
others of a like mind, such as John Campbell, afterwards of
Kingsland Chapel, London, and John Aikman, threw himself
into aggressive Evangelistic work at home, only to find that
the Moderatism which had frowned on Foreign Mission
enterprise abroad was quite as unfriendly to energetic forward
work in the field of Home Missions. So it came about that
the Missionary cause for which they laboured was extruded
from the Scottish Church, and soon the movement proved to
be the head waters of most of the Independent Churches of
Scotland. In this connection a number of tabernacles were
built at strategic points, and as an active Evangelistic
and Missionary movement the community of the Haldane
Independents became a force that had to be reckoned with.

James Haldane, who became the pastor of the tabernacle
in Edinburgh, interested himself in restoring the life and
conditions of the Apostolic Church, but without the Pentecostal
endowment. And with the bias that was given him by the
extrusion of his zealous activities from the National Church
he became in some sense a forerunner of the type of Church
fellowship which in the next generation took the shape of
Brethrenism. At last he and his brother Robert became
Baptists in their sacramental views. This change on their
part split the tabernacle movement into two almost equal
parts. It was the first step in popularising Baptist views in
Scotland. It was not, however, quite the beginning of the
Baptist movement any more than of the Independent Churches.
But we might trace far the greatest part of Baptist
propaganda in the country to the changed convictions of the
Haldanes.

It might be urged that the changes which came over the judgment of these good men, and of James in particular, argued a certain shiftiness or instability of mind. This, however, was more in appearance than in reality. They were at first amateurs in Theology. Yet in regard to the cardinal verities of the Evangel there were few men whose record was as consistent as that of James Haldane. His contemporaries, M'Crie and Andrew Thomson, would bear ready witness to the soundness of his teaching as to the Way of Life and to the blessing that rested on his clear preaching of free Justification by Faith alone. When in his later years his erstwhile partner in his Independent days, Ralph Wardlaw, swerved from the accepted Reformed view of an effective Atonement or one that secures the salvation of those for whom it was made, James Haldane struck a thoroughly sound note in his little work on the Atonement and so showed himself to be well grounded in the Evangelical doctrine that he had preached from his early days. Where he was off from the Reformed Faith was in his defective view of the Old Testament Dispensation. He looked upon it as being one that was radically of such a carnal character as to shut out the recognition of a really high attainment in spiritual life on the part of the saints who lived under its system of shadows. This was quite in keeping with his position as a Baptist.

James A. Haldane was an Evangelist. His elder brother, who could hardly be spoken of as a preacher at all, though he did preach at times, was a thinker and a student in Theology. He had become a Baptist when his brother did. Yet he came to lay little stress on denominational differences and to give so little prominence to the points on which he diverged from the common teaching of the Reformed Faith that his Continental friends spoke of him as a Scots Presbyterian. Indeed, in his last years, with the exception of his brother, he held no men in such high esteem as some of the Evangelicals in the reviving Church of Scotland who were most outspoken in their adherence to the full Reformed Faith, such, for instance, as Dr Robert Gordon, who was one of the most revered leaders of the Free Church of Scotland at the Disruption. He had found that they stood by him most loyally in the decisive battle that he fought, which was the main work of his life. He had done a great and remarkable work on the Continent of Europe among theological students at Geneva and elsewhere, so that he became, as it were, a second father to the revived Evangelical Churches in France and in French Switzerland. But he was to do a greater work at home.

The crowning work of Robert Haldane's life was his defence of the Canon of Holy Scripture. This was work that he felt himself called upon to do as one of the active friends of the Bible Society. He found that those who held the reins of the Society's management in their hands had embarked on a policy of circulating the books of the Apocrypha in the editions of the Bible which they sold in the countries of Continental Europe. This he held to be out of keeping with the principle on which the Society had been founded. The managers defended their practice on the ground of expediency, holding that unless they gave with the Old Testament the Apocryphal Books they could not sell their Bibles in the lands overseas. A controversy began which lasted for years, and in the course of it loose ideas in regard to the inspiration of Scripture and to the integrity of the Canon were freely put forward by some of the defenders of the policy to which Haldane took exception. This might be said to be the first token of the working of an unbelieving leaven as to Holy Writ in Evangelical circles in Scotland. It was at work to some extent among English Nonconformists, and the leaders of the New Light movement among the Seceders felt the infection. On the other hand, Mr Haldane had the powerful backing of Dr Andrew Thomson of St George's, Edinburgh, who opened the pages of his *Christian Instructor* freely for such a good cause. The issue of the long and painful conflict was that the English-speaking world was furnished with the unadulterated Protestant Canon of Scripture as its everyday possession, a thing that was by no means universally the case before; and for over a century it is with such a Canon that it is familiar. To no man under the hand of God are we more indebted for this state of things than to Robert Haldane.

In questions of a generally apologetic or defensive character Haldane was much more interested than was the ordinary devout Evangelical of his age. With a feeling of the coldness and aloofness of what were then the recognised apologetical works, such as Butler's Analogy and Paley's Evidences and Watson's Letters, and with the conviction that when such Apologists had occasion to touch on the substance of the Faith they presented it in a very defective way, he set himself the task of writing on the subject of Christian Evidences that he might put the good case that the cold defenders made in a warmer manner than they did, and when he dealt with the teaching of the Scriptures he might shun the doctrinal errors into which the current Apologists had fallen. This work saw two editions. In the presentation of the internal evidence that Scripture contains in its bosom as it sets forth the way of the Gospel, this work is of a value that is not tied down to the needs of his age. A little work of his, which first came out as a large pamphlet in the Apocrypha controversy, saw quite a number of editions. In it he ably discussed the inspiration of the Scriptures and defended the strict and Apostolic doctrine which Scripture itself teaches and which in later years was set forth by one of his disciples, Louis Gaussen of Geneva, in his Theopneustia. The Scripture Doctrine of the Inspiration that belongs to its pages and that extends to its words is to be learned from its definite statements, and among these in particular from the use that is made in one part of Scripture of the words of earlier Scripture. In fact it is arrived at from an induction and comparison of the statements that we find the Apostles and Prophets making about their own work and writings. In this respect it is the result of a conspectus of relevant Scripture material just as is the case with any other of the great doctrines of the Faith.

Speaking of Robert Haldane and his theological work, we ought not to leave without mention his massive Commentary

on the Epistle to the Romans. In it we have in permanent
form the teaching that he gave to the theological students
of Geneva when, after Waterloo, he spent a winter in the
city of Calvin. In his informal meetings with the young men
he unfurled again the banner which the Reformer had
unfurled almost three centuries before; and the results of
his action in so doing told on a wide scale on the Churches
in which his young converts were called to labour. This
Commentary has gone through a number of editions, one of
them as late as more than thirty years after the death of
the venerable author. The work appeared both in French
and in English. For those who wish to know what the
Apostle taught in his great doctrinal Epistle this exposition
ranks with those of Calvin or of Hodge. In book form it is
Robert Haldane's stone of memorial.

VIII.
NEW LIGHT AND WHAT IT HAS DONE
I.
WHAT IS NEW LIGHT?

IT has been said that the various branches of the Church
of Scotland have sprung from the main trunk, making the
profession that in taking up their separate position they did
so only to adhere the more faithfully to the truths that were
held by the Church as a Confession of Faith or to its
professed principles. In such a statement there is a good
measure of truth. If it were always and altogether thus,
there would be little or no room in making such separations
for the working of New Light except by unfaithfulness to
truth already professed. The separations, whatever they
may have been to begin with, did not all by any means hold
fast their integrity; and in spite of the profession of
adherence to the unabated Confession of the Reformed Church
their record will show that after a while there was, on the
part of many, an easing off of the intenseness and of the
conviction with which the old truths were held and taught.
The working of such a tendency to drift from the old moorings
was claimed to be but obedience to New Light which made
it impossible or impracticable to make the full profession
that was formerly made. This accession of light brought
into prominence what had formerly been in the shade. So
it was looked upon as imperative to give it a regulative
place, if men would show themselves loyal to what they looked
upon as fresh truth.

1. CAMERONIANS AND RELIEF WELCOME IT

As a term, New Light came especially to be used in
connection with the change that took place in the thinking
of the Seceders towards the end of the 18th century. At

an earlier date a change had taken place in the teaching of some of the Reformed Presbyterians. But though the innovating Presbytery may have been at some times spoken of as the New Light Party, the term did not take root, nor did it meet with such a vogue as it got in connection with the Seceders. For that movement soon came to naught.

At a somewhat earlier date than among the followers of the Erskines and Gib the views that were to be later the distinctive teaching of the New Light Party in the Secession found a place in the Synod of Relief. This Synod, which to begin with was a Presbytery, was founded to relieve the grievances of parishioners who felt the pinch of Church patronage, and who were left the choice of separating from the Church if they would have a ministry after their own mind, or of putting up with an unacceptable presentee as their pastor. In the earlier days of this Relief Body, which avoided tying its hands for the future by a profession such as the Seceders made that they would adhere loyally to the old Covenanting position, it met with strenuous opposition, especially from the more militant branch of the Secession. The Relief champion, Patrick Hutchison of St Ninian's, had to fight for them in print against the assailants who attacked them from the Secession position. That views of a more or less revolutionary character should be found among the Relief was not so significant of change as that they should find a welcome in the ranks of their more conservative neighbours. For from the outset of their separate existence the Relief Party were in sympathy more with the Calvinistic wing of the Methodist movement than they were with the older Reformed school of teaching and worship. In saying this we do not mean to say that the early ministers of the Relief were not orthodox in holding the Evangelical verities of the Reformed Faith; for they were. But as a class they were little disposed to be fighters. They had among them some good Evangelical theologians, such, for example, as Thomas Bell of Dovehill, Glasgow, who was the author of a Treatise on the Covenants, and of a volume of solid doctrinal discourses. He also translated into English, with

notes, the *Animadversiones Irenicae of Hermann Witsius*.
This last bit of work he carried out, if not on the suggestion,
at least with the encouragement of Dr John Erskine; for the
working of the leaven of revolutionary thought had not yet
drawn the Relief people into a position of militancy against
the State Church as a religious establishment, nor estranged
them from their Evangelical friends within its borders. Indeed,
it was not until about the end of the period of Moderate
ascendancy that the Relief Church took steps to educate its
own students for the ministry. Until then it accepted for this
end the Theological Curriculum of the Established Church
in the Universities.

2. THE SECESSION SYNODS

A good while before the end of the 18th century the
ministry in both the Secession Synods began to a considerable
extent to hold looser views of the relation of Church and
State to each other, and on the whole subject of National
Religion and Covenanting, than were undeniably those of their
fathers and founders. In taking up the new opinions they
put forth the claim that they were hospitable to the teaching
of New Light, and that it was their duty not to quench such
light. This last position goes without challenge, for it is a
man's duty to do justice to the light that he has. No one
was disposed to deny this. But, if what was claimed to be
light was not light at all, things looked somewhat different.
And the crux of the situation was in regard to the duty of
the men who had given such definite pledges as the Seceder
ministers had done. They had got their place as rulers and
teachers in the fellowship of the Church in virtue of the
pledges that they had given. Could they in honour use the
place, that they had got on such terms, as the officers of
the body in whose ministry they served, to release themselves
from the obligation which of their own accord they had
undertaken? Was not such action suspiciously like the
exercise of the power put forth by the Vatican to dispense
with oaths and vows? It was not to be wondered at that
there should be an old guard of Orthodoxy who were not

prepared to alter the terms of association on which they held fellowship in the Church.

The fact that the change of opinion that had taken place was not in the region of those Gospel verities that bear at once on the business of personal salvation gave to the problems which had to be discussed a far-off aspect, so that they were not felt by many to have an intimate connection with the main concern that is the everyday interest of the Evangelical Church. From the early days of the Secession there had been a controversial interest in some of these problems. For one of the early Seceders, Thomas Nairn of Abbotshall, had gone over from the Secession to the Cameronian position.[1] His action in doing so called for an examination on the part of the brethren that he had left of the reasons that he gave for the step. So the Seceders had to look into the matter, and they drew up an elaborate document dealing with the questions at issue between themselves and the Reformed Presbytery. This Presbytery, indeed, as a matter of fact, came into being by the very step that Mr Nairn took in joining John Macmillan of Balmaghie, who for well over thirty years had been the only minister among the old Hill-folk. There continued to be intermittent controversy between the Anti-burgher Body and the Anti-Government Party, as they called their opponents.

Those who are curious on these matters will find vigorous polemic writing in old pamphlets of John Goodlet of Sanquhar on the Secession side, and John Fairley, the champion of the Cameronians.

3. ADAM GIB

Among the Covenanting Seceders, Adam Gib held a dominant place. The whole Secession had renewed the Covenants in a bond suited to their situation, that is, as a

---

[1] After some time Mr Nairn quitted his new connection with the Reformed Presbyterians and retraced his steps to the State Church. It is told that when he applied to the Presbytery for readmission, he was asked by the Moderator if they were any better now than when he had left them. He thought they were, for he was now looking at things from another angle. The Moderator, however, went on to assure him that they were not one whit better.

Church and not as a thing done in a national capacity. But after the Breach in 1747, which split the Seceders into two Synods, it does not seem that the Burghers repeated the renewal, so that their rivals might be called the Covenanting Seceders. They had their quarrel with the type of theocracy for which they held the Cameronians to contend. And the Synod's Answers to Nairn, which bore the mark of Adam Gib's hand, made statements in regard to the nature of civil government and the principles by which it was to be guided which got different interpretations when controversy arose in the ranks of the Secession itself. The charge made by the Seceders was that the Cameronian doctrine meant that magistracy is founded in grace and does not belong to the order of nature. This would make out that on this matter the Cameronians had taken up an old Erastian position. Such may have been the case with the New Light Reformed Presbytery, but the Reformed Presbytery itself expressly repudiated such teaching. They held, on the other hand, that it is founded in nature and that its sphere is cut out for it by natural principles. It had, however, been taken over into the realm of grace and made subject to the Mediator of the Covenant of Grace to be at His disposal. What was founded in nature had its sphere of operation determined for it by its original constitution; and though it was made subject to the Lordship of Christ for His own ends, this did not endow the civil magistrate, as such, with any rights or authority in the holy things of the Kingdom of God. So, then, any intrusion on his part on the domain of Church rule was an unholy invasion of the sacred region that is made subject to the Head of the Church, and under Him to those whom He has called to bear rule in His Kingdom. On this reading the Seceders were but the champions of the old Reformed view of things. But their position of separation from the National Church was one that was fruitful of jealousies; and they felt the movement of the age which applied old Revolution principles more in keeping with the current fashionable political philosophy of France than with the ideal which had found its embodiment in the Scottish Covenanting movement. This tendency in French thought told on the young States of America. It was telling, also, on the younger ministry of the Nonconforming or non-Established Churches of the old country. It was of such a complexion that those Seceders who gave place to it ceased to be mere Seceders and became, what they had not been before, Dissenters. They now dissented from so much of the Confession of their National Church. This movement was the true progenitor of Voluntaryism in the Churches. It took up and gave point to the teaching of John Glas.

The Secession in its zeal for propagating its witness did not confine itself to Scotland by any means. It had a strong hold, as we have seen, of the north of Ireland, where it might be said to be in the strength of its following not much behind the older Synod of Ulster. It had its congregations in England. These were outposts which proved to be the parents of many of the Churches of the present English Presbyterian Body. It had its congregations, too, in America, which have in various branches their successors to this day. It was from one of the English outposts that the earliest significant voice was heard to plead for something like what the New Light Revolution brought in. This was a volume by William Graham of Newcastle-on-Tyne, which dealt with the propriety of having such a thing as Churches established by the State. It appeared in 1792. A work of this kind was only a symptom of the change that was on foot. While Adam Gib lived he held the reins of his Synod; and though some of his own sayings were open to a construction that favoured the views which were emerging over the horizon, there was not so far any marked movement in the way of change. Gib died in 1788. He issued his Display of the Secession Testimony as late as 1774. Yet change was in the air, and when in 1796 Thomas M'Crie was ordained to a charge in Edinburgh, he indicated that he had difficulty in accepting some of the statements in the Confession bearing on Church and State. He had his difficulties, but he came out of them. He was allowed by the Presbytery to enter the ministry with what might be called a reserve or a modified subscription. The

course of his thought and study led him to the acceptance
at last of the full teaching of the Confession, which was
also that of the Secession fathers. The truth which he found
hard to reach he learned to prize highly.

One might almost be disposed to say that when death
removed Adam Gib from his leadership of the General
Associate Synod, that body heaved a sigh of relief; not that
it did not miss him and value him and mourn for him; but
he had held it in so tight that now that he was in it no more
to control its business, it was in danger of taking an overdose
of the wine of freedom and having its fling. When one of
a sober cast of mind, like M'Crie, was, in his earlier years,
so far carried by the popular stream, its current would easily
sweep off their feet men of less solidity. It was his honesty
that he showed in giving intimation of the difficulties that
he felt. That he was allowed to proceed to ordination after
such an intimation, told that the court which ordained him
was prepared to make the things that were difficulties to him
a matter of forbearance, or so many open questions.

4.   Change of Testimony—Anti-burgher

In those days there was a movement afoot to bring the
Testimony of the Synod abreast of the needs of the time.
Among the Seceders a Testimony was neither a kind of
formula of subscription to bind the subscriber to the Church's
standards, nor was it exactly a Confession of Faith.   It
was rather an official exposition of things that had been
called in question as to which the Church felt itself called
upon to bear witness. It was thus not unlike a supplement
to the Confession of Faith. It was a document that could
be curtailed or extended according to the need of the day,
and that without doing hurt to the Confession, unless, indeed,
it sought to teach something out of keeping with the
Confessional statements. Thus it was possible that a Testimony
might be so amended as to bring it into conflict with truth
formerly confessed. In due course the New Testimony
appeared. It was found to be a document that was pregnant
with evil consequence for the stability of the Confession.

There were several of the ministers of the Synod who were themselves of Old School convictions that failed to see the significance of this Church deed, though M'Crie, Bruce, and their friends did, who had given special study to the nature of the changes made. On its adoption, Professor Bruce and his brethren stood aside and formed what they called the Constitutional Presbytery. The innovating Synod promptly deposed them, and even excommunicated M'Crie, such was the drastic tradition of discipline among the Anti-burghers. The newly formed Presbytery entrusted to M'Crie, who was the youngest of its members, the task of writing a Statement of the Differences between the new Testimony, which gave place to New Light, and the old Testimony, which was set aside. This work was published in 1807, and it is perhaps the ablest work extant that deals with the Confessional teaching on the subject of National Religion. As a publication it fell flat from the press at the time; for those who were not of the Anti-burgher Body would look upon it as but part of a squabble among a race of squabblers. For the Anti-burghers had an established reputation for militancy. In later years, when the name of Thomas M'Crie was made as the biographer of Knox and Melville, and the expositor and defender of the principles of the Scottish Reformers and Covenanters, the book was sought out and reprinted more than once in whole or in part.

The results of the change of his denominational Testimony which M'Crie and his fellows had foreseen and anticipated were such as to justify their forecast; for in the later years of his life the burning questions in Scotland were those that dealt with National Religion. The beginnings of a formed opposition on a large scale to the national acknowledgment of the Christian Church were in the change of Testimony which took place on parallel lines in the two branches of the Secession; and by 1830, before the Secession was a hundred years old, this opposition took shape in the Voluntary agitation which kept pace with the national movement for political reform. The new system which aimed at displacing the old one was one that would solve the problem of the inter-

relation of two Divine institutions by bidding them stand
apart so that each might leave the other to itself.   Thus,
instead of loosing, it would at one stroke cut the Gordian
knot and treat the State or the corporate unit of the nation
as though it had its sphere of functioning only in the business
of that world which lies in the Wicked One.   Such a view
of things would put a fool's cap upon much of the contendings
of the Reformers and the Covenanters.   Their martyrs had
died in vain.   They had been mistaken in what they shed
their blood for.

5.   THE BURGHERS CHANGE TOO

We have just said that on parallel lines similar changes
of Testimony took place in both branches of the old Secession.
We have spoken of the new Testimony of the Anti-burghers;
their old rivals took a way of their own to do the same
thing.   Among the Burghers the movement in the way of
change, by means of a new Preamble to the Ordination
Questions, was made in the same years as that among the
Anti-burghers.   It had a singular beginning.   Fraser of
Auchtermuchty was himself in his personal views in agreement
with the Testimony as it was.   But he found that the younger
ministers of the body had given up the old ground and he
sought, instead of trying to bring them back to loyalty to
the Testimony of their Church, a thing that he despaired of
being able to do, to have some correspondence between the
actual thinking of the Synod and its avowed profession.   The
movement that began when he mooted such an idea met with
a strenuous opposition among his brethren.   It was but as
yesterday that John Brown of Haddington, their old Professor
of Divinity, had died, in the year 1787, and to the end he
had held the old doctrine of the Confession and of the first
Seceders on the subject of the duties that the State owes to
the truth and Church of God.   His successor, however, as
Professor of Theology, was George Lawson of Selkirk,
another like himself looked upon as a " dungeon " of learning.
But Lawson was a hot advocate for change, and in this he

was very much a man of his own generation. The younger
folk were working for a revolution and they got their way.

The leader of the Burghers on the Old School side was
William Willis of Greenock, who wrote with great force
and with as much zeal and conviction as did M'Crie on this
subject among the Anti-burghers. Willis and William Taylor
of Perth, who became the Professor of Divinity to the Old
Light Burghers, were really good divines, worthy of the best
days of the Secession, as was also Mr Willis' son. This was
Dr Michael Willis, who became in 1843 one of the Disruption
fathers, and who in after years was one of the ornaments
of Presbyterianism in Canada as Principal of Knox College,
Toronto. The opposition to New Light among the Burghers,
though it was vigorous, did not meet with great success, for
apart from a score or two of congregations the Burgher
Body came to hold very much the same ground with the
majority of their old rivals. Those who are curious in
regard to the byways of Church history will find a considerable
pamphlet literature that was called forth by these discussions.
It is still to be met with, though it is now scarce. On the
Anti-burgher side there is not only M'Crie's statement, but
an elaborate and detailed history of the change from the
pen of Archibald Bruce, and two very capable and business-
like statements of their views from the pens of Hog of Kelso
and Chalmers of Haddington. On the New Light side Mr
Allan of Coupar-Angus wrote a large pamphlet; nor was
Robert Culbertson of Leith idle. He appears in Professor
Bruce's narrative as pretty much the villain of the piece.
On the Burgher side, Fletcher of Bridge of Teith and Willis
were prominent as pamphleteers, while George Thomson, once
of Rathillet, who had been with the New Light Cameronians,
took the field again. And George Lawson of Selkirk wrote
with vigour on the New Light side. The men who set themselves in opposition to the New Light changes got the name
of Old Lights. That name in its Scots dress is better known
in recent days in Scotland in the region of fiction than in
that of fact or history. They were Barrie's " Auld Lichts."
His Kirriemuir " Auld Lichts " were of Anti-burgher descent.

6. Fixed or Fluid

In connection with the controversies that attended the changes of which we have spoken, the whole question of the fixity as over against the fluidity of a Church's doctrinal constitution came up for discussion. In substance the same line of argument is taken by the advocates for change or indifference as to the very core of the Christian Faith as had to be met by M'Crie and Willis. Neither the multiplication table nor the proportion that a majority bears to a minority can solve the problem in morals—Is it permissible for men who have come to hold office in a Church by giving pledges, which in turn they have exacted from other entrants to the ministry, to make use of the vantage ground that they have so secured for the end of overturning the full and unabated profession of the truth that they have pledged themselves to maintain? In this connection there came up for decision the substantial issue of the whole subscription controversy, a latitudinarian solution of which wrote the death warrant of the post-Puritan Presbyterian Church in England. When it took the line of non-subscription this Church was easily the greatest part of the important Nonconformist Body, which in that country represented those confessing Puritans that the Act of Uniformity had shut out from the Church of England.

There is a well-worn tag to the effect that the Lord has yet much light to break forth from His Word. As to this no devout believer has any more doubt than had John Robinson. At the same time as believers have no doubt in regard to this matter, it holds of them in the measure in which they are well instructed and established in the knowledge of the Word that they are equally confident that the further light that is to break out will not cancel nor challenge nor detract from the brightness with which the light of the Word already shines. What is new will only intensify what is old. It will not darken it nor throw it in the shade. It will not open up the light or message of another Gospel than that which our Lord and His Apostles have left us. It will be a thing of detail and not of wide-sweeping principle.

We need not, then, look for results of a revolutionary kind as the outcome of the shining of New Light if it is light indeed. Old Light of this kind is better than pretended New.

We need not fear for the Faith as it has been confessed from the first that it shall be shaken or overthrown. It is too well grounded in the sure warrant of the Divine Word to run any such risk. And as for the discovery of further truth such as will modify what is embodied in the Reformed Confessions, the system taught in the Reformed Faith is so truly an echo of the Apostolic word that those who hold it need not be put about in their mind nor give place to craven fears that it shall ever be set aside. It may meet again and again with what it has often met already, cavillings and perverse disputings of men that were not willing to take and keep their place at the footstool of Him who by His Apostles has left in their writings the final norm of the Faith. The truth already known may be known more fully and perfectly. It may be seen better in its own setting and in the connection and relations of its various parts. Its power and its beauty and its sweetness and its glory may be more richly known. Yet those who have learned the Gospel of the Glory of the Blessed God may rest assured of this, that any further truth which as light will break forth from the Word will have no quarrel with the truth and the proportion of what they have already come to know. They may well keep their windows open to the east to welcome the light that a new day brings with it; but no shining of the rising sun will do more than confirm them in the knowledge and faith of what their confessing fathers learned from the Apostles—what, indeed, in Holy Writ is set forth with great plainness of speech. The great outline of the Word is not a thing of yesterday.

The possible emergence of New Light, then, that will set aside the historic faith of believing Christendom may be set up as a bugbear to deter the Church from bravely and simply and steadfastly professing, as truth known and ascertained, what he who runs may read. This has been set down for all time in the Word which crystallises and perpetuates the ministry of the Apostles. As that ministry was one of witness we need look for no new facts in the record of our Lord's work, nor for any new words to add to the message with which the New Testament has already come. As their ministry was one of teaching we need look for no other exposition of the facts of the Gospel or of the work of the Lord than they have already given. Divine truth does not contradict itself. The return of the Reformation to the regulative authority of the Lord as He speaks in the Word which He has given was of such a *bona-fide* character that not only is the general substance of the Faith as confessed by our Reformers in keeping with the Rule of Faith, but the system of truth in the mutual connections of its leading parts is the truth that the Divine Word itself has set forth. The offence that as a matter of fact has been given by the Calvinism of our Reformed Faith is an offence that is taken at the truth of the Word in regard to the Sovereign Grace to which we trace up the hope of Eternal Life that is to be found in the Son of God Incarnate.

7.   AGGRESSIVE ENCROACHMENT

The region of Divine Truth that was affected in the claim to a right to change, put forth by the school who broke away from the old teaching of the Confession and the early Secession documents, might be said to be remote from the heart of things. Yet if men change their views on what they had confessed as the truth of God they should have the manliness to acknowledge that such a change has taken place and to refuse to stay in what is now to them a false position. This, however, was not what was done. And what was done first in regard to truth that was on the periphery was soon to be done in regard to truth that lay near the heart. The principle was the same in each case. The significance of the change, however, came out more clearly when it aimed at the centre of things.

When the two branches of the Secession had each in its own way decided no longer to exact a pledge of close adherence to what their fathers had held, and by doing so parted company with their former brethren who kept by the old profession, they soon took steps to unite, and when they became the United Secession, they adopted a Testimony which was revised to fit in with their new situation. In connection with the adoption of this document in its final form, there came to be difficulties raised in the course of a few years. What was at stake now was a truth which lay much nearer the heart of the Faith than the doctrine of the duty of the State. It was nothing less than the matter of what is the true nature of our Lord's Atoning Work. A form of words was adopted in this Testimony of 1830 wittingly, it is alleged —and this may have been the case—on the part of those responsible for the drafting of the document, but unwittingly and by oversight on the part of others, if, indeed, it was not done behind their backs. This form of words permitted the introduction of that view of the Atonement against which Adam Gib had waged what for the time was a successful warfare, and which seemed to have had no recognition accorded to it in the other wing of the Secession. The presence of these words in this Testimony came into prominence in the case of James Morison.

8. Morison and His Professors

Morison of Kilmarnock, who became the founder of the Evangelical Union, a body that were called after him in popular speech the Morisonians, was a minister of the United Secession Church who made himself conspicuous by preaching an Atonement that was universal. He was subjected to discipline for this doctrine. The issue of the trial was that he was condemned and deposed. He became more and more Arminian in his teaching so as to verge on Pelagianism. He and the movement which he led were zealous and vigorous in their propaganda. When he paid a visit to America he met with a very warm welcome from the Cumberland Presbyterians. Probably he had gone further than they did in his revolt from Calvinism; yet he and they had a common bond that bound them to one another; it was their feud with Calvinism.

When Morison was being tried by the United Secession Synod, his old Professors, John Brown and Robert Balmer, stood by him and did what they could to shield him. This held especially of Dr Brown. In the proceedings of the case it came out that Morison's doctrine of Universal Atonement was what he seemed to have learned from his Professors. So attention was turned to their teaching. In the course of the endeavour to bring them under discipline, Balmer died, and when in the end a finding was reached in the case of his surviving colleague, he was exonerated. This virtually opened the way for the teaching of a doctrine of Atonement which admitted of a double substitution, one that was effective and redemptive, and the other that was provisional or conditional, or, as the issue would prove, ineffective. Thus the end of the record of the " Marrow " tradition in the largest body of the Secession went so far to justify those who from the first connected it with the teaching of a Redemption that was universal. The first exponents of that tradition disclaimed, and with truth, any such doctrine. But an extreme way of saying to the unconverted, Christ died for you, or, the Saviour is dead for you, was forced by a kind of logical necessity to justify its own statement by holding not only that Christ who died to redeem His people is ours in the overtures of peace that the Gospel makes that we may take and have Him as our own, but that He actually died for each and all to whom the Gospel comes when its Word calls upon us to believe.

9. John Brown, Tertius

Dr John Cairns sets it to the credit of Dr Brown that he liberalised the Theology of his Church. If he had only rescued exegesis from undue subjection to formulated dogma and taken a less provincial view of the Faith than was to be had in the exclusive groove of the " Marrow " teaching, it would have been a change that would bring the Body into line with the Reformed Confession on terms that would cordially recognise the value of the " Marrow " presentation of the openness of the Gospel way, while they would not exclude true Calvinism of a more inclusive outlook. This, however, was not what he did; he gave up the old " Marrow " Calvinism and paved the way for a halting compromise which patched up a concordat with the laxer Evangelism of later New England. He did make a change, but it was more or less of a revolution.

The influence of Cameron's teaching, though it might work indirectly on his thinking, told on Dr John Brown. He was a student of the writings of the Huguenot school of the 17th century which followed the lead of Cameron and Moses Amyraut. And when he adopted what was in substance Amyraut's view of the Atonement, his indebtedness at one remove to Cameron came out. We have already noted Mair of Orwell and his follower, Thomson, as at least possible disciples of this school the best part of a century before Brown; and in the case of Thomson we have seen how, in a quiet and unobtrusive way, this kind of teaching may have had a small following among the Burghers, to which wing of the Secession body the Browns belonged. In the course of the controversy in connection with Morison when Dr Brown was brought under discipline, Robert Wilson, one of his keenest critics, seems to charge him virtually with having tampered with the Testimony of his Synod when the 1830 edition of it was being prepared. The charge is that he got it changed in the direction which led away from a definite doctrine of the Atonement as efficacious, the doctrine for which the Secession had historically borne witness.

The finding of the United Secession Synod that cleared Dr Brown from the charge of unsound doctrine, which had been laid against him by Dr Hay of Kinross and Dr Andrew Marshall of Kirkintilloch, did not hinder the Union of 1847, by which the Synod of Relief joined with the United Secession to constitute the United Presbyterian Church. The former of these two bodies had always been understood to profess that it was less strict than the latter, so that it did not take amiss the action of his Synod in Dr Brown's case. To say the least, this decision left ambiguous the relation of the largest body of the Secession to the Confessional teaching in regard to such a doctrine of a genuine Atonement as their previous Testimonies had helped to buttress.

10. ANDREW MARSHALL

The significance of the decision which acquitted Dr Brown may be seen in the light cast upon it by the action of Dr Andrew Marshall. He refused to enter into the Union of 1847 that his relation to the Orthodox doctrine of the Atonement might be kept quite clear. He was a sturdy fighter in any cause that he took up. In the Voluntary controversy which raged in Scotland from 1829 to 1833, and even later, he was the protagonist of the policy which aimed at cutting out all national recognition of a Church on the part of the State. In this movement Dr John Brown was one of his strongest supporters. But when the question arose as to what the nature and extent of our Lord's Atoning Work is, Marshall was adamant in the stand he took for an Atonement which did indeed atone. He believed in an Atonement which put away sin and won life and acceptance for those on whose behalf it was made. With his views on national neutrality in the Church sphere, he was for the rest of his days left to draw a lonely furrow as he could not accept the doctrine in regard to Church and State which was held in the other Presbyterian Churches, and which was optional in the Body which he refused to join. The laxity, in regard to the cardinal doctrine of the Atonement, which he held to prevail in that Body, precluded for him, with his strong convictions on the subject, the possibility of his associating himself with it. The old warrior in his loneliness was a pathetic figure.

II.

NEW LIGHT AT WORK

In the decision arrived at in Dr Brown's case, the main body of the Secession in effect acquiesced in extending hospitality to a type of teaching that came down from John Cameron. New Light was coming nearer the citadel of the Faith in its disintegrating results. At this point, among a considerable section of professed Evangelicals, the key that admitted to the fortress of a true and efficacious Redemption was given up; and this had a close relation to practical methods in preaching and pressing home the Gospel message. It meant a new approach to the case of the anxious sinner when he was told that our Lord had died for him, and that he must right off receive this as the good news of salvation. This method of approach to him hid from the enquirer that when it said that the Saviour had died for him it might prove that He had died either in vain, or with no intention to effect his salvation. For the Universal Redemption which it taught was on its own showing a Redemption that did not secure life. In this respect the method of treating the anxious played with the use of deceitful terms, and did not compare well with the method that had been formerly in use. This older method told the sinner of a Saviour Who had died to save His chosen and called ones, and Who was now calling and inviting him to make proof of His saving power by taking Himself as the Lord his Righteousness, and so sheltering under the covert of His sacrifice and the shield of His inter-cession. The older Calvinism did not seek to assure the sinner that Christ had died his death until he had first, in the obedience of faith, closed with Him as a Saviour in His office as Mediator. It could, as *The Marrow* put it, tell him that Christ, Who died the Just for the unjust, was his for the taking, and that when he took this Christ as his own, he was in doing so guilty of no presumption. Methods that were borrowed from organised, almost mechanised, American Revivalism began to be so common in dealing with enquirers for salvation that they came to be looked upon as part and parcel of aggressive Gospel work. This holds in particular of such effort for the last sixty years and more since the great Evangelistic Campaign conducted in Scotland in 1873-74 by D. L. Moody and Ira D. Sankey.

The beginnings of the New England revivalist influence can be traced back for more than a century. The school that stood by Dr Brown felt early in the 19th century the impact of the teaching of Andover Theology, and this was only a modified Calvinism. In England, the teaching of the great Edwards had told on both wings of the Independent movement. Andrew Fuller, for example, was in much of his teaching one of his pupils. In his doctrine, however, of the Atonement, though he might be said to follow Davenant, he seems to have felt the influence of the next generation of New England teachers in regard to the extent of Redemption. So the view that he took of this cardinal mystery was virtually the Hypothetical Universalism of the New Methodists of 17th-century France. Fuller's teaching told powerfully on those Baptist Churches which gave up the position of close communion. It told, too, on the Dissenters in Scotland. At the same time the Independent Churches yielded to a great extent to the Modern Calvinism of Edward Williams, whose *Equity and Sovereignty* was perhaps his best-known work. He, too, was of the school of Edwards, yet was in sympathy with the developments of New England Theology in the generation which followed Edwards. A governmental type of thought in regard to the provision of the Atonement was what found favour with the men of this tendency. They came under the spell of Grotius.

1. RALPH WARDLAW

Among the Independents in Scotland who embraced this modified type of Calvinism was Ralph Wardlaw, one of the partners in labour that the Haldanes had in their Evangelical Campaign of the early years of the 19th century. Dr Wardlaw was of Secession extraction, and he and John Brown of Edinburgh had a close likeness to one another in their attitude to the Evangel as set forth by the Reformers and the Puritans. They yielded to the same innovating influences. Dr A. A. Hodge was more than charitable to Dr Brown in taking his position to be practically that of the " Marrow." Either that, or he was less than charitable to the " Marrow " in respect to the consistency of its Calvinism. Dr William Cunningham was definitely of the opinion that Brown and his friends had given currency again to what was substantially the system of Amyraut. Dr Wardlaw and his kinsman were full of confidence in what was their teaching on this subject. They looked upon it as a decided improvement on older methods in dealing with sinners. This came out in particular in Wardlaw's clever, though unconvincing, attempt to parry the damaging criticism that Dr William Symington had passed on his doctrine of the Atonement. With the innovators it was a matter of Method, just as it had been with the innovating Huguenots.

2. Hugh Martin on Wardlaw

When the Morisonian movement, with its militant Arminianism, began to tell on the Independent Churches, Wardlaw, with the Glasgow Churches of his order, felt called upon to apply discipline to the neighbouring Churches that showed such sympathies. In this connection he was the author of an important Church letter dealing with the saving, effectual work of the Holy Ghost. In the correspondence he indicated clearly that the Calvinism which he held was one that was mainly concerned with the application of Redemption. With him Redemption, which he held to be universal, was in its fruits, and in the good of it, confined to God's elect people whom He calls and keeps. In regard to his doctrine of the Covenant of Grace, Dr Hugh Martin uses the pungent words: " Under the pretence of enlarging the aspects of grace it achieves most effectively a precisely opposite result. For to bring in a Covenant of Grace in order to limit the application and circumscribe the effectual results of an Atonement in its own nature and accomplished merit unlimited, is surely one of the most perverted and perverting schemes that could be adopted. . . . To introduce a Covenant of *Grace* as an instrument for the *limitation* of Grace is at once an insult to the human understanding and a travesty of the Divine wisdom. In any such view of its nature and extent it must assuredly cease to be called a Covenant of Grace. The grace is all in the prior arrangement or achievement, which it has been agreed on this scheme to call the Atonement; and the covenant is a covenant circumscribing the grace into limits narrower than its own. It is therefore a Covenant not

of grace but of alarming judgment.   Nay, more : it is a
Covenant of reasonless, arbitrary and capricious judgment. . . .
And a Covenant coming into play . . . to exclude in point of
fact vast multitudes from all beneficial effects of an Atonement, which, in its own nature, had as beneficial bearings on
them as on any and all of those who are ultimately to be
saved—a Covenant such as this, it is utter folly to call a
Covenant of Grace.   It is not a Covenant of Grace in any
sense, but a Covenant of Judgment; and not a Covenant of
Sovereignty, but of arbitrary and reasonless and terrific
judgment."

The later New England school, which, in the interest of
the doctrine of a governmental Atonement, told on English
Nonconformity and along with it on Wardlaw and his friends
in Scotland, told also in a more developed form directly on
Scotland through the wide circulation of Dwight's Theology,
and the attention that was aroused by reports of the Revivals
in the New England and other American Churches.   Dwight
and Finney told on James Morison; and Dr Brown was
thrown into close contact with English Independents in the
interest which they had in common in their opposition to an
Established Church.   For the New Light Seceders became
aggressive and militant on behalf of their Voluntary theory,
so that they aimed at the abolition of all State Churches.
This association with Baptists and Independents, who held to
a Universal Redemption, affected both the Synod of Relief
and the United Secession.   Robert Hall told on Robert
Balmer; and the reissue by the latter with a recommendatory
preface of Edward Polhill's Essay on *The Death of Christ*
was significant of change.   It threw light on where he stood.
The decision reached in the case of Dr Brown certainly did
not hinder the union of the two Synods.   It may have even
paved the way for the step that they took when they came
together to constitute the United Presbyterian Church in 1847.

3. MACGREGOR ON AMYRALDIANISM

The question of the attitude of the United Presbyterians
as the heirs of the New Light Seceders to the doctrine of

the Atonement came into the field of discussion again when
the Old School minority of the Free Church, in their critical
attitude to proposals for the union of their Church with the
United Presbyterians, raised the matter.   In the course of
these negotiations there was published, over and above an
earnest tract from the pen of Dr J. Julius Wood of Dumfries,
an elaborate pamphlet discussing the subject from the pen of
James Macgregor, who was one of the school of Cunningham.
In this work, from the standpoint of the older Calvinism, he
treats of the situation created by the decision arrived at by
the United Secession Synod in the case of Dr Brown.   He
was of one mind with his master, Cunningham, that on the
side of Brown and his friends there was a renewal substantially of the tendency of Amyraut and his school in the
French Protestant Church of the 17th century.   These are
the terms in which Macgregor canvasses and criticises the
value of the Amyraldian scheme : " The more malignant
aspects of Amyraldianism are as follows :—First, the notion
of any saving purpose of God that does not infallibly
determine salvation; or, in other words, of a frustrated
intention or disappointed desire of His; this notion is not
only on the face of it unscriptural, but, in the heart of it,
offensive even to our natural reason, because inconsistent with
the very nature and perfections of Deity.   Nor does the
notion gain anything, in respect of spiritual seemliness, when
transferred from God's eternal decree to the execution of
that decree in time on the Cross.   For the notion of any
substitution of Christ that does not infallibly secure by
purchase the salvation of all for whom He died, is deeply
dishonouring to the personal work of the adorable Substitute.

" Again, the two notions alike (or the notion in its two
applications alike) must, when seriously entertained, tend to
undermine the believer's assurance of hope.   For that
assurance is ultimately founded on the truth, that all God's
purposes are unchanging and effectual, and that no sinner
can ever perish for whom Christ gave His life on the Cross.
The assurance, therefore, is fatally undermined by the
notion, that there is a changeable or ineffectual purpose of

God, and that many of those for whom Christ gave His life shall nevertheless fall into death eternal.

"Once more the two notions alike (or the notion in its two applications alike) must tend, when seriously entertained, to prevent unbelievers from coming to God in ' full assurance of faith.' It is at this third point that the Amyraldians deem themselves strongest. Hence, as I have said, in France they assumed the name of *Methodists* under the impression that their doctrine constitutes a method or way, more excellent than had previously been known among Calvinists, of leading sinners to salvation through faith, and particularly of helping them over the difficulty, already referred to, in the way of believing. And it is at this point—their strongest—that I find them weakest."

4. PRESENT-DAY EFFECTS IN EVANGELISM

In present-day Evangelistic work it is the common thing in various circles and communions to employ the method that harks back to Cameron's attempt to find a middle way between the teaching of the Synod of Dort and that of the Arminians. This in effect works out to the result that the Arminians are left the masters of the field.

III.

OLD LIGHTS STAND FAST

While things took the course they did in the larger section of the Secession body, the conservative wing that had the leadership of M'Crie and Stevenson of Ayr held to the old school Calvinism of the Secession fathers. Dr M'Crie we have already met as a champion of the old order of Church and State, the order which was aimed at as a goal in the programme of the Reformers and the Covenanters, the order, indeed, that sought to give effect to the teaching of John Calvin in his Institutes. He was one of the most capable theologians, as he was the greatest man that the Secession produced at any time. His Sermons survive as a monument of his massive and powerful pulpit work. He and Dr

Stevenson were entrusted with the drawing up of the Testimony of the Original Secession in 1827. The historical part is from M'Crie's hand, the doctrinal from Stevenson's. Dr George Stevenson was one of the best-equipped theologians of his day. He is the author of a choice little work on the Atonement; and from such a pen one would look for good Theology in his account of the doctrine to which the Testimony bore witness. There is also extant a valuable work of his own on *The Offices of Christ,* which is a capital exposition of the subject. He kept his eye on the theological movements in transatlantic, and particularly in New England circles; and he saw the danger of the development of Hopkins' teaching which ensnared so many of the generation.

IV.

NEW LIGHT LEADERS

The men who developed the application of the principle that hospitality should be extended to New Light, in spite of pledged engagements to be true to the Faith with which the New Light joined issue, were the leaders of the innovating parties in the Secession along with their abettors. The application of this principle to a realm of Christian truth that is nearer the heart of things than is the region of the duties to Christ and His Church which lie upon kings and magistrates, was made by the Professors of the United Secession, backed by their supporters in the Synod discussions. They met with decided opposition. Yet most of the opposition subsided, and that to such a degree as that the older school of thought virtually consented to give quarters in their fellowship to the looser type of Calvinists who sympathised with Dr Brown.

V.

MISCELLANEOUS

Before John Brown — Tertius — became Professor of Theology to the United Secession the office was held by John Dick of Glasgow, who has left a System of Theology in four volumes that would do credit to the best days of the Secession.

It is true that he was a Voluntary, and that he favoured a laxer view of the inspiration of Holy Scripture than was the accepted Reformed teaching on the subject, but his systematic presentation of the Faith in his lectures on Theology was reckoned by such a good judge as Archibald Alexander of Princeton as being the best System extant in the English language. With such a standard of theological erudition as was reached by Dick or M'Crie or Stevenson, we are warranted in laying stress on the kind of thought in the region of divinity that prevailed in the different branches of the Secession. In regard to John Brown of Edinburgh, it would not be fair to pass over without notice his good work in the region of exegetical study. Spurgeon, as an outsider, could speak of him in his *Commenting and Commentaries* as a modern Puritan. He did as much as any man in his day to advance the credit of that type of interpretation— the grammatical and historical one—which prevailed at the Reformation with Calvin as its most illustrious exponent, but which subsequently passed under an eclipse owing to the length to which divines tended to go in applying the Analogy of the Faith to the decision of questions in the field of Exegesis. It is, as we have indicated, an instance of undue and overgenerous charity on the part of Dr Archibald Hodge when he ascribes Brown's attitude to the teaching of Universal Redemption to his exegetical conscience, exclusively of the other elements that contributed to his breakaway from the sound hereditary Calvinism of his family, of his Church and of his country. When we mention him as a commentator we should not forget the good work done in the same department by his colleague, Dr William Lindsay, who had been one of the Relief theological teachers in his massive exposition of the Epistle to the Hebrews. It is a monument to his sound scholarship. From 1847 onward Brown and Lindsay were colleagues in their respective Professorial Chairs. There was another of the Relief men that we should not wish to overlook, though he did not attain to the eminence of the first three. This was Neil Macmichael. He may not have been perhaps a great theologian; but he had a tart way of putting things

that made them stick in the memory. Here is an illustration :—He was applying what the Apostle says of the
fathers who were all baptised unto Moses in the cloud and
in the sea and he said : " 1. The Israelites were baptised, both
adults and infants ; for the Apostle declares it.   2. They were
not immersed, a fact which Moses and other inspired writers
testify.   3. The Egyptians who pursued them were immersed.
4. The Israelites had baptism without immersion, and the
Egyptians immersion without baptism.   5. The baptism of
the Israelites was salvation, and the immersion of the
Egyptians drowning."

VI.

THE ISSUE OF THE NEW LIGHT TENDENCY

The New Light movement has virtually found its culmina-
tion in the present constitution in the Church of Scotland,
which leaves that Church with a Confession which no one
of the ministry is bound to treat as his own creed.

The incautious hospitality extended to New Light has thus
proved it to be a powerful solvent ; and in review of its
record of achievement as such we should not fail to observe
the moral issues that are raised in regard to the loyal
maintenance of pledges given to be faithful to Creeds and
Confessions.   These call for very deliberate study and consideration before they are adopted.   They call equally for
honourable treatment on the part of men who have avowed
them as their own.   In spite, however, of what yielding to
New Light has done, we should not forget that the fundamental
obligation lies upon every teacher in the Church of God to
be true to the full circle of truth as the Apostolic and
Prophetic Revelation has brought it before us.   This truth
has been entrusted to the Church to be held fast in its
integrity, and it is no bondage to be laid under the obligation
to honour such a trust ; and this is what is meant by the
exaction of a strict pledge of loyalty to the Confession of
Faith.   Nor can it be well spoken of as an advance in Christian
freedom for the Church to loosen the bond that binds her
rulers to hold fast the whole truth of God as His Word sets
it forth.

IX.
THE EVANGELICAL SCHOOL AND VICTORIAN ORTHODOXY

I.

THE EVANGELICAL REVIVAL

THE epoch of the French Revolution was a time of crisis in the Scottish Churches. We have seen that a new principle began to assert itself among the Seceders whose traditional part was to be the guardians of old Orthodoxy. At first the New Light tendency did not show itself at work except on the outskirts of the Christian profession. It seemed to touch only the fringe. Ere long, however, it showed how revolutionary it was in its ultimate issues. At the same time as this New Light began to work, a warm breath came which revived the cause of the Evangel and so of sound doctrine. This told powerfully on the State Church. It did not come like a quick spring-tide with a rush and an instantaneous transformation and renewal of the face of things. But it wrought none the less powerfully that it wrought slowly and quietly. It was not so much a wind that rent the rocks as the sound of a still, small voice.

We have seen how in the days of the Moderate ascendancy the banner of the Gospel was still upheld by the hands of men who were distinguished for the soundness with which they held the Faith to which their subscription to the standards of their Church pledged them. Their witness was to rise from the dust. It was to receive the accession of a goodly and worthy host who should take it up as their own. They had a remarkable succession. Revival came to the cause of the Gospel, and when it came it came from more quarters than one as its proximate source. In the highest sense, of course, it came from above.

255

The awakened interest in the spread of the Gospel all over the earth took practical steps to find an outlet for its energy when it was frustrated in its effort to enlist the Church as a whole in the service of Foreign Missions. Two or three Missionary Societies were set on foot and at the same time a friendly hand was stretched out to the English Missionary organisations. The movement represented by the brothers Haldane was a symptom of what was at work and it contributed its quota to the resurgence of the Evangel in the ministry of the National Church. The appearance of the *Life of John Knox* from the pen of Thomas M'Crie was the signal for the revival of an interest in the Reformation and, what was more, in the Faith for which Knox and his successors fought. Andrew Thomson, as a younger member of the Evangelical school, was the centre and the moving spring or live wire of what in modern political speech might be spoken of as a " Ginger Group." He and those who thought with him were not content to lie under the incubus of that system of policy and compromise and despotism and subservience for which Moderatism had so long stood. In his *Christian Instructor* he provided an open forum for the discussion of matters bearing on national righteousness, Christian witness, and the duty of the Church.

Soon after Thomson took the warpath the conversion of Thomas Chalmers and the marvellous popularity that attended his early ministry told powerfully on the side of the revived Evangel. It was the age of Societies for all kinds of good objects, for the circulation of the Scriptures and of Tracts, for the education of the less-favoured parts of the land, and for benevolent purposes of every description. The same success that attended the cause of the Gospel in England was met with in Scotland too; and many men of ability and standing in the ministry, who, like Chalmers, had begun their public work as members of the Moderate Party, were converted and came to be leading men on the side of a sound and a lively Gospel. Stewart of Moulin has been already referred to as one of these. Robert Gordon and John Bruce, two of the most influential men in the Edinburgh

pulpit, belonged to this class. These were men whose
ministry was richly blessed to the conversion and upbuilding
of students for the ministry; and the conversion of these
young men was attended with a revived and deepened and
abiding interest not only in the practical everyday Evangel
which they faithfully proclaimed, but in the whole circle of
Christian truth. A generation of able theologians was being
raised up such as Scotland had not seen since the group that
were the ornaments of the second Reformation age. In his
student days, Robert M'Cheyne waited on the preaching of
John Bruce, while there were two in particular who felt the
power of the Gospel in its freshness under the preaching
of Gordon and who became prominent in their generation
as Orthodox and Evangelical forces. William Cunningham,
than whom a greater divine has not arisen in Scotland, was
one of the two. The other was the devout and cultured
Alexander Moody Stuart, whose ministry in its turn was
one of the most fruitful that Edinburgh has seen. These
were outstanding specimens of what was going on, but they
were only specimens. And by the time that these two began
their public work the revival of religion and of sound doctrine
in the Church had already made great headway. It advanced
in the teeth of social persecution and opposition of every
kind. The ranks of the Gospel preachers in Scotland were
being recruited.

II.

EXCESSES AND EXTRAVAGANCES

It is no strange thing that there should be a boiling over
or an effervescence when a movement of revival is on foot.
This there was in connection with the great Scottish movement of over a century ago. It took place in the errors of
doctrine and the irregularities in worship and Church life
that attended the kindred movements associated with the
names of Edward Irving and John Macleod Campbell. The
latter of these was minister of the parish of Row or Rhu—
spoken of as The Row—in Dumbartonshire. He taught
something more than an Atonement that was universal. His

message was one of Universal Pardon which warranted on the part of all who hear the Gospel an assurance of full forgiveness and of the Divine Fatherhood. Campbell was tried and condemned and deposed from the ministry. Years afterwards he published his work on the Nature of the Atonement in which he sets forth and expounds one of the many Broad School perversions or evasions of the cardinal mystery of the Faith as a message of Redemption. He resolves the atoning work of our Lord into an adequate repentance such as no one but the sinless Saviour could render or bring forward. This view held implicit in its bosom the Deistic teaching that an adequate repentance is the only Atonement that is needed. The penal, the forensic, the judicial aspect of the great transaction was spirited away. It melted into the thinnest of thin air. Campbell's follower and friend and supporter, Thomas Erskine of Linlathen, became as an amiable Broad Churchman the centre of a circle of revived Moderatism which, while it claimed to be religious, broke away from the mysteries of the Evangelical Faith. Its engrossing doctrine was that of a Divine Fatherhood which is quite universal. To this the fervid hyper-evangelism of the Row teaching burnt itself out and it left not even the ashes of the Evangelical Faith behind.

Irving, with his extravagance of doctrine and worship and Church organisation, broke himself as a power in the Church and bequeathed to the world as his legacy only that system of Catholic Apostolicity, as it called itself, which rested for authority on the basis of ecstatic utterances of half-hysterical speakers with tongues. The effervescence of the first days of his movement wrought itself out. But the very excesses of the doctrine of Campbell in regard to assurance of pardon and of Irving in regard to the imperfect character of the manhood of the Incarnate Lord and the restoration of Pentecostal conditions in response to the faith of a penitent Church—these excesses and extravagances shook the mind of the Church, not out of its dogmatic slumbers, but out of the disregard into which the various aspects of relevant truth had fallen which were impugned by the exhibition of perfervid heterodoxy. The mind of Scotland, which was awaking to the great truths of the Evangel, was not left to rust for want of exercise in regard to the true doctrine of the mystery of godliness and of the mystery of reconciliation. So the issue of these outbursts of extravagance and folly was by way of reaction a confirming of the Church in its hold of the doctrine of the Person of the Incarnate Saviour and of the work that was given Him to do that He might win life for His people.

III.

A DEFENCE OF CATHOLIC VERITY

There is one monument that survives to tell of the theological conflict that was waged with the views put forth by Irving when he denied the sinlessness of the manhood that our Lord in His Incarnation took into union with His everlasting Person. The human nature that this doctrine ascribed to Him was man's nature as fallen. Yet it was held that such was His control of this fallen nature that in fact no sin was allowed to raise its head. The monument referred to we have already mentioned. It is a treatise by Marcus Dods of Belford, of whom we have already spoken incidentally, on The Incarnation of the Eternal Word. Though the writer lived on the English side of the Border his spiritual home was Edinburgh. He also, we believe, was one of those who began their ministry as adherents to the Moderate Party and became out-and-out Evangelicals. They were arrested by the grace of God. In the later years of his ministry he was an Evangelical of the Evangelicals. In the course of his masterly work in criticism of Irving's views there is the chapter to which we have already referred from the hand of his friend Maclagan. It was the work of a man high above the average. Now it says much for a country audience that they should follow and prize preaching of such a profound character. But Dods took part in an earlier controversy.

IV.

DEFENCE OF THE CANON OF HOLY SCRIPTURE

Before the Row and Irvingite questions became matters of hot discussion there had taken place the Apocrypha controversy of which we have already spoken in connection with Robert Haldane's work. There were two Scotsmen who at this juncture did good service to the defence of the Canon of Scripture by standing faithfully against the circulation of the Apocryphal writings with Old Testament Scripture. Haldane was one of these; Andrew Thomson was the other. But Andrew Thomson had a number of lieutenants in his set and perhaps the most eminent of these was the minister of Belford. In the sad strife in regard to this Apocrypha question it was not to be wondered at that the Anglican friends of the Bible Society were to such an extent disposed to favour or to wink at the circulation of those books bound up with the Bible. For though in their Articles the Apocryphal Books are clearly excluded from the Canon of Scripture, yet in those same Articles they have so much recognition given to them that we are told that they are read for " example of life and instruction of manners." The Anglicans, however, were not unanimous on this matter, for not a few of them sympathised with Haldane and Thomson. What was more ominous for the defence of the Scripture was the attitude of men like Pye Smith and other leading Nonconformists in England who had their echo in Scotland among the Independents and the New Light Seceders. They were yielding to the Rationalism that had made itself a home in the Continental schools and that had found a foothold in the circles of the laxer 18th-century school of Apologists. And this attitude of theirs was the forerunner of the portentous falling away of the younger ministry of the Scottish Churches in regard to Holy Scripture as that began to come to light in the discussions over the Higher Critical views of Dr W. Robertson Smith. Of the Evangelicals in the reviving Church of the era of that controversy there was no eminent name who took the side of the managers of the London Society in

conniving at the circulating of the Apocrypha but that of
Henry Grey, and he came to be embroiled in the quarrel, I
take it, without his own seeking. Dods, however, was
perfectly unambiguous in his attitude on the question. In
the course of the war of pamphlets called forth by this
conflict he wrote what was perhaps as good a statement as
the age saw of the case put forward by those who stood for
an undiluted and a thoroughly inspired Canon of Holy
Scripture. In this work he took part with right goodwill.
The pamphlet referred to is *A Letter to the Corresponding
Board or Remarks on the Bible, 1828*. In this letter there
is found a very remarkable piece of writing in its last long
paragraph than which there are few more moving passages
that one can read in the theological literature of the English
language. It shows how the writer's heart was in his task.
Though the passage is, as I have said, long, it is well worth
quoting and here it is :—

"I regret to look back on the length of my discourse;
but my text was the Bible—a Book from which many have
learned much more than I have done, but which few have
had reason to regard with a more profound veneration, or
to cling to with a more pertinacious grasp. Should my views
of that Book be erroneous, they have, at least, neither been
rashly formed, nor lightly adopted on the authority of other
men. If I maintain them warmly it is because I have won
my way to them painfully. My own experience abundantly
proves the truth of the maxim—*nihil tam certum quam quod
ex dubio certum*—and it also abundantly testifies the power
of the Bible to afford the most effectual support, in that hour
when support is most urgently needed, and most difficult to
be found. Few have passed so far into the domain of death
and been permitted to return. I have felt the breath leaving
me, that I expected not again to inhale. I have counted the
dull, heavy throb of my heart, as it grew fainter and fainter,
fully anticipating at every pulsation that it would ' heave but
once more and forever be still.' I have gazed on the faces
of those dearest to me, till my eye grew dim in the blackness
of death, and I could no longer see; and I have listened to

the soothing voice of affection, till my ear grew torpid in the apathy of death, and I could no longer hear; and I have felt the icy chilliness of death shooting through my veins, arresting the current of life in its course, till sensation itself forsook me, and I could no longer feel. And while thus placed on the very line that separates time from Eternity, what was it, that under a deep consciousness of manifold guilt, enabled me to look forward in the momentary expectation of passing that line, calm and tranquil as I am now? Gentlemen, it was just that Bible, of whose Divine inspiration I once as foolishly maintained the low view that prevails, as, I thank God, I have now long and cordially renounced it. I consider the opportunity afforded me, of bringing it to so severe a test, as one of the richest blessings of my life. And, recalled as I have been to longer days, I wish to consider every day lost which does not add to my knowledge of its contents, or deepen my experience of its value. I am well aware that the trying hour will return; and, when it does, one of my most anxious wishes will be satisfied if the prolongation of my life be made a means, however humble, of extending the knowledge of the Bible, of maintaining its integrity, and preserving its purity. But while recollections never to be forgotten rush on my memory, and feelings never to be effaced, crowd upon me, and all in perfect accordance with the principles which my reason approves, and which the Bible, as I understand it, teaches; I find it altogether impossible to accede to your views, or to unite with you in conduct, by which you are giving—unwarily, I believe, undesignedly, I am sure—currency to principles of the most dangerous tendency. While, however, I feel it a duty to reprobate these principles, and to protest against that line of conduct which you have felt it your duty to adopt, the worst I wish you at parting—is, that each and all of you may daily, while you live, enjoy more and more of the riches of the Word of God, and, when you come to die, may by it be enabled to look forward with a ' hope full of immortality,' to that land, where our every doubt shall vanish in the unclouded light of heaven, and our every difference terminate in the all-pervading influence of Divine love."

That the son of such a father beginning at the outset of his career with the avowal of his father's Faith should end his course in the fogs of a barren and self-sufficing Rationalism is one of the tragedies of our Church life. It is but a piece, however, of the history of declension from the high and spiritual life and doctrine of the revived Church of Scotland and the early Free Church. It came down in two generations from its height of attainment in faith and fellowship to the morass of questionings and doubts and halting uncertainty that by the opening years of this century had become the fashion of unfaith. As to the type of life and doctrine of the Disruption Church in its prime it won the encomium of Dr C. H. Waller, the Principal of the London School of Divinity, who was examining chaplain to the excellent Bishop Ryle of Liverpool, as he said once to his students that the nearest approach that he knew of in the history of the Church universal to Apostolic conditions of faith and living was what was to be seen in the Free Church of Scotland in its early days.

We have remarked that some of the New Light leaders in Scotland took the other side in the Apocrypha discussions. This was the first occasion in the country when men of a generally Orthodox and Evangelical character showed an inclination to go away from the tradition of the Reformed schools on the subject of Holy Scripture.

The matters at issue in the discussions over the Canon and Inspiration of Holy Writ were commented upon in his own eminently judicial fashion by Dr Cunningham in his Theological Lectures which saw the light in 1878. This volume from his hand gives the course which he delivered as college lectures in his first Chair. For before he became the Professor of Church History in the Free Church College, Edinburgh, the position with which his name and memory are most closely associated, Dr Cunningham was colleague to Dr Chalmers in the Chair of Divinity, and in this capacity he lectured for two sessions. When there took place, nearly a score of years after his death, the serious outbreak of Rationalistic Criticism, of which Robertson Smith was the chief exponent, the survivors of Cunningham's old students took steps to have his early lectures published. They wished the Church and the world to know how such a master in the field of theological learning dealt with the type of questions that were now thrust upon them for solution. In this volume there is an altogether admirable commentary on the first chapter of the Westminster Confession of Faith as it deals with the Rule of Faith, the Canon and Inspiration of Scripture. In the discussion of the Rule of Faith these matters bearing on what are the books of Holy Writ and what is the nature and extent and proof of their Inspiration come under review. This had been one of the great battle-fields of the theological centuries and then the witness of the Reformed teachers was clear. When these lectures were written the Apocrypha controversy was a recent memory, and it is a matter of some importance to have the judgment of a divine of the capacity and calibre of Cunningham writing in the maturity of his powers in regard to the questions at issue. For if there was one thing more than another in which he excelled it was in setting forth the real issue at stake. His great aim was to find out and set forth so as to clear the discussion from irrelevancies the precise *status quaestionis*. In teaching, as he did, a high doctrine of Inspiration, he was in full sympathy with the conservatism of Haldane and Carson among the non-Presbyterians and Chalmers and Marcus Dods of Belford and Andrew Thomson among his comrades, fathers, and friends. Chalmers, who was not naturally disposed to screw principles or questions up to the last turn, teaches an equally high doctrine in his work on the Evidences when he deals with the subject of Inspiration. He could approve of Haldane on Inspiration as fully and as cordially as he did of the same valuable writer in his Commentary on his Epistle to the Romans.

The latter years of Chalmers' life were a time when a singular group of masters in Theology was raised up in the Church of Scotland previous to its Disruption in 1843.

Contemporaneous with them there was a similar group raised up in the American Presbyterian Church who were the recognised leaders of the Old School when the breach of 1837 took place. These were the days of the Patriarchs of Princeton, Archibald Alexander and Samuel Miller, and of such pre-eminent men as Charles Hodge and his younger colleague, Joseph Addison Alexander. Then there were the Breckinridges, Robert and John, and George Junkin, who was a protagonist in resisting the New England Theology of Albert Barnes and his fellows, while in the south W. S. Plumer of Richmond and J. H. Thornwell of Columbia with his friend, B. M. Palmer of New Orleans, were the standard-bearers to be followed by men like Moses D. Hoge, J. L. Girardeau, R. A. Webb and R. L. Dabney, just as in the north the succession passed into the hands of the younger Hodge and Shedd and Patton and in a later generation to the beloved B. B. Warfield and Machen. Just such a galaxy of stars adorned the reviving and reforming Church of Scotland in the second quarter of the 19th century, and it was from their number that the staff of the Free Church Colleges in their early days were chosen.

V.

THE SPREAD OF THE REVIVAL

Even at the end of the first quarter of the 19th century the Evangelical Revival had made great and rapid advances. Yet at that stage Dr M'Crie, in correspondence with Sir George Sinclair, expressed it as his mind that sound Evangelical preaching had been still quite as abundant, if not more abundant, at the epoch of the Secession in 1733 as it was in the year 1825 in which he was writing. It is, however, just possible that M'Crie, well informed as he was, being an outsider and looking upon the National Church with thorough goodwill, but from the angle of a Seceder, might know less of how things were in his own day than of how they had been a century before. In particular, the outsider would be likely to hear more about the unsatisfactory kind of teaching that still prevailed among the Moderates than of the many cases in which the banner of the Gospel was flying again in pulpits to which it had been long a stranger. The tide had begun to flow about 1790 and it did not quite begin to ebb for more than half a century. Indeed, even when the flower of the Evangelical ministry cast in their lot with the Free Church in 1843, they left behind them a considerable body of Orthodox and even Evangelical preachers in the State Church, and the ranks of those that might be classed as Evangelical Erastians continued to be recruited for years so that in the seventies of the 19th century in a city like Glasgow it could be said that it did not matter very much to which congregation a man went, for in almost any one he might look for a sermon that spoke the message of Evangelical Orthodoxy. This, however, did not hold by any means of the country as a whole.

The leavening of the National Church with the Evangel was not then a uniform process. There were some country Presbyteries where the tradition of unevangelical Moderatism lived on. Dr James Cooper, writing to a friend early in this century, spoke freely of a " rigid Calvinism," by which term, we take it, that a high Sacramentarian like him meant the teaching of his Church's Confession; and he says that he had never heard it preached. The Moderates had killed it largely by means of the Paraphrases. These had helped to set aside the old metrical Psalter as the matter of public praise. He speaks in this letter of the agitation of the Ten Years' Conflict which led up to the Disruption as a revival of pseudo-Covenanting violence, and referring to the state of things that prevailed in the Established Church for years after 1843 he spoke of the timid bigotry of those times and a Calvinistic recrudescence. In his circle in his native Morayshire old Moderatism was strongly entrenched. Indeed, it might be said to be almost stagnant as part of a settled order of things so that he had little chance of hearing in his early life the message of Evangelical Calvinism. Yet in large areas, as we have seen, much of the preaching in the State Church was Orthodox, earnest and Evangelical.

VI.

THE "CALVINISTIC RECRUDESCENCE" IN THE STATE CHURCH

With such a state of things as we have indicated in the Establishment it was not to be wondered at that there should be found in its ministry a few quite good divines who, while tainted, it might be, by Erastianism or prepared to yield to its aggressions, were quite competent Calvinistic theologians in other respects. It was of this type that T. J. Crawford of Edinburgh or Dr William Muir of the same city was, or Dr Alexander Hill or Dr Robert Jamieson or Dr John Muir of Glasgow was, or Principal Haldane or Dr A. F. Mitchell of St Andrews was, or Dr Daniel Dewar of Aberdeen. Dewar was a prominent Evangelical. His Systematic Theology inclined to be more Biblical than dogmatic. Dr Mitchell was the man who did such good service in connection with Westminster Assembly and its work. As a student of old documents he won the high praise of that master in the department, Dr Hay Fleming, that he knew no one more trustworthy in the use that he made of his documents than Dr Mitchell. He was a divine of whom one has the feeling that he was more in line on the subject of the extent of the Atonement with Ussher or Davenant than with the stricter school of Calvinists. He recognised, however, in William Cunningham the outstanding theologian of Scotland in spite of what then ran very high, the tide of estranged feeling that was due to their denominational difference. Mitchell's work on behalf of the Westminster documents was done with none the less keenness that he had as his neighbour and colleague, Dr John Tulloch, who was the recognised leader of the newer type of Moderatism. Principal Tulloch had a high-brow contempt for theological Confession of the Orthodox Faith. His best work was done in his *Theism*, a book dealing with rational common Apologetics. It had considerable vogue until it was eclipsed and replaced by Robert Flint's Baird Lecture on the same subject which has held the field since it appeared about 60 or more years ago.

Dr Hill at Glasgow kept up the type of Orthodox tradition that was in his own day associated with the teaching of his father, Principal Hill of St Andrews. His colleague in the Chair of Church History was Dr J. Seaton Reid, who wrote the standard History of the Presbyterian Church of Ireland. Muir and Barr and Jamieson and Macduff and Elder Cumming were representatives of varying shades of the Orthodox or Evangelical school in Glasgow and the West. At Edinburgh, T. J. Crawford made his name the best known of the divines of his Church as a sound and able theologian. His book on the Atonement is of standard character. And his discussion of the Fatherhood of God was a vigorous criticism of R. S. Candlish's Cunningham Lecture on that subject. It is one of the most important contributions to the literature on a side of Christian truth that was very widely discussed in the third quarter of the 19th century by different schools of Theology—Broad and Orthodox alike. These men were representatives of Theology in the State Church.

VII.

Dr CHALMERS

We have, however, passed from the group of divines who adorned the early years of the Victorian age. Dr Thomas Chalmers was far the most celebrated of them all. His celebrity he achieved as a preacher. As a theologian he was largely an Apologete and in this respect he resembled in his output the work of Flint, only that in proportion he is less devoted to the borderland region where philosophy and theology meet. His *Institutes of Theology* show him to have been a fresh and original worker in the region of revealed Theology rather than a theologian of learning. That work was distinguished by the order in which he attacked his subject. His natural bent was to the study of the sciences, exact and metaphysical both. This helped to colour and to determine the course of his thinking. He followed the line of the inductive rather than the deductive. He was, as his colleague in the New College, John Duncan, put it, a great theologue, while Cunningham was a learned theologian.

VIII.

DR WILLIAM CUNNINGHAM

Cunningham, whom we have mentioned time and again, was, as a theologian, the most eminent of the group of Evangelical divines of his age. He was at home in the different departments of his subject. Indeed, he was one of the foremost theologians of the Reformed school in the widest sense. His friend, disciple and admirer, Dr Hugh Martin, bracketed his name, as we have seen, with that of Thomas Halyburton as one of the two greatest divines that their country has ever produced. His collected works speak for themselves. The greatest of these, in two solid octavo volumes, is his *Historical Theology*. This reproduces his course of lectures in the Chair of Church History, which deal with the various schools of Theology and the leading erroneous or heretical perversions of the Faith. This work is like an elaborate and luminous judicial charge by a master of his subject addressed from the Bench to the jury of Christian students who may well avail themselves of the judgments of so penetrating and comprehensive a mind. In particular, the work is of supreme value for the thoroughness of the treatment that it gives to the Theology of the Church of Rome. It gives great prominence to the Council of Trent and to that Tridentine Theology which owes its dogmatic shape to the teaching of the schools of the Middle Ages. Over against the avowed Theology of Rome he sets historical Calvinism as it speaks in its most mature utterances. These he found in the documents of the Westminster Assembly. And the Theology which they embody is that set forth, analysed and defended in the *Theologia Elenctica* of Francis Turrettine. Cunningham was nothing, if he was not thorough. He devoted the fine judicial quality of his mind to the balanced and considered exposition of the Faith that he had first analysed. His handling of the Socinian and Arminian systems is that of a great doctor of the Church. This *magnum opus* will remain as a masterpiece in the field of historical Theology in which from the standpoint of a loyal acceptance of consistent Reformed teaching he passes the thinking of the Christian centuries under review.

Cunningham took a leading part in the inception and in the conduct for its early years of the *British and Foreign Evangelical Review*. Indeed, he might be said to be the moving spirit behind it. To this quarterly organ he contributed in quick succession near the end of his valuable life a series of Essays dealing with his favourite field, *The Reformers and the Theology of the Reformation*. These Essays appear under that name as the first of the four volumes of his collected works as they were edited by his literary executors, who were his colleagues, James Buchanan and James Bannerman. In these collected writings, volumes 2 and 3 are devoted to his *Historical Theology*, while the fourth volume is made up of his Reviews and Pamphlets. This last volume is entitled *Discussions on Church Principles*. As a writer he had been in the front rank in the warfare about Church questions and the contributions that he made to the cause for which he stood were so marked with his fullness of knowledge and his fairness of judgment as to be worthy to be grouped with the fruits of his more mature pen. We have already noted the final volume issued in the 'seventies. Besides a volume of his Sermons, edited with a biographical sketch by his friend John Bonar, there is another valuable volume in which Cunningham's work is found. It is his edition of Stillingfleet on Popery. The value of the original work may be said to be fully doubled by the extensive notes which he as editor supplied. Few men were so conversant as he was with the vast literature of the Roman controversy and so there were few so fitted to furnish such notes as enrich this edition of Stillingfleet. Among his various works perhaps the effort that shows his powers at their best is the Essay reproduced in *The Reformers and the Theology of the Reformation*, in which he treats of Calvinism and the doctrine of Philosophical Necessity. Here he is at once comprehensive and acute, full of information and balanced in statement. The interest taken in the subject that is dealt with in this Essay may be much less to-day than it was in his days; but for all time this Essay remains as a weighty deliverance of a prince of divines and thinkers. Hodge, by the way, and Cunningham were great friends and each was very much the admirer of the other. Each looked upon the other as the foremost Reformed divine of their day.

The story is told of one of Cunningham's students who had thoughts of taking a session at Princeton with Hodge. He was a canny Scot and wanted to make sure beforehand that a session taken overseas would count as part of his Divinity course. So he went to see the Principal about it. He stated his case. Cunningham when he heard it, took a pinch of snuff—for he was a snuffer—and then gave his answer. He had a question in his mind about this business. But here was the shape that it took. His only question about the matter was whether a session taken with Hodge ought not to be counted as equal to two.

IX.

Dr R. S. CANDLISH

There was a man in their own generation whose name was often coupled with that of Cunningham as a leading Scottish Churchman. There was no comparison between the two in regard to weight of judgment or breadth of learning. Yet the companion name was that of one of the ablest Churchmen in an age in which able Churchmen were not few. Robert Smith Candlish was the minister of one of the select congregations of what was in his time a great Evangelical city. He was a wonderfully electric preacher of the Evangel; and in his public prayers, as he led the devotions of his people, he was described by Addison Alexander as praying like an inspired Hebrew prophet. It may have been the case that he had his own share of the suppleness and elasticity of the typical ecclesiastic. His was an adroit mind that was fertile in expedients. He was a manager of men and liked to have his own way. This brought him under the lash of the pen of his formidable contemporary, Hugh Miller, who did not spare his victim when he had him in his grip. Here are some of the things that Miller had to say of him :—" It seems all too characteristic of a mind greatly more adroit in preliminaries and detail than sagacious in the master businesses to which the preliminary should lead and the details belong—a mind skilful in coasting along shallow bays and miniature promontories, but that, when it launches into the open sea, lacks both compass and rudder, and carries with it no nicely graduated sextant by which to determine lines of bearing or points of position." Or again :— " This I shall dare say—that were I disposed to make sport to the Philistines, I could find in the recorded thinking of Dr Candlish not a few magnificent immaturities with which to amuse them. There are some minds that from a certain structural idiosyncrasy lie peculiarly open to animadversion. . . . I might perhaps find exercise for ingenuity in the dissection of one special intellect of this character, that, like a summer in the higher latitudes, produces much, but ripens little—that is content often to acquiesce in its first hasty conclusion, without waiting for what the second cogitation may produce—and that bears on its incessant stream of thought, ever copious and sparkling, many a fragile air bell, that, though it reflects the rainbow hues of heaven on its surface, owes all its dancing buoyancy to a lack of weight and is singularly hollow within." A man of Miller's powers when he was minded to be candid could hit right out from the shoulder. And the other man would remember the blow.

Dr Candlish was a fine Evangelical in his preaching. He was, however, a quick thinker rather than a patient divine. As a man of shifts and expedients he was a marked contrast to the Master in Theology whom he succeeded as Principal of the New College. Though Cunningham could be precipitate and hasty when aroused in the heat of conflict, he was a man whose movements were slow when compared with those of his successor. Candlish was the first to lecture on the Foundation which was established soon after Cunningham's death, which took place in 1861, to commemorate the great divine. He chose as his subject, " The Fatherhood of God and the Sonship of Believers." Instead of taking the line of historical review of a subject which had been thrashed out in the region of polemics, the lecturer took a doctrine or cluster of doctrines in which it was possible for him to do what was more or less pioneer work; for the subject of Adoption had not received anything like the full treatment that Justification had. His lectures met with a mixed reception. His own circle of friends were divided in the estimate that they formed of their merits. In the pages of the *British and Foreign Evangelical Review* Hugh Martin gave a cordial welcome to Candlish's work. In the main, he agreed with him, but he made some reservations. These, however, dealt more with details than with the main theme of the lectures. Crawford, however, his neighbour in the Theological Faculty of the University of Edinburgh, had much more to say by way of criticism. There was an interesting passage-at-arms between the two, in the course of which the lecturer catches his critic out on some points, as, for example, in regard to the distinction between person and nature. Yet with respect to man as he was made in the likeness of God to hold fellowship with his Maker, most folk agreed with the critic in seeing in such a creature a child of God. All, however, that Candlish affirmed was that man at the first was not *in the proper sense of the word* a son of God. On this he laid stress, in view of the teaching of the school of F. D. Maurice as to the universal Fatherhood of God. In regard to the sonship for which Crawford pleaded there was the question : Was it one that was or was not amissible? Martin agreed with Candlish in denying the true standing of a son to Adam unfallen. It might be said that the leaders on the two sides disagreed at bottom in regard to their definitions and that their conflict was in the main a verbal one. With their definitions of the nature and contents of sonship, whether that definition was in black and white or merely operative as influencing their thinking, Martin and Candlish found no difficulty in denying a universal Fatherhood of God with a corresponding Divine sonship of man. Crawford pleaded for such a Fatherhood and sonship. Candlish maintained that the sonship which believers receive in adoption is an entirely new relation for any one of the race of man. He regarded in this sense the Gospel as doing more than making good the loss brought on our race by sin. It was more than a remedial or restorative provision. But he went on to maintain that there is virtually only one thing that should be truly called sonship, and as the salvation of the believer is in the Son of God he becomes in his union with his Saviour a sharer in the Sonship of the Everlasting Son. To this teaching it was that many of his best friends took most exception. They held that the mysterious relation of the Son to the Father in His Everlasting Sonship is entirely a thing *sui generis,* a relation that is unique and incommunicable. It was then on their reading of the situation the uttermost that one is entitled to go that we should say that in union with God's own Son as a public Person in His office as Mediator, an honorary standing of Sonship that is inamissible is conferred on those for whom the way to this rank is opened in their acceptance as they are justified by the Blood of Christ and who are prepared for the life of sons by their New Birth and the sealing by the Spirit of the Son. This is the Adoption that is held out in the Son of God as Saviour and that as regards relative grace is its very crown. It is the supreme expression of the saving love of God, for this is the kind and measure of love that the Father has to His chosen ones that they should be called the sons of God. When He gave His Son for them they were not only to be freed from the guilt of sin, they were to get the standing that they should never lose of sons in the house of His Father Who is now their Father too. Crawford seems to us to do less than justice to the truth that the sinner in his sin is a child of wrath, is of his father the devil, and a child of disobedience. And his defence of the common teaching of Reformed divines, that in a certain diluted sense fallen man is still a son, though an apostate son, of God, might stress more than it did the exiguous character of the content of this universal Divine sonship for which he pleads. Both sides might be unduly straining the methods of Systematic Theology in dealing with a problem in the solution of which Biblical and Exegetical Theology had much to say. For the precise content of various portions of Scripture required that justice should be done to them, and the same terms in different writers or contexts did not of necessity always convey precisely the same shade of meaning.

His venture in these lectures to advance the bounds of Systematic Theology is Candlish's chief contribution to the exposition of the Reformed Faith, though his work on the Atonement is a fine and able treatment of the subject. His method of tackling his theme tells of his dash and his versatility and his fearlessness. In the features of his intellectual equipment we might say without invidiousness on the one side or on the other that in their respective spheres of statesmanship, the one political and the other ecclesiastical, he and David Lloyd George were very like each other. We have ranged Candlish alongside of Cunningham because of how in the public mind they were associated as the two ablest Churchmen who came to the front in the Ten Years' Conflict in the Church of Scotland which ended in the Disruption of 1843.

As theologians there were some of less name among his fellows who were more remarkable for the reach and compass of their attainments in the field of Divinity than Dr Candlish was. There were two of his special friends who took divergent views of his Cunningham Lectures for example. One of these was William White of Haddington, who was distinctly critical of them. He had the hereditary Theology of the Secession. Candlish felt sore that he had not earned the approval of White. The other, William Alexander of Duntocher, to whom he wrote about White's unfavourable judgment, decidedly approved of his positions, told the lecturer so, and won his gratitude. It may have been the case that the leaning in the direction of Supralapsarianism which readers have detected in the *Fatherhood* may account for the welcome that Alexander gave the book. For he was a very definite Supralapsarian at the same time as he was a very militant Calvinist. These two of Candlish's friends were divines of good standing. But there were many such that we need not name.

X.

Dr MACLAGAN

We have already spoken of the friend of Marcus Dods whose sermon he embodied in his work on the Incarnation. James Maclagan did not publish much, but he was known to be one of the finest scholars and ablest divines of his Church and age. It was this that led to his appointment as Professor of Theology to the Free Church students at Aberdeen. He died in 1852. We have already spoken of his published lectures, for the form of which his friends and not he were responsible. The recognised merit of the contents of this volume which gave to the world the writer's *Academic Prelections* was such as to lead John Bruce of Edinburgh, no mean judge, to say that such a work was ample justification for the Church's action in providing facilities for northern students to study Divinity at Aberdeen and for sending Maclagan there to teach. Hugh Martin speaks with a special commendation of his lecture on the Righteousness of Christ. In the author of these Lectures we have recognised a man of Maclaurin's mould in whom clearness of insight and reach and compass of thought kept pace with one another.

XI.

Drs GORDON AND BRUCE

The names, too, of Robert Gordon and John Bruce of Edinburgh have been before us already; yet, influential as these worthy divines were, they need not delay us long. The very fact that men of their ability began their public work as strangers to the power of the Evangel meant that ere they came to hold Gospel truth as they did, they must have devoted their attention to its credentials and character and contents. They were men of fine mental powers and highly competent theologians. Indeed, so far as mental output went, Cunningham said of Bruce that he put more brains into his pulpit work than any other man in the Edinburgh ministry. All, however, that these worthies did with their mastery of sacred truth was to put it into use in their fruitful ministries. This they did to some purpose. They raised up in the cultured circles of their city a generation of solid instructed Christians.

XII.

M'CHEYNE AND THE BONAR BROTHERS

Among the young men of that epoch who profited by the studies of such divines in sacred truth there was none that left his mark on the Evangelical Churches more than Robert Murray M'Cheyne of Dundee, whose sermons have had as wide a circulation as any of the Scottish pulpit. These show in their clear and solid statement of Christian teaching how sound the Theology was that lay at the basis of his preaching; and he was only a specimen of a large class. Of that class, a few were taken up with Premillennial ideas and this affected their preaching to a greater or less extent. The members of this school were men like the brothers, Andrew Bonar, who wrote the Life of M'Cheyne and who edited Rutherford's Letters, and Horatius Bonar, the hymn writer; these were the best known of the Chiliasts. In the formative years of their college career they came under the spell of the meteoric message of Edward Irving before his excesses in doctrine had led him far away from the beaten track. And as he laid stress on the Premillennial dating of the Second Advent they imbibed this form of the Chiliastic hope. Among the Scottish Evangelicals of their age they and their fellows were regarded as being in this respect peculiar. But the mere fact of their holding such an expectation as they did was not looked upon as being in itself a matter of much moment. Modern Chiliasm had not yet learned to cut and carve the ages into dispensations with the cocksureness it has now reached. It had not found out the elaborate system that overturns the true character of the dispensation of law that is gone. Nor had it yet mapped out the field of the unfulfilled prophetic future until the expected dispensation of the Millennial presence and vision of the Returned Lord which will modify seriously its message and dispense salvation on

other terms than those which the Gospel now sets forth. It
is true that even the milder Premillennialists must hold that
the message of salvation in Christ and the means of grace
will be materially modified in the age to which they look
forward by that manifested presence of the Lord which they
believe will then be vouchsafed. And consequently the hope
of His Advent will not find a place in the expectation of a
world or a Church that has Him already in its midst in
the glory of His Second Coming. Perhaps we might have
to ask their pardon for speaking of a Church in this connection.
So many of them hold that the Church of Christ has been
completed at His Advent, and that the saved of the Millennial
age have no place in His body.

It may have been by way of somewhat slighting reference
to this school and its fanciful hopes that the older Evangelicals
used to call the young Premillennial set The Evangelical
Light Infantry. They certainly held the Premillennial hope;
yet Andrew Bonar as an old man could say that he subscribed
the Confession of Faith because he believed every word of it;
and this was his attitude toward the Confession to the last.
The members of this school used to claim that Chalmers was
in sympathy with their outlook. He, however, and most even
of themselves, did not shift the centre of gravity of the
Gospel message from the Word of the Cross to the hope of
the Crown. A man would not be far out in saying that the
ordinary Scottish view of the glory of the First Resurrection
of Revelation 20 was that given in substance by James
Durham in the 17th century, which saw in it the resurgence
in power of the truths and the principles for which the
martyrs had laid down their lives.

XIII.

DAVID BROWN AND PATRICK FAIRBAIRN

Of the literature produced by the discussions in the early
Victorian period in regard to our Lord's Coming Again
perhaps the most influential book was the post-Millennial
Treatise on Christ's Second Advent which was written by

Dr David Brown when he was a minister in Glasgow. Dr Brown died as Principal of the Free Church College at Aberdeen. His brother, the godly Charles J. Brown, was with Dr Moody Stuart, the special experimental divine of the Edinburgh pulpit, down to about 1880. David Brown was the friend and biographer of Dr John Duncan. In his early life he had been assistant to Edward Irving in London and shared in his prophetic views. With his change of judgment and conviction on these contested questions he became, by reason of his volume on *The Second Advent*, the leading opponent of the Premillennial reading of unfulfilled prophecy. This work of his ran into some seven editions and it is a book of permanent value. It was reprinted in America by Carter of New York. On the same side of these questions there was to be heard another voice which perhaps carried more weight than even that of Brown. It was the voice of Patrick Fairbairn, who became Principal of the Free Church College in Glasgow. He was the writer of the standard work on the Typology of Scripture and also, among other works, of an important volume that deals with Prophecy. The works of both these writers stood high in the esteem of their contemporaries of the Princeton school. In their own departments—that of Fairbairn was the more comprehensive—these divines ranked with the foremost men of their generation. The two Bonars and Walter Wood of Elie wrote from the Premillennial standpoint.

XIV.

MISSIONARY ACTIVITY

1. DUFF AND WILSON

The age of the Evangelical Revival was one of marked Missionary activity; and the roll of honour for Scotland is adorned with the names of Alexander Duff and John Macdonald of Calcutta, with that of John Wilson of Bombay among its Missionaries to India, of William Chalmers Burns of China, and John Duncan, Missionary to the Jews. The eloquent Duff was the pioneer agent of his Church as a

Missionary organisation in its corporate capacity. Wilson, who did a work at Bombay equally striking with that of Duff at Calcutta, was on the Foreign Field before the Church as such had a Foreign Mission scheme. He served in India to begin with, and, indeed, until after 1843, as an agent of one of the Scottish Missionary Societies. It was as such an agent that he acted until the Free Church of Scotland took over so much of the Missionary work of the older Missionary Boards. These Boards were founded after the Assembly of 1796 flung away the opportunity of initiating Foreign Missionary enterprise as part of its normal programme. They were interdenominational and their agents were ordained by their respective home Churches. However jealous those Churches were for the welfare of their own schemes they were large-hearted enough to have no quarrel with the voluntary associations for the spread of the Gospel which were independent of their control. Indeed, for about 50 years, this interdenominational Board system functioned, and for almost a score of years the Church scheme was working side by side with it. This came to an end only when the home Churches came to an agreement as to the delimitation of their areas and the control of their agents. Even after the partitioning out of the fields of operation took place, there was widespread support in Scotland, and there is yet, for the Presbyterian Missionary work in China, which is under English control. There was no attempt made to concuss the membership of the Churches to be so exclusive in their Missionary loyalty as to confine their benefactions to those of their own denomination. And this holds in the strictest circles of Presbyterianism in regard to such a Mission as the China Inland Mission and different Missionary Societies that are at work in the South American field. These, though not under the control of the Churches, are regarded with favour as fellow-workers in the Gospel harvest field. In Scotland it was when Moderatism was about the lowest ebb of unbelief that the Moderate Party became the greatest sticklers for Church authority, which, indeed, meant their own autocracy. History has a way of repeating itself.

2. JOHN MACDONALD OF CALCUTTA

We have named in the company of noted Missionaries John Macdonald of Calcutta. His Life by W. K. Tweedie used to be a well-known Missionary biography. It is the life of an unusually saintly man. In the Memoirs of the devoted John Milne of Perth by Horatius Bonar, Dr Bonar tells of how Milne in his Calcutta days—for he spent some years there as minister—loved to trace out the steps of John Macdonald whose memory he revered. He mentions that when Macdonald was lying unconscious nearing his end he was visited by the veteran Swiss Missionary Lacroix, who said as he looked at the dying man : " There lies the holiest man in India." John Macdonald, like his father before him, had an uncommonly brilliant academic record. But like his father again, he counted all things but loss for the knowledge of Christ. Father and son were both of them theologians of the practical kind of exceptional competence. The father, known as Macdonald of Ferintosh, was the great Evangelist of the Scottish Highlands. The son, who died at Calcutta, was an orthodox Richard Baxter, with all his zeal and without his erratic orbit in Theology. His grandson, as a civil servant of the Indian Government, has done remarkable Missionary work in the closed land of Tibet. And now that he is retired, he is busy at Kalimpong at the translation of the Bible into Tibetan.

3. W. C. BURNS

William Chalmers Burns is the most outstanding man that Scotland has given for the work of the Gospel in the Far East. He went out to China as the agent of the English Presbyterian Church. But he was born in a Scottish manse, the son of one of the worthy Disruption ministers. His deep burning zeal consumed him in his work and he was honoured to mould and influence the early years in China of J. Hudson Taylor, whose work is his monument. Almost

as soon as Burns began to preach there were great awakenings
in the places where he laboured. He took M'Cheyne's place
for a few months, and before the godly pastor came back the
great awakening that continued under his ministry had begun
under that of Burns. There was no uncertain note on the
awful things of God struck by these faithful witnesses.
M'Cheyne on his last Sabbath in his pulpit preached—and,
we doubt not, tenderly—on the words in Romans ix. 22, 23.
" What if God, willing to shew His wrath, and to make His
power known, endured with much longsuffering the vessels
of wrath fitted to destruction; and that He might make
known the riches of His glory on the vessels of mercy, which
He had afore prepared unto glory. . . .? " In respect of
the solemn truth that he preached, Burns was not a whit
behind his friend of Dundee. He bore the stamp of the
rich teaching he had heard in Glasgow. One of his converts
used to tell of how he spoke at the close of the last service
that he held in Perth in John Milne's congregation after a
time of refreshing there. Addressing his hearers he said :
" If you have got any good from my teaching you may trace
it under the Lord's hand to that man of God in Glasgow,
John Duncan." It was under Duncan's ministry that Burns,
in his student days, was nourished and moulded, instructed
and built up.

4. JOHN DUNCAN

This John Duncan, of whom we have spoken more than
once, was one of the first Missionaries sent by a National
Church to bring the Gospel to the Jews. And since the days
of the Apostles there is hardly on record such a striking
work of grace among the Jews as took place in the days
of his labours in Buda-Pesth. It was to that time of
refreshing that the Christian Church owes the ministry and
work of Adolph Saphir and Alfred Edersheim. John Duncan,
better known as " Rabbi " Duncan, was taken home by his
Church from this work in Hungary to be the first Professor
of Hebrew and Old Testament in the New College, Edinburgh.
He was at once one of the most profound and versatile of

scholars, one of the humblest of believers, and one of the most erratic and absentminded of men. His Theology was the choicest of the Reformed school. Though he left his mark on many of his students by his words, he left next to nothing in writing. There are, however, some books in which so much of his teaching is treasured up and preserved; and there are scarcely any books of their generation in Scotland that are even yet more greedily sought after than these. He had a genius for epigrammatic wisdom, as any one may see who will read Dr Moody Stuart's *Recollections of John Duncan* or William Knight's *Colloquia Peripatetica*. The first of these books has been described as "a man of genius depicted by another." The latter has run through about half a dozen editions. Dr Duncan had a circle of admirers and disciples who were so distinctive as to represent what was almost a "Rabbi" Duncan cult.

John Duncan as a preacher and divine was recognised by the admirers of Dr John Love as the Elisha on whom the mantle of their master had fallen. This told of the great subjects that he handled, of the spiritual manner in which he dealt with them, and the chaste eloquence that marked his treatment of the most profound and high themes. While thus he had strong meat for the mature he had milk for the babes in Christ, and there were few at once so faithful and so tender as the beloved "Rabbi." His Life, as we have mentioned already, was written by his old friend, David Brown of Aberdeen, who also edited a volume of his Addresses from the Pulpit and at the Communion Table. These two volumes are indispensable for those who would come to a just estimate of the man. Over fifty years after his death there was issued still further a substantial volume of *Rich Gleanings from "Rabbi" Duncan*; and it soon went through two large editions.

Let me introduce you to him in one of his Communion Table Addresses which a hearer took down in shorthand. It is John Duncan all over :—*Mount Sinai and Mount Zion.* "Jehovah He is the God. He is a wonderful God; He is a wonder-working God, God quickens the dead, God opens the blind eyes, and unstops the deaf ears; and the quickened soul has a voice wherewith to respond to the call—'Call unto Me and I will answer thee and show thee great and mighty things which thou knowest not'; and the opened ear can hear the voice that says, 'Look'; and the opened eye can look.

"I have been lately, and methinks I still am, at the foot of Mount *Sinai*; and I heard a *voice*, and this voice spake of wrath; the wrath of God, which is revealed from heaven against all ungodliness and unrighteousness of men. God thundereth with His voice—who thundereth with a voice like Him? I heard the sound of a trumpet, and the voice of words, concerning which the Scripture saith, 'so terrible was the sight that Moses said, "I exceedingly fear and quake."'

"And the Lord showed me a *biography*: a biography written defectively in the memory, which at the best is ever treacherous, but written perfectly in the book of God's remembrance. And the voice said, 'Come, and read this biography.' I said, 'O Lord, how can I read it?' 'I have read it,' said God. 'And you must, you must.' And when I had looked, still the voice came, 'Turn thee yet again, and I will show thee greater abominations than these.'

"And not a biography only—he showed me *a heart*. 'There are seven abominations in a man's heart'—seven being the Scripture number for completeness. And my eye was fixed on that with horror. I speak not now of godly sorrow and repentance, but of horror; and with something that is surely worse, with shame. For it was not simply my eye fixed on the heart but God showing me His own eye looking on it. 'See thy sin under My eye; see, My eye sees that.' God be merciful to me a sinner!

"Now I heard a voice, at first distant and mysterious; but it came nearer, *a still small voice*, proclaiming salvation —a voice which came from Zion, the city of our solemnities, the city of our God—a voice publishing peace, proclaiming the salvation, which comes from Zion—a voice proclaiming, as salvation, so also a Saviour—'Behold I bring you good tidings of great joy, for unto you is born in the city of

David, a Saviour '—and not merely a Saviour, and a Saviour on earth—Emmanuel, God with us, God among us, God for us—but a Saviour slain.

" Methought then I stood on *Calvary* and heard these words, ' It is finished.' God said, ' Look into the heart of Christ and behold Him in His vicarious death. Behold Him, and know the grace of the Lord Jesus Christ, that, though He was rich, yet for your sakes, He became poor, that ye through His poverty might be rich.' The greatest depth of this poverty being not in His incarnation—though that was a wondrous depth—look at it in His death.

" Then methought also that God said, ' Come by the blood to the Mercy-Seat.' And I heard a voice speak from the Mercy-Seat from between the Cherubims. And what voice was that? ' This is My beloved Son (not merely with Whom, but) in Whom I am well pleased, hear Him,' said He from the Mercy-Seat, from between the Cherubims. ' The Lord is well pleased for His righteousness' sake,' said He from the Mercy-Seat, from between the Cherubims. ' I, even I, am He that blotteth out thy transgressions, and will not remember thy sins,' said He from the Mercy-Seat, from between the Cherubims. Sweet invitation to me, a departer, ' Return unto Me,' God assigning to the sinner the saving clause, ' For I have redeemed thee.'

" Then methought the Lord said, ' I know heart secrets.' And I said, ' Lord, show me *a heart which thou knowest.*' And methought the Lord showed me a heart. Whose it was He did not say, and I do not know; but a heart which God knows. He showed me something of it.

" It was a heart into which He had put a *new song.* The soul was making melody, attempting to make melody to the Lord. Where it was I do not know; but I heard it singing about the middle of its song. It had been singing other songs before this. It had been singing, ' What profit is there in my blood when I go down to pit?' It had been singing the 51st psalm : and Jehovah had put a new song into its mouth; He had done it, and it was trying to sing; and I heard it in the middle of its song. It had been reading

Revelation v., and trying to sing some of its numbers; and now it was at these words, 'For Thou wast slain.' And oh, how it was sobbing and breaking, how it was melting and breaking with a joyous grief, and a grievous joy! It could not get its song sung, though it would have liked it. Oh how it faltered when it tried to sing, 'And hast redeemed us to God by Thy blood.'

"It was the song of a soul known to God; and many such there are. It was the song of one to whom much had been forgiven, and who therefore loved much; and many such there are. But it was the song of the chief of sinners; of the one to whom *most* had been forgiven, and who loved *most*.

"Yet it *faltered* and made wrong music; it jarred, and there was discord; and it grated on its own ear; and pained it. And God was listening to it; the omniscient God, Who knows all things. But the song was presented through and by the Mediator of the New Covenant; and if there was discord, it was removed by grace in atoning blood, by the sweet accents of intercession; for it came up as music in Jehovah's ear; melody to the Lord. It was not discord in heaven.

"I would know, O God, what soul that is! O God, let that soul be *mine*! And tell me of it. Let it be mine! Put a new song into my mouth; teach me to sing it. Teach me to sing it on earth; and to sing it when earth shall be no more."

There is a specimen of the eerie, unworldly sayings of the Rabbi who said that he should like to sit at the feet of Jonathan Edwards to learn what true godliness is and at the feet of Thomas Boston to learn how to reach it. The stories are almost without number that are still told of him, though it is now a little more than seventy years since his sun went down. He was colleague in the Free Church College with Chalmers and Cunningham and that fine historical scholar and divine, David Welsh, who, as retiring Moderator, read the Protest of 1843.

XV.

A GREAT SENATUS

The first Senatus of the Free Church College was a galaxy of men of the first rank; and when blanks were made by death their first successors were worthy of the place that their predecessors adorned. Cunningham succeeded Chalmers as Principal and Welsh as Professor of Church History. He had as his new colleagues James Buchanan and James Bannerman, and at a later stage George Smeaton. They were all men of the Disruption generation, the last of them being the most eminent scholar of the set of young men who with M'Cheyne and the Bonars sat at the feet of Chalmers.

James Buchanan was a highly accomplished divine. He had been a spiritual power in the pulpit and was one of the most popular practical writers of his age. But he was more: he adorned in turn the Chair of Apologetic Theology and that of Dogmatics. As the second lecturer on the Cunningham Foundation he delivered a most valuable course on *The Doctrine of Justification*. It is about as full and accurate, well-informed and well-balanced a book on the subject as can be consulted. His work as an Apologete has left behind it two monuments. One is a pioneer treatise in which he essays to deal with the Logic of Analogy and the uses to which it may be put. It is of solid worth, as is also his other work on Theism which appeared in two volumes—*Faith in God and Modern Atheism*. Dr Buchanan was a very clear thinker and a good writer. He had a mind of a texture at once firm and fine. The most important of his other works is the volume that he devoted to the subject of the Holy Spirit. This is written in a popular way and is spoken of by Warfield as worthy of the best traditions of the Puritan school which made a speciality of the Spirit's Person and Work.

On the theme of the Person and Work of the Spirit Buchanan's younger colleague, George Smeaton, in his mature years, wrote his Cunningham Lecture. This Warfield brackets in the same encomium with Buchanan's work on the Holy

Spirit and he describes it as handling that subject in a more academic style, while Buchanan's work was of a more popular kind. This volume of Smeaton's we might call invaluable within its own range. Next to Cunningham he stood as our foremost student of the history of the Reformed Theology and when he gives the conspectus of the development of a doctrine and the varied handling that it met with he does very fine work indeed. This is seen not only in his account of the history of the Doctrine of the Spirit, but also in the historical sketch that he gives of the doctrine of the Atonement in the volumes which he has devoted to that subject. These inductive studies in regard to the Atonement are works of the highest value. One of them deals with the doctrine as it is to be learned from the statements bearing upon it made by our Lord Himself in the Gospel; the other deals in like fashion with the doctrine as found in the teaching of the Apostles. Both of them are works of standard quality. They will wear and stand the test of time in respect of neat and accurate statement for all who take a serious interest in the study of the subject. Dr Smeaton was the master of a very clear and unobtrusive style of expression. Even when one does not agree with the details of his Exegesis one cannot but take note of the wealth of sanctified learning that he brought to bear upon his theme.

Dr Duncan, when his junior colleague, A. B. Davidson, began to show signs of going off on rationalistic lines, which to begin with were of that character only cautiously or tentatively, called in the help of Smeaton to do what he could to reclaim him. The best meant of efforts were in vain; and Davidson's teaching, and even more than his positive teaching, his hints and suggestions, became the source of an alien infusion in Old Testament studies in Scotland. Robertson Smith caught the infection and spread the plague.

Though Smeaton was far from being an ecclesiastic in the ordinary sense of the word, yet he took a deep and lively interest in the subject of National Christianity, and his pamphlet on this matter in connection with Scriptural Union of Churches is one of the fullest and most luminous expositions one can see of the historic Scottish Reformed view of Church and State or of National Religion. It was his interest in this side of things that led him to issue a new edition of M'Crie's *Statement*. He was very much at home in the discussions in former days of these topics. Smeaton was a scholar and divine of the same mould with M'Crie, whose fellow-countryman he was. His work as a theologian still awaits a worthy appraisement. He was as modest and unassuming as he was thorough and painstaking. A man can take his word in regard to any theme that he handles as soon as that of any writer on theological subjects. His talented junior colleague, James Macgregor, said that Smeaton had the best-constituted theological intellect in Christendom. When he died in 1889 he was succeeded by the second Marcus Dods. Between the two men there was a yawning gulf.

The other name we have mentioned as having a seat in the New College Senatus in its great days is that of James Bannerman. He was the author of two works that bespeak his quality. One of these is an elaborate treatise in which he handles the Inspiration of Scripture. In it he teaches a high doctrine on the subject. In reading this book one should attend with care to the definitions and to the use of terms in keeping with these definitions. There was a contemporary book in high repute on the same subject by Archdeacon Lee which used the leading terms Revelation and Inspiration in a different way, so that Bannerman and Lee could be set the one against the other, so far, at least, as mere words went. The first fruit of F. L. Patton's work was his little book which deals with Inspiration, in which he shows that the difference between Lee and Bannerman was largely, if not altogether, a verbal one. The work, however, with which Bannerman's name will be most associated is his treatise on the Church of Christ. This appeared after his death and it gives the teaching which he delivered in his lectures in connection with the Doctrine of the Church. It was so much of the work of his Chair. This treatise is worthy of being regarded as a standard one as it deals with the Reformed Doctrine of the Church in its various aspects, especially as these came into prominence in the chequered record of the Church in Scotland. In his treatment of his subject, Dr Bannerman reminds one of Cunningham. He is comprehensive in his outlook and acute in his distinctions. He is full and clear in his treatment of the various topics that came under his notice. Indeed, these volumes, although they deal with their subject to a great extent in the light of Scottish historical conditions and discussions, are more than a classic work of one of the Reformed Churches. They give weighty deliverances that are illuminating for the Church life of the whole family of these Churches and for an even wider circle.

Dr James Bannerman's work on The Church was edited by his son, D. D. Bannerman, who was himself the author of an important and elaborate Cunningham Lecture dealing with The Church. This lecture shows more of the apparatus of scholarship than the father's volumes. It deals with Church questions as they were discussed in Anglican and German circles; and, apart from an occasional show of undue deference to a type of criticism to which the father would pay little heed, this lecture of the younger Bannerman is a worthy product of the Scottish theological scholarship of his generation.

The doctrine of what the Church is, in one shape or other, has been the most vexed one in the ecclesiastical history of Scotland. A veritable library of pamphlets, large and small, deals with the subject as discussed in the second quarter of the 19th century alone. Among them no mean place belongs to the fugitive work produced by Andrew Gray of Perth. He was a clear and trenchant writer. His pamphlets were masterly. So when the Free Church, soon after 1843, decided to prepare a Free Church Catechism he was entrusted with the task of drafting this modest yet clear and careful exposition of Scottish Theology in regard to the Church. With him we might bracket as a defender of Presbytery against Independency and as an assailant of high Episcopal claims the name of another who was one of the senior men of the Disruption race. John Brown of Langton was a most vigorous and well-informed writer.

XVI.

THE PURITAN TRADITION

Dr Warfield, in his introduction to the American translation of Kuyper on The Holy Spirit, speaks of the Free Church ministers of the Disruption generation as carrying on the Puritan tradition—and it was a side of truth that the Puritans specially wrought out—in their handling of the doctrine of the Person and Work of the Holy Ghost. This was indeed one of the salient features of their pulpit work as the Evangelical Revival was swelling to full tide. They were eminent in this department; but it could hardly be said to have anything like a monopoly of their attention. For they did a large measure of justice to what is most specifically and directly the objective message of the Evangel. Indeed, they were equally distinguished for the fullness and clearness with which they set forth their teaching in regard to the Person and Work of the Son of God. The doctrine of the Atonement or of Christ crucified, with its intimate relation to the free justification of the believing sinner, was perhaps even more their theme than that which told of the application of redemption. This can easily be seen from a perusal of the abundant sermonic literature that shows what the burden of their message was. They laid almost equal stress on the sinner's need of a change of state and of a change of nature. Thus they avoided the peril of an ill-balanced teaching which laid too much stress either on the subjective and introspective side or on the exclusively objective side of Christian truth, as it is called, when they set forth God's gracious call and spoke of the forensic justification which rectifies the standing of man as fallen.

XVII.

Dr A. MOODY STUART

We have already spoken of Moody Stuart as one of those who in their student days owed their souls to the ministry

of Dr Robert Gordon. Early in his own ministry he came
to a new Edinburgh charge while M'Cheyne was still a student.
This young minister struck a note that brought the future
Evangelist of Dundee to be one of his steady hearers. That
note marked the message of Moody Stuart to the end of his
long ministry. That ministry was an eminently spiritual one
and there are few ministerial biographies that are better worth
reading than his Life by his son. His Church became a
rallying centre of the most exercised Christians of his
generation in Edinburgh, and with so many of this class in
his audience it was not to be wondered at that the handling
of the divers needs of such hearers was a marked feature
of his preaching. He was an expert in case divinity and the
experimental and searching element entered largely into his
message. Yet, though it was prominent, it did not displace
the more directly Evangelical note. He may be taken as a
specimen of the most studious type of the old cultured Gospel
ministers. With his yoke-fellows in the Evangel, men of
like mind, John Macrae and Charles Mackintosh, he was wont
to spend one day each month in private brotherly conference
and prayer. When trouble arose in connection with the case
of Robertson Smith he showed his quality as a student of
the questions in debate as fully as any that took part in the
discussions. But this critical interest was for him only a
thing that came in by the way. The attitude that he took
up in regard to questions of that nature was one that was
altogether to his credit.

XVIII.

THE SYMINGTONS

We have spent so much time in telling of the theologians
of the Evangelical Revival and particularly of the ornaments
of the Edinburgh ministry and professorship. Of the same
age, however, there were two names of mark in one of the
smaller branches of the Presbyterian tree. They represented
the survival of a true and deep Evangelical strain in their
own body. They were the two brothers, Andrew and
William Symington, of the Reformed Presbyterian Synod.

The former of these was Professor of Divinity to his denomination and was a very sound and able exponent of the Puritan Theology. In the Reformed Presbyterian Synod the teaching of John Owen had come, from the days of John Macmillan, to hold a special place; and to it Andrew Symington adhered. His brother William was an even more popular divine and he was equally able and orthodox. In the Atonement controversy in early Victorian days he took a very active part. This was to be looked for from the author of such a valuable work as he has left dealing with the Atonement and Intercession of Christ. As might be reckoned upon in one who was of the school of Owen, he looked on the Atonement as a transaction or provision that definitely secures the salvation of those on whose behalf it was made; and his review of Wardlaw shows how strong his grip was of the subject in debate.

Ralph Wardlaw as an Independent was responsible as fully as John Brown, if not more so, for the vogue secured by the Hypothetical Universalism of the school of Amyraut. Some of his old pupils went the whole way with Morison in the Arminian direction; and it was in defence of what was virtually his last ditch as an Evangelical Calvinist that Wardlaw wrote his important circular correspondence on behalf of the Glasgow Congregational Churches, whose case he set forth when they took action by way of cutting off from fellowship the Arminian Congregational Churches of their neighbourhood. In this correspondence he lays just stress on the need for the effectual work of the Holy Ghost in the application of salvation. Symington, in argument with him on the subject of the Atonement, was not such an adept in sword play as his antagonist; but on the solid merits of the controversy he bore away with him the honours of the field. With such devotion on the part of his denomination to the teaching and writings of John Owen it was not a thing out of the way that the task of editing the final edition of Owen should be entrusted to the care of W. H. Goold, who succeeded Symington as Professor of Divinity to the Cameronians. Goold, whose sister was the wife of George

Smeaton, was himself a thoroughly respectable divine of the
school of Owen. In this respect he was true to the tradition
of his denomination, though he saw reason to give up their
distinctive attitude as the old political Presbyterian Dissenters
of Scotland.

XIX.
Dr GUTHRIE

We have said so much about the remarkable group of
divines and preachers who adorned the early Victorian age.
There was one, and he one of the most popular of them all
as a preacher of world-wide name, that we have not yet
mentioned. This one was Thomas Guthrie, a man who held
a unique place in the pulpit of his day. More than almost
any he drew the crowd. His strength was that of a master
player on the emotions of an audience. He was a large-
hearted friend of the poor. It could hardly, however, be
said of this prince of pulpit oratory that he was much of a
divine; and no more was his colleague, Dr William Hanna.
Both of them were, however, Evangelical, though the latter
was deemed to have too great a fondness for the Broad school
and did not stand high on the Evangelical scale. It may
have been only that he was so far in advance of his day
that he was emancipated from the shackles of ecclesiastical
rivalry. He was the son-in-law of Dr Chalmers and he had
his own following. Guthrie had a son in the ministry who
was, it may be, more solid as he was less eloquent and
interesting than his father. This son, David, took one day
his father's services and there was in the audience one of
the congregation, an old washerwoman, who was somewhat
of a judge of pulpit form, a reputed sermon taster, as the
phrase goes. Friends came to her to get her measure of the
young man. She let them have it: " He has mair deeveenity
and less deevairsion than his faither." Yet for all his popular
rhetoric and his blaze of illustration, Guthrie's doctrine was
sound Gospel truth. It was orthodox Evangelism that gave
tone to the prevalent type of Church life for the first half
of the Victorian age. The Calvinism might be mild and

non-aggressive. But it was fundamentally a Calvinistic kind of Evangelism that might be looked for as the message of the Scottish pulpit.

XX.

CHANGE AHEAD

When we thus describe the typical Scottish preaching we do not mean that the Moderatism of a former age had vanished to the limbo of forgotten things. Nor does it mean that forces were not at work which were to produce a rejuvenated Moderatism which would scarcely own its kinship with the old order of the same essential character that had gone into disrepute. There was, as there always is, change at work; and before the passing of the old Queen the change had asserted its character and dominance. And it was change that was not confined to one branch of the Church. It was a change, or it was more than one change, away from the old Evangelicalism and it moved in more than one direction. The bright day of the Evangelical Revival seemed to recall to the Church the traditions of its best days. These were valued not in an indiscriminate way, but with a sense of the final authority of the norm of the Word; yet at the same time with a sense of their worth and tried quality. They were a proof in illustration on the field of national history of the power of the Gospel in moulding a people's character and outlook and in determining their ideals. It is easy to err in judging the measure of attainment and to look upon its record with undue complacency. But in what it had to do to establish itself and in what it did by way of evident fruitfulness the record of Evangelical Calvinism in the early Victorian age is one that will speak for itself.

X.

LATER DEVELOPMENTS—THE EBB-TIDE

By the time that the impetus of the Evangelical Revival was sensibly less in evidence and during the regime of the early Victorian Orthodoxy there were tendencies at work which made for the disintegrating of the Reformed Confession.

I.

MORISONIANISM AND INDEPENDENCY

We have seen already that the Morisonian movement which took shape in the early forties of the 19th century was one that called forth great zeal and that zeal was attended with an intensity of moral earnestness. This showed itself especially in its keenness in regard to total abstinence from the use of alcoholic liquors as a beverage. It had a corresponding propaganda in favour of avowed Arminianism which shaded off into something very like out-and-out Pelagianism. The way must have been paved for the ominous advance of this doctrinal movement by a decay or collapse of the conviction with which the older Faith was held. And this advance took place largely in the constituency and at the expense of the New Light Secession Church. The process of this decay must have been at work on a somewhat extensive scale. It was just in the days when this definitely heterodox movement began that Scotland had a visit from one of the great divines of America. This was James Henley Thornwell of the Southern Church, which was then only the Southern wing of the Old School Presbyterian body. Dr Thornwell took note of the beginnings of what was a new Theology in the West of Scotland. For him it was not a new one at all, but the transplanting to the Orthodox land of the Covenants of a kind of teaching with which he was familiar in the development of a line of New England tradition. He spoke of its leaven as the working of the spirit of speculation in religion and he augured ill of the spread of such a speculative spirit in theological subjects if once it got under way among the Scots. There was no telling where such a tendency would stop. What met his eyes was to him a token that Evangelical Scotland was beginning to drift from its old moorings. The question might soon be put—Stands Scotland where it did?

The Morisonian movement affected not only the United Secession but also the Independents, who, until this stage in their history, were looked upon as a body in which Evangelical Calvinism prevailed. The growth of the Evangelical Union, for such was the name that the Morisonians took as their own, was rapid, for in less than half a century they had come to have about 100 Churches. In this respect they were running neck to neck with the Baptists. In the year 1896 the two Unions—the Congregational and the Evangelical— coalesced. This meant that a creedless body, such as the Congregational Union was, saw no reason why they should not absorb, or be absorbed by, another body which was almost creedless too—it was virtually creedless, only it had not abjured its war with Calvinism. This movement, though of enough importance and significance in its own place, did not affect the country as a whole, for in Scotland the Churches of the Independent order have always been only a small minority. The true inwardness of the thing was that Churches which still would claim to be Evangelical forsook Calvinism. Fifty years before, even the modified Calvinism of Wardlaw broke fellowship with the early Morisonian movement among the Independents, and much more at that stage would men like David Russell of Dundee hold aloof from fellowship with Arminians. He maintained fellowship with Wardlaw, whose Calvinism was diluted, but he would draw the line at out-and-out Arminianism. In the correspondence of J. W. Alexander of Fifth Avenue Church, New York, we find that he came across a book by David Russell in which he met his own type of Calvinism. He did not know to what body

in Scotland the writer belonged, but hazarded the guess that
he was of one of the smaller Presbyterian bodies. This was
not the case: he was an Independent minister in Dundee.
In his volume of Letters, practical and consolatory, he
reminds one of John Newton of Olney. His Letters, however,
are more like Sermons and are less readable than those of
Newton. In his Evangelicalism, Russell retained the standard
of that old Scottish Calvinistic Orthodoxy which belonged
to the first days of the Haldane movement. As long as Dr
W. Lindsay Alexander lived, though he was more or less of
a free-lance, the Calvinistic strain had not quite passed away
from the Congregational Union. But when it merged with
the Morisonians that could hardly be said to be the case any
longer. Thus it was that the stream ran its course, the head-
waters of which Thornwell saw in 1841. In these days of
ours, while Calvinism is virtually unknown among them, so
also is systematic doctrine of almost any kind. Their
alignment is with modern critical movements and with political
and social reform and betterment movements of every sort.
The stream of change, however, had more channels than one
in which to flow.

II.

OTHER INFLUENCES TELLING ON THE CHURCHES

Of greater significance and importance than the movement
which has affected the Independents has been the growth in
the Presbyterian Churches of both Broad Churchism and
High Sacramental Doctrine. There was alongside of the
recrudescence of Calvinism, of which Dr James Cooper spoke
as a feature of the post-Disruption life of the State Church,
a resurgence of essential Moderatism. This was of the same
generic type as the old brand. It came, however, in a new
dress. It owed something to the remoter results of the Row
teaching; and the influence of Thomas Erskine of Linlathen
promoted it by giving it the religious appearance that older
Moderatism had thought it safe to cast off or lay aside. The
older brand had run to seed in unblushing worldly living.
The newer brand presented itself in a more respectable guise

in so far as Thomas Erskine's influence told upon it. His Universal Fatherhood was its leading doctrine. Among the promoters of this tendency a leading place belonged in somewhat different ways to Robert Lee and John Tulloch.

1. BROAD CHURCHISM

(1) *Lee*

The Broad Church movement in the Church of England told upon this parallel movement in Scotland. Lee passed away just at the end of the first half of the Victorian era. He had pursued a definite policy which was the outcome of the situation in which he found his Church. Weak and shaken and depleted in its numbers as it was by the loss which it incurred in 1843, it presented a fine target to the Voluntaries and the Liberation Society who aimed at the abolition of all State Churches. So it occurred to Lee that the wise course for his Church to take would be to come into as close a relation to the Church of England as could be secured. He initiated a programme of reform for the Church of Scotland which was to begin in the department of worship. Here he advocated liturgical services which would be a colourable imitation of the English Liturgy and the adoption of which would break the national prejudice against organised worship of such a type. This approach to the Anglican ideal was to secure the goodwill of the defenders of the Church of England so that the defence of the State Churches as such might be a common interest on each side of the Border. Thus he meant to counter and to frustrate the aims of the Radicals who were out against the national recognition of religion by Church Establishments. His proposals for reform in the region of doctrine and Confession of Faith did not see the light. But it was shrewdly suspected that Lee had personally wandered far from the Orthodoxy to which his place in the Church pledged him.

As to this matter of doctrine the question was never put to a test. But Lee's policy along the line of worship was a success; the result of it is to be seen to-day in the revolution of fashion that has almost banished from Scotland its time-honoured and Apostolic and Puritan plainness which in public worship a century ago was virtually universal. This part of Lee's programme had the hearty concurrence of those whose divergent interest drew them along the line of High Church Sacramental teaching. These were men who had felt the influence of the movement in the direction of high ritualism in which Edward Irving's ministry ran to seed, or they were caught in the eddies of the Oxford Movement of Keble and Pusey; for that movement was telling through Scottish Episcopacy in the ranks of the aristocracy. And what was fashionable in these circles percolated to social strata with an inferiority complex.

(2) *Tulloch and Caird*

As a leader of the Neo-Moderates Tulloch wrote from the standpoint of a kind of superior philosophic divine who rose high above the doctrinal quarrels of a systematic age. He had no place for the definiteness of the Reformed Confessions, but bowed his shoulder to the mode of fashion as it ruled in the schools of contemporary thought. He and John Caird exercised a controlling influence on a wide circle of State Churchmen. They were both of them more of the philosopher than of the divine—the former the expositor, and so far the successor, of the Rational philosophic divines of the English school, while the latter bowed his neck to the yoke of German Idealism. They and their followers might not see eye to eye as to what they held and taught on the positive side. They would agree better as to what they reacted against; for they had a large measure of common antipathies. The tendency that they stood for broke away from a definite confession of Christian truth as it was embodied in the symbolic documents of the Reformation. These were to them pretty much the outgrown manifestoes of a rabble of parties and factions which had their day and ceased to be. So they would let the dead past bury its dead. These hermit crabs would gladly cast their shell; it irked their urge to be free. Indeed, they extended scant hospitality to the Theology that they had pledged themselves to teach and to defend. For they, too, had signed the same formula as the rest of the ministry of their Church and that formula pledged them unambiguously to the historical Reformed Faith. Yet from that Faith they broke away.

(3) *Norman Macleod*

Before the second half of the Victorian age Norman Macleod showed himself to be clearly on the side of the Broad party. He had, though a hereditary Erastian at the outset of his ministry, taken the line of an Evangelical of the popular school that was in fashion in those times. He came, however, under the spell of the followers and friends of Arnold and Stanley in England and he was responsive to the stimulus of the influences that emanated from the court. He was a *persona grata* with his Queen almost beyond any Churchman of his day on either side of the Tweed; and court influence, although it was Protestant in a latitudinarian Lutheran sense, did not tell in favour of Norman's earlier Orthodoxy. It was in particular in regard to the Westminster doctrine of the Law of God and the Scottish practice as to how the Lord's Day is to be observed that he did his worst disservice to his country. His outburst on this subject told more disastrously upon Scotland than did anything else of the age. He let loose forces that he could not control and that have wrought a revolution from which we might well believe he would himself have shrunk back. He was a man of great native kindliness and immense personal popularity. But in regard to the nature and obligations of law in its bearing on the Christian and his life he adopted and taught views that were in their real nature Antinomian. This came about in his effort to dislodge the obligation of the Fourth Commandment as a part of the abiding code of moral law from the place it held in the Confession of his Church and in the mind of his countrymen.

This outbreak on the part of a court chaplain was a challenge that could not be left unanswered. There was, it is true, enough good, sound Scottish literature dealing with the Sabbath law expounding and defending the Church's Faith in regard to it. In particular, there is a work dealing with the subject in a full and judicious fashion that was published in 1861, only a few years before Norman Macleod made his attack. It is a book written in a modest spirit. It is thorough. It is well informed. It is painstaking. The writer was James Gilfillan of Stirling, a minister of the United Presbyterian Synod, who belonged to its right wing which still held the old Orthodoxy of his family and of the Secession in matters of special Scottish doctrinal interest. This work is as convenient a thesaurus as there is in our language of information and argument in regard to the Sabbath and its moral obligations. This, however, was not the work called forth by Dr Macleod's attack on the sacred day. The champion who took up his challenge and who produced another work worthy of the traditions of Scottish Theology was the brilliant, though erratic, James Macgregor. His book on the Sabbath Question deals with Norman's teaching as only an expert in theological literature and in the realm of polemics could handle it. It is conclusive in argument, vigorous in style, and it has in it a bite that is almost the hallmark of that streak of genius which is found in the author's work. But social standing such as that of a court chaplain and personal popularity such as his opponent had told mightily in the direction of furthering the abandonment of Orthodox ideas in the subject of what had been a leading feature of distinctly Scottish religious life.

2. High Sacramentalism

We spoke of not only Broad Churchism which gave a new lease of existence to old Moderatism in a new guise. We mentioned also High Sacramentarianism as a thing that has grown. The High Church party represented by the Scottish Church Society has had among its leading men Dr Sprott of North Berwick, Dr Leishman of Linton, Professor William Milligan of Aberdeen, and, above all, Dr James Cooper of Aberdeen and Glasgow and Dr John Macleod of Dunse and Govan. The last of these was first cousin to Dr Norman Macleod of whom we have just spoken. He was a devout admirer of the Edward Irving tradition, particularly along its sacramental and priestly lines. To an early conference of the Scottish Church Society, of which he was one of the leading spirits, he contributed a long, elaborate and very confused paper which ran in its printed form to about 200 pages. In this he tried to establish his favourite doctrine of Baptismal Regeneration. It is now more than 40 years since he did this and the Society has never repudiated his teaching. It met with a very effective trouncing from an anonymous ministerial critic who signed himself Dr Theophilus. This exposure of the priestly line taken by the high faction is in short compass a careful bit of work that follows the lines of the undoubted Reformed doctrine of the Sacraments which is taught in the standards of the Church.

The High Sacramentarian school may be spoken of as both high and narrow. So far as getting away from the Puritan ideal is concerned, that ideal which gave law to the plain worship of Presbyterian Scotland, this school was quite prepared to work hand in hand with Robert Lee's movement. They represented, however, a tendency to get away from more than the worship of their fathers, they revolted from the Reformed teaching as to the nature and place of the Sacraments, while, in regard to the ministry, they favoured a priestly reading of the office and special work of the ordained presbyter. Thus their Church principles were those of Order and Sacrament, whose new presbyter was only old priest writ large.

In regard to baptism the Church Society sought to make out that the Reformed standards teach a doctrine of baptismal grace which issues in the actual regeneration of the baptised through the sacrament as an instrument. This they did oblivious of the twofold fact that the statements of those standards deal primarily with what baptism is in the normal instance of its administration, that is, in the case of believers who are baptised on their own profession; and that the baptism of children as members of Christian households, though thoroughly well warranted on its own grounds, is not the normal and regulative example of the administration of the sacrament. Such a baptism is due to the fact that, born in Christian homes, the children of believers enter life within the circle of the holy nation, the visible Israel of the New Testament. Thus from their birth, even before they are baptised at all, they are entitled to be reckoned to be members of the Visible Church. They have such a title, for the children of professed believers are looked upon in the Apostle's language as holy. It is as being from their birth the members of the Church that they ought to be thus looked upon, for they are holy inasmuch as they are set apart by the Lord as His own to have a place among His people at whose hand He makes a demand in keeping with the special privilege that He bestows upon them. It is thus that they have a right to be recognised by the Church as its infant membership. In their case their baptism can be regarded as in the full sense a seal of their oneness with Christ only when the time comes that they indeed take His yoke upon them. Then, and not till then, have they the righteousness of faith of which their baptism is a seal; and it is meant to shut them in to yield the obedience by which they shall come to have the righeousness of faith. This being so, they are to be taught the truths of law and Gospel, that they may know themselves and their need and the Lord and His fullness. It is only when they yield to His claims, taking Him as their own, and giving themselves to Him, that their baptism comes to its full meaning. They get the good of it just as they respond in a living faith to the appeal of their privileged position by taking Christ as their own and giving themselves up to Him to be for Him and not for another.

In regard to the ratification of the Baptismal Covenant of those who are baptised in their childhood, the High Church school has hankered after the Anglican rite of Confirmation. Indeed, they have made clear enough that they would gladly see the restoration of a prelatic Episcopacy. This being so, it is not strange that they tend, in keeping with the teaching of the higher Anglicans, to magnify unduly the priestly character which they assign to the Christian minister when he officiates at the observance of the Lord's Supper. In doing so, they forget that whatever there is of a priestly character inhering in his obedience to the will of his Lord in this service is equally present in the service of each of the participants. And when he and they partake of the sacramental Bread and Wine neither of them can be said to offer a sacrifice other than that of praise and obedience. With the men of this tendency their special stress laid upon the office of the Presbyterate shows how they are caught in the stream of a backwater of Mediaevalism. They must find it a hard problem to solve what the standing in the Church is that belongs to the presbyter who only rules and does not teach, for he is ordained as a presbyter to be a ruler in the Church. This school is high in doctrine and it aspires to be higher still, yet it is not so much strict in doctrine as narrow in fellowship. The attitude that its members take to the valid standing in the ministry of those who are held to be ministers among the Methodists and the Independents is the outcome of just such an exclusive Churchly tendency as is at work in the high circles of the Episcopal Communion. This narrowness of Catholic fellowship has gone hand in hand with the claim that these men put forward to be Catholics and with their failure to make a stand on behalf of Catholic truth when that is obscured or set aside. For in regard to the doctrine of the Person of our Lord they have allowed with no sustained or effective protest the witness for it in the Catechism to be cut out from the Church's scheme for religious instruction in the State schools of Scotland. Of course, this might be let go at default, as the scheme also cut out from the Catechism its definite Calvinism and in particular that Calvinism as it is to be heard speaking when the Catechism bears its witness in regard to the Redeemer and calls Him the only Redeemer of God's *Elect*; for this last word is itself enough to awaken their antipathy. The natural genius of a system which makes the Sacraments efficacious of themselves has no love for the sovereignty of

grace that comes out in the mention of God's election of each
of His redeemed people to life everlasting whatever shape
that mention may take.

The Scottish Church Society's policy was not so much
conservative as reactionary and its reaction was away from
the most characteristic feature of the Reformed Faith. In
this it aimed at getting behind the Scottish Reformation,
however much stress—mistaken stress it is true—it laid for
its own ends on the sacramental statements of the Confession
of 1560. The working of such a leaven did not make for
faithful adherence to the standards to which the Church and
its ministry had pledged their allegiance. So when an
agitation took shape to have the Ordination pledge altered
it was a case of *non tali auxilio nec defensoribus istis tempus
eget* as far as help was to be looked for from this professedly
conservative wing of the National Church. Its help was a
broken reed to lean upon.

As distinct from the obscurantist mediaeval school the
newer Moderatism of which we have spoken, and which, by
the way, was the precursor of, if it was not identical with,
what we have come to speak of as Modernism, had no quarrel
with the Moderatism of a former age of any serious kind,
though its votaries might at times criticise the older thing
for its more obvious and glaring faults. The two types
agreed in their repulsions. They both had an antipathy to
what is truly supernatural in the Christian scheme; for both
of them were radicated in an unbelief that would not bow
to the authoritative yoke of Holy Writ as the Word of God.
This kind of thing is but the reaction of the natural man
to the things of the Spirit of God. The men that we have
named as the leaders held their place in the movement as it
was at work in the State Church. But the same movements
that made for change were at work in the larger Presbyterian
Churches which were not established just as the drift wrought
in the Churches of the Congregational order. The revolutionary tendency has its quarrel with the unmistakable
Calvinism of the Scottish Confession.

III.

CHANGE OUTSIDE THE STATE CHURCH

1. U.P. SYNOD

In the United Presbyterian Synod the leaven of doctrinal revolution was definitely at work. In this body it was so far the logical working out of the policy of yielding to the claims of New Light to which indeed that Synod might be said to owe its distinct existence. The principle of indefinite change to which it had opened its doors tended to claim the mastery of the house. It sought to have the bonds relaxed that still held the Church bound to the National Confession. A man like John Cairns, who was at bottom Orthodox and Evangelical, was glad to find about sixty years ago that the storm which had long been brewing and which broke at last did not prove more serious than it did. A *modus vivendi* was found by the adoption on the part of the Synod of a Statement or an Act Declaratory of the meaning of the Confession on certain points. Of this Act, Dr George Smeaton remarked to a friend : " There are good Calvinists in the United Presbyterian Synod; but I should not find it difficult to prove that in its Declaratory Statement the Synod has taken up Arminian ground." If this was so, a sufficiently heavy ransom was paid to satisfy the agitation for change. It was the working out, however, of the policy of concession to the demands of New Light which meant indefinite change. And the Ordination pledge was changed to make this Statement operative.

There were a few of the Broad Churchmen such as David Macrae and at an earlier stage George Gilfillan who left the fellowship of the Synod as the place was too strait for them. The literary tradition of Robert Burns, the easy good fellowship of a kind of Freemasonry that was reminiscent of old Moderatism, and a touch of Modernism before its time were at work in the extremists. They found a new Apocalypse in the Larger Hope of the would-be seers of the Anglican Broad school and a publicity manifesto in the Eternal Hope of F. W. Farrar. It was only the old quarrel of the mind of the flesh with the Law of God. For the men who in heart are estranged from God, His law is too strict in its precept and too awful in its penalty. The sanction they hold to be quite out of keeping with the evil that they see to be in sin. One of John Duncan's sayings is to the point here : " The only heresy is Antinomianism," that is, the sinner's quarrel with the authority of God. The modified Calvinism of the United Presbyterian Synod had in its later years, after the death of John Cairns, its most prominent representative in James Orr and he, in his Doctrine of Inspiration, shows himself less than quite fair to what Scripture has to say in regard to what itself is. In the case of George Adam Smith, Orr, in the United Free Assembly of 1902, followed Rainy as his seconder in finding a place for the teaching in his Church of a kind of Wellhausenism which had a veneer of supernatural profession. In this business a man like him, of whom better was to be expected, was held by many to have virtually sold the pass.

2. THE BROAD SCHOOL IN THE FREE CHURCH

The Broad tendency was also at work in the Free Church. In its early days its most outspoken exponent was William Knight, who could see his way to hobnob with the Socinians and drop suspicions into men's minds in regard to the consistency of prayer with Natural Law. He, however, became a professor in the University of St Andrews and found in his new office a freedom from confessional bonds that he could not have as a minister in Dundee. Of his generation was Walter C. Smith, who, like Knight, had some reputation as a man of letters. He ventured a little bit of the way with Norman Macleod in his attack on the old order. But this business was patched up. In later years he was a centre of Broad Churchism in a select coterie in Edinburgh. The first generation of the Free Church ministry was not quite the environment for men of their tendency. Things, however, were shaping in a different way for the succeeding generation. For the spirit of a new age was abroad.

It was so much of the irony of history that a Church which had prided itself on the place that it gave to the Reformed Faith should so soon become the home of that revolutionary movement in Theology which has transformed the whole aspect of the religious life of Scotland. The other Churches, too, were feeling the changed spirit of the age. But it was reserved for the younger ministers of the Free Church to take the lead in the abandonment of the Faith of their fathers. They were the party of movement. Behind them there was in their Church a tradition of having things done. And with the conceit of leadership they were bent on showing how things could be done. Their country had become, with the improved means of communication in the 19th century, much less isolated and self-contained than it was before. So the teaching of the German theological schools began to tell upon its younger ministry. Without well knowing at first what they were doing they borrowed to begin with from the Liberal Evangelicals and then from the Rationalistic schools of Germany the kind of theological ideas that found favour among them. Those being on the whole so far Lutheran as distinct from Calvinistic, and unbelieving as distinct from Christian, were at war with the underlying principles on which the Orthodox Faith of the Reformed Churches builds. The hospitality that was given to such ideas led by degrees to the forsaking of the ground which from the Reformation onwards had been held by the Evangelical teachers of Scotland's Reformed Church. The freedom of thought, and of utterance for it, that was common in Protestant Germany came to be envied, to be copied, and at last to be freely practised. In one of his essays William Cunningham had passed a disparaging judgment on the theological insight of even his own day. The really distinctive features of various systems were not clearly enough recognised in his opinion. The next generation was to show what a measure of reason he had for cherishing such a low estimate of the theological competence of the men about him. They were too much at sea in judging the true differentia of systematic schemes of thought.

The decisively revealing proof that brought out how far the spirit of compromise and cowardice was ready to go in making concession to radical change came to light in the Robertson Smith critical trial. The question at issue was whether or no the Alphabetic fissive documentary hypothesis of Wellhausen which applied the evolution that was in the air to the history of religion in Israel was to find a foothold in an Evangelical Church. There was no clear stand taken against the kind of criticism for which Smith pleaded. In keeping with the early tradition of their Church he and his followers claimed to be earnest Evangelicals. Indeed, the plea was put forward that in Calvin himself there was to be found a free type of critical work and they claimed that they were in this kind of succession. While they turned the fabric of its history upside down to make the pyramid rest on its apex they dared still to profess that the Old Testament was inspired Scripture. It was this sort of plea that called forth the scornful question of Thomas Carlyle. He could hardly be thought to have a bias in favour of the Faith to which he bade farewell in his early days and to which he never came back. Yet he knew what that Faith was and what underlay its teaching. Nor could he be looked upon as being ignorant of the stream of German thought. On one occasion when this trial was on Dr James Begg of Edinburgh, the leader of the Conservative school of the Free Church, was in London and, as he was wont to do, he called on Carlyle. The latter, though long away from Scotland, took a lively interest in what was going on there. So the conversation turned to the claim that the budding Rationalists were making to be called Evangelicals when Carlyle thundered out : " Have my countrymen's heads become turnips when they think that they can hold the premisses of German unbelief and draw the conclusions of Scottish Evangelical Orthodoxy? "

In his later years Robertson Smith came to see, what a man of his powers of mind ought to have seen from the first, that his attitude to Holy Scripture was quite out of harmony with the Westminster Confession. This it was both in regard to the teaching of its first chapter and the place that the Confession accords from first to last to Scripture as the Word of God and the principium of the theological system that it elaborates and sets forth. The leaven, however, of unbelieving criticism had now begun to work strongly, and hand in hand with it went the spirit of speculation in religion. The issue of this state of things was that to a large extent the ministry, and, in particular, the men of the rising generation not only in the Free Church, but also in its sister Churches, came to stand in a false relation to the Confession by the avowal of which, as the Confession of their personal faith, they had come to hold their office in the various denominations.

IV.

AUTHORITY OF SCRIPTURE AT STAKE

Even men who, in their own thinking and teaching, held to the old Faith were to a great degree at a loss. The age with its questionings launched them on a great sea of critical difficulties. They were not at home in these things. They saw the little minutiae of detail that were pressed upon their notice. But they could not see the wood for the trees. They were in the midst of a thicket and could not take their bearings. Nor had they a strong enough hold of the principle of Apostolic authority which would have taught them to relegate objections and difficulties to the subordinate place to which they belonged. With the recognition of the authority stamped upon the witness of the Apostles and their teaching they would have taken the Old Testament books as our Lord and His authenticated representatives did. This would have kept them from holding parley with a type of teaching in the Christian Church that was a denial of the *bona fides* of the narrative or the historical framework of the Old Testament books. This denial was the outcome of the application of naturalistic principles to the question of how the religion set forth in the law and the Prophets was given and grew. Some who were afraid of holding a too high doctrine of the Inspiration of the Scriptures made the attempt to restate it by starting at the wrong end. They began with the array of difficulties, and ended with the attempt to adjust the statements of Scripture on the subject of its own origin to the impression that their preoccupation with what were in truth subordinate details had given them of the subject as a whole. This, of course, involved them in confusion.

Like any other of the great doctrines of the Word of God that of its own Inspiration was to be derived directly from the statements which we find it making on the subject. Thus it is that we reach a doctrine of the Person of Christ or of the work of the Holy Ghost or of Justification by faith. It is when the various statements of the sacred writers are carefully weighed and compared that on these subjects we come to a decision as to what on a conjunct view of the evidence should be held to be the Christian Faith. Rays of light from a variety of texts and contexts are seen to converge or to come to a common focus. This gives us the truth that is regulative for Christian thinking. The doctrine of Inspiration is in no different category. Like all the other doctrines of the Faith it can be profitably formulated only when we are sure of our ground in authority. For as a doctrine it is to be discussed as a thing possessed with authority only among the believers in the witness of the word. What the word teaches controls the faith of the Church, or at least it ought to do so. In controversy with avowed unbelievers it is not on the inspired character of Scripture but on its truth that Christians first lay stress. It is only when their opponents come to own that truth that they will accept its witness when it tells about itself. The campaign of opposition to the doctrine of the fully inspired character of Holy Writ when it is carried on within the Churches proceeds logically on a refusal to accept the truth of the claims which the Apostles made on their own behalf. In taking this line it not only aims its blow at the common faith of Catholic Christendom in regard to the inspired and consequently divinely authoritative character of Holy Writ; it strikes also at the substantial truth of the Christian archives. It is only when we set aside the witness and authority of the Apostolic word that we refuse to own Scripture as the Word of God.

The Churches of Scotland were but ill prepared for the day that had overtaken them. As they wavered and halted they let a tendency that was inimical to their ancestral Faith find a home in their bosom. For they lost sight of the essential simplicity of the Christian position. When John tells us that he wrote his Gospel that we might believe, with the record of his signs, that Jesus is the Christ the Son of God, and that believing we might have life in His name, he thought that the witness borne by his fellows and himself was ground enough for the faith of Christians to build upon. Christian faith has through the ages responded to this claim and this claim was that not only of the Apostle, but of the Holy Ghost who spoke in him. For it is undoubtedly the mind of the Spirit that the evidence which he thus bore to the truth as it is in Jesus should suffice as a ground of faith for the Church of God to the end of time and to the ends of the earth. What was thus in the Gospel claimed by an Apostle for the witness of his writing, he and his fellows could claim for their teaching in the Epistles. They spoke not in the words which man's wisdom teaches but which the Holy Ghost teaches. This was what Paul could say, and we find John in the same vein adding: "We are of God, he that knoweth God heareth us: he that is not of God heareth not us." Not to hear the Apostles proves that one is not of God. Now claims of this kind were in full keeping with the promises given to the eleven by their Lord in the Upper Chamber at Jerusalem.

There has been from the beginning a Holy Catholic Church—define it how we may—to whose care and keeping the New Testament books were committed, and from whose hands in successive generations its children have received them as being alike in their witness and in their teaching the crystallised and perpetuated ministry of the Apostolic band. As many as are willing to sit at the feet of the Apostles, as they thus by their written word continue to bear witness and to teach, will learn to treat the Old Testament Scriptures as it is plain the Lord and His Apostles did. They will accept both Testaments as the Word of God. Here we have the common view of Holy Writ as it has been held throughout historical Christendom. It is on this view that the whole structure of Church Confession and of Christian Theology is built. To maintain the superstructure we must defend the substructure.

With the change of attitude and of message, too, on the part of so many of the rising ministry the puzzled Christian public, the rank and file of the Churches, might feel that something had gone wrong. What that was they could not very well say. A strong and definite lead in the acceptance and defence of the fundamentals of the Faith was sorely needed among the younger men and for the rising generation. For the purely Scottish tradition came to be regarded in the light of a provincial peculiarity. The young bloods in the ministry let go the Faith of their fathers. They would pray to be excused from bearing its reproach, and losing sight of the fact that their fathers, as the lawful successors of the Reformers, were fitted to teach those who had gone astray from the Christian Confession, they learned to look upon those fathers as narrow and benighted.

V.

A STRIKING FORECAST

Such a state of things could hardly be said to tell of a healthy condition of the body politic of the Church or of a high level of Christian life. It looked like the fulfilment of what, when uttered in 1820 by Thomas M'Crie, might be thought to be a too gloomy forecast. These were his words: " A vague and indefinite evangelism mixed with seriousness into which it is the prevailing disposition of the present age to resolve all Christianity, will, in the natural progress of human sentiment, degenerate into an unsubstantial and incoherent pietism, which after effervescing in enthusiasm will finally settle into indifference; in which case, the spirit of infidelity and irreligion, which is at present working and spreading to a more alarming extent than many seem to imagine, will achieve an easy conquest over a feeble and exhausted and nerveless adversary."

The healthy and vigorous Christian life which was rooted in such an acquaintance with the Word of God as results from the sealing illumination of the Holy Ghost was, in many instances and on a wide scale, replaced by the outcome of a fitful and sensational revivalism which produced excitement and aimed at giving speedy peace and securing immediate results in the profession of conversion. It often issued in hasty profession. Its method of short cuts and the warfare that it waged with the solid and serious introspective type of godliness that attended the Puritan tradition did not encourage the large and searching and generous attention which the earlier Evangelicals had paid to instruction in Christian doctrines set forth in judicious proportion and in systematic array. Those who were the advocates and the fruit of this newer kind of Evangelism could scarcely be reckoned upon in the day of battle to stand as the champions of the Reformed tradition. There was thus a weakening of the hold that Confessional teaching had on the converts of the newer Evangelism as compared with those of the older generation. The fact of the matter was that the tide of fashion had turned and those who were its votaries were carried along on the bosom of the stream.

VI.

A TYPE OF UNION POLICY AT WORK

But over and above the sporadic action of individuals of a Broad tendency and the widespread working of an unsettling leaven in regard to questions of Criticism and Bible Authority there was another movement that was telling in the direction of breaking down loyalty to old Confessional Orthodoxy. This was the action that was taken to promote ecclesiastical union by the creation of open questions, that is, by making truth which had been already acknowledged as matter of faith to be only a matter of free opinion in a

larger fellowship. The manner in which this movement was
conducted made for the fluidity and not the stability of
doctrinal profession. The man whose name is most closely
associated with this line of advocacy is that of Robert Rainy.
His predecessors in the Free Church of Scotland in pushing
for such union were R. S. Candlish and Robert Buchanan.
In their days the effort to carry their policy proved futile.
The resistance of old Orthodox men was too much for them.
They had to leave their ploughshare to rest and to rust in
an unfinished furrow. Rainy, however, lived to give effect
to his leading principle which recognised the Church's right
to go back on the pledges by the giving and taking of which
a standing in the office of the ministry was secured. This
at its root is to bid farewell to all guaranteed continuity of
doctrinal witness. For in good logic one cannot distinguish
between one doctrine and another as worthy to be preserved
in its unviolated integrity. As a matter of fact Rainy's
policy opened afresh the questions which were at issue over
two centuries ago in the controversy in regard to Subscription
among the English Nonconformists. Those who took sides
against Subscription have left as their representatives the
Unitarian body in England. James Martineau was their
outstanding man for the greater part of a century; and we
find him putting the argument for refusing to exact a pledge
from our successors in a letter that he wrote in 1859 to
S. F. Macdonald. These are his words: " My protest is
against a *Church* fixing its creed, i.e., against a prior
generation of life tenants prejudging the convictions of a
posterior and using their own rights to the restriction of
their posterity's. I know well that to believe a thing true
is to believe it immutable; that earnest conviction naturally
excludes all suspicion of possible change and carries in it a
confidence of spreading to other minds and attaining universal
recognition. Within the limits of his proper rights I would
have every man surrender himself freely to these impressions,
utter them and act upon them. But limits there certainly
are to his proper rights in this respect; arising partly from
the presence around him of his fellows with precisely similar

feeling attached to different beliefs; partly from the certainty of successors whose faculties and opportunities are not his to mortgage."

That is to say, men may think for themselves that they have found the truth, but the Church must be ever learning and never able to come to the knowledge of it.

Martineau was an advocate for hospitality to be extended to New Light. Those who have learned the truth of the Gospel have no fear that any new light that will break forth from the Word will do otherwise than intensify and heighten the light that has already shone upon them. It will not quarrel with what went before. The truth that they have learned they can each one for himself and also all of them as a body acknowledge, and those who share their faith are their rightful heirs in the Church of God. They lay no obligation on others to avow as their own Faith what is not their Faith. Those only who hold their Faith for themselves are their legitimate heirs in the Christian succession. The witness of the Church of God has a continuity of its own.

The principle in regard to a Church's Confession which would always keep the window open to the east for new light to welcome a sun that is to arise was one held in common by two men so different as James Martineau and Robert Rainy. It allowed the former to put in a claim to legitimate succession from Richard Baxter and Oliver Heywood and Daniel Williams and even Matthew Henry. These men were undoubted Trinitarians and most would acknowledge that they were Evangelicals, yet Martineau and his fellow-Socinians hold the chapels or the endowments or the historical relics of those early Nonconformists and in particular the Dr Williams' Library is in their hands. This only shows how insecure a doctrinal heritage may be when it is not guarded by a strict Subscription to a Confession and that Subscription is honourably observed.

Those who took Dr Rainy's side and view of things as regulative of the Church's freedom and duty felt that the strictness of the terms of Subscription which the Free Church exacted was a galling yoke. They set about the task accordingly of freeing themselves from its obligations. They took steps along the lines followed in the United Presbyterian Synod. They adopted Declaratory legislation on the subject, but left the terms of the old Questions and Formula for ordinands unaltered. In taking this course they tried to do what was incompetent for them. For any Declaratory legislation to be *intra vires* would need to declare truly what the teaching of the Confession is. The thought of turning to such a device in the State Church to meet the clamour for relaxation of Subscription was considered and set aside. For its competence so long as the Confession remained the Church's avowed Confession to which its office-holders were pledged by their own engagement was found to be restricted to very narrow limits. On matters in regard to which the Confession is either ambiguous or silent it might be employed. But in view of the place held by the Confession in its constitution the Church had no power by Declaratory Acts or otherwise to modify, abridge, or extend any article of the Confession. Its possible use in regard to topics that were outside the scope of the Confession could not relieve Subscribers from any share of the full obligation to own the doctrine of the Confession to be the true doctrine to which they pledged themselves constantly to adhere. In the case of the State Church the national legislation of 1690 to 1693 and of 1706 and 1707 must be altered to allow the other party to the concordat to relax the bonds which held it bound to the terms of the Revolution and Treaty of Union settlements.

In the case of the Declaratory legislation of the Free Church, as the declaration must be one of what indeed is the teaching of the Confession, any other kind of Declaratory statement was inept. It was indeed null and void. If it was a statement of what was beyond the Confession's teaching it could not modify the full pledge given at Ordination to hold to the whole doctrine of the Confession. For no competent addition to the Confession could modify its considered statement so long as the terms of adherence by Subscription were left unchanged. Legislation, then, in the

Church courts of such a kind as to secure the change which was sought was incompetent by a mere Declaratory Act. It was *ultra vires* for the courts of a Church which commissioned its Assembly representatives to sit, vote and deliberate according to the Confession of Faith. It was as being thus incompetent that such innovating legislation was null and void. The pledge given at Ordination was fundamental to the whole Church life and acting of the man ordained. For it was in virtue of it that he held the office with all its privileges to which he was ordained because he had given his pledged word.

VII.

MONCREIFF'S FEAR

As far back as 1868 Sir Henry Moncreiff expressed the fear that an attempt might be made as part of the policy of the Moderate party to relax the Formula of adherence in the State Church while the Act of the Scottish Parliament of 1690 was left intact. This was the Act which ratified the Confession as a document nationally accepted. So he called upon the friends of sound doctrine to be on the watch lest their opponents should find a favourable chance of stealing a march by pulling down the standard of an unambiguous profession of the Faith on the part of the Church as by law established. This was the apprehension of the head of one of the great legal families of Scotland and Sir Henry was for many years principal clerk to the General Assembly of the Free Church. He sensed how things might go; and in the end what he feared took place. It took more than a generation, however, before such a change came about, but it did happen in 1905. And what took place in that year was confirmed and strengthened in 1921. This was the remote outcome of Dr Rainy's policy. It wrought out at securing the legal right to make almost indefinite change; and this is now the recognised constitution of the Church of Scotland. For years the efforts of Dr Rainy were put forth to disestablish that Church. The issue of events was that the Confession was disestablished while the Church was left to enjoy its privileged status and the way was thus opened for such a union as took place in 1929 which brought the vast majority of the Presbyterians of Scotland into one communion. The measure of unity that was thus secured was bought at a price. The old endowments were left with the State Church as her own possession while the Formula of adherence to the Confession, which was the outcome of the legislation of 1905, is the document in the reconstituted National Church that links that body to its avowed Confession. In this Formula the subscriber to its terms, while he subscribes the Confession of Faith, does so with the declaration that he accepts it as the Confession of the Church and that he believes the fundamental doctrines of the Christian Faith contained therein. He thus does not explicitly contract himself out from avowing the Confession to be the confession of his faith, but he definitely pledges himself to the belief of no more than the fundamental doctrines of the Christian Faith that the Confession contains. As to what these fundamental doctrines are, there is no definition given. The nearest approach to such a thing that one can find is the first of the Declaratory articles sanctioned by the State in 1921, the terms of which are worthy of attention.

VIII.

ARTICLE 1 of 1921

" The Church of Scotland is part of the Holy Catholic or Universal Church worshipping one God Almighty, all-wise and all-loving in the Trinity of the Father, the Son and the Holy Ghost, the same in substance, equal in power and glory, adoring the Father infinite in majesty of Whom are all things; confessing one Lord Jesus Christ, the Eternal Son, made very man for our salvation; glorying in His Cross and Resurrection, and owning obedience to Him as the Head over all things to His Church; trusting in the promised renewal and guidance of the Holy Spirit; proclaiming the forgiveness of sins and acceptance with God through faith in Christ, and the gift of eternal life; and labouring for the advancement of the Kingdom of God throughout the world. The Church of Scotland adheres to the Scottish Reformation, receives the Word of God which is contained in the Scriptures of the Old and New Testaments as its supreme rule of faith and life, and avows the fundamental doctrines of the Catholic Faith founded thereupon."

There is beauty and dignity in the wording of this article; few, however, would dare to say that it is a worthy or an adequate representation of what is distinctively and historically the Faith of the Reformed Churches. Yet it is all the indication that one can detect as to what the fundamental doctrines of the Christian Faith are to which those who subscribe the Confession are understood to pledge themselves. The undefined mention of those doctrines in the end of the paragraph does not, however, seem to point in the direction of saying that its previous statements are designed to set forth or indicate the doctrines that are to be deemed fundamental. Before these Articles of 1921 were drawn up an opinion was given as to the meaning of the Formula which, as the outcome of the Churches Act of 1905, was adopted in 1909 and is still in use. This was the judgment of Dr William Mair of Earlston, who was long looked up to as the leading ecclesiastical lawyer of the Established Church. In *The Scottish Churches,* 1914, he wrote of the changed Formula of Subscription which was then almost a new document: " It requires us to believe no more than the fundamental doctrines of the Christian Faith, if these are in the Confession, and we need take no account of any amplification or explanation of these given by the Confession." This throws light on the flux of doctrine, and it seems to be a fair account of how the matter stands.

The Articles Declaratory of the constitution seem in Article 8 to give permanence to what Article 1 sets forth. Yet in the context that calls for consistency with the provisions of Article 1 the claim is made to modify or to add to these Articles. Further, the adherence to Article 1 itself is limited by the words, " as interpreted by the Church." The sentence reads : " The Church has the right to interpret these Articles,

and subject to the safeguards for deliberate action and
legislation provided by the Church itself, to modify or add
to them; but always consistently with the provisions of the
first Article hereof, adherence to which, as interpreted by
the Church, is essential to its continuity and corporate life."
This does not seem to give much of a guarantee in practice
for steadfastness of adherence to even the early creeds. Thus
it has come about as the outcome of Dr Rainy's long advocacy
of an undefined reserved right to change that such a right
is now in effect the recognised constitution of the National
Church. In substance, though not in form, the scheme for
which he fought has been accepted; and with this acceptance
has gone by the board the traditional and age-long stability
of the Church's avowal of the Faith.

The Broad Church movement which has reached its goal
in the new order of things that replaces the old fixity of
doctrinal profession is the result of the confluence of more
streams than one. It found the head-waters of one of its
channels in the discussions of the students of the New College
in Edinburgh in the days when Cunningham was its Principal.
Men like John Veitch, afterwards Professor of Metaphysics
in Glasgow, who was the biographer of Sir William
Hamilton, Alexander Nicolson, a kindly genius, who, after
a long apprenticeship as a briefless advocate, got a subordinate
post as Sheriff-Substitute, and Alexander Taylor Innes, who
became a Chamber Counsel of some repute in Edinburgh
and wrote *The Law of Creed in Scotland*, carried into their
theological classes the kudos of heading the philosophical
section, especially Hamilton's class, in Edinburgh University.
They brought with them also somewhat of a spirit of
conscious superiority to the older order of things and none
of them finished his course for the ministry. These three were
but representative names. There were others who found it
possible by some legerdemain to sign their Church's Confession
and pledge themselves to assert, maintain and defend its
whole doctrine, while their ministerial career was marked by
the ease with which they salved their conscience in holding
their office, while at the same time they went back on the

pledge that gave them a title to it. The tale of organised change is not one that reflects credit on the godly sincerity of men who took such a line. Even if they went on to abolish the pledge of any subscription to Confession or Catechisms they could not free themselves from the bonds laid upon them by their profession to be Christians and by their position as avowed Christian teachers to accept and hold in its fullness the message which our Lord has left for His disciples to hold fast and to hold forth as His Word of salvation. The old strict Subscription was meant to secure that the Church was satisfied that its rising leaders and teachers held the Faith and at the same time, if only honour prevailed, it gave the rank and file of the Church a guarantee as to where their teachers stood. The new order does not seem to make provision in any adequate way for such ends or, indeed, to concern itself about them.

IX.

Dr MARTIN ON FREEDOM TO CHANGE

If the Churches Act of 1905 is the pivot on which the subsequent ecclesiastical history of Scotland turns, the issues at stake were read aright in the course of the long-drawn-out negotiations for union between the Free Church and the United Presbyterian Synod in the years from 1863 to 1873. There was a protracted journalistic duel between the organs of the Union party in the Free Church and of the opponents of the Union proposals. Dr Rainy was the leading figure in guiding the policy of *The Presbyterian*. Its opponent was *The Watchword*, which was edited by Dr James Begg. Begg had as his right-hand man in the running of this magazine Dr Hugh Martin, much of whose most pointed and valuable writing was done for its pages. The real crux in this warfare was in regard to the claim as a constitutional thing for a freedom to change over after the pledge of loyalty has been adhibited to the Confession and at the same time hold the position that the giving of such a pledge has secured. The champion of the old guard of Orthodoxy once put his case thus, and Martin did it in his trenchant style: "I am ordained into this Church, resigning, we shall say, all other life prospects which I might be warranted to cherish and devoting to her service all my energies and interests, embarking on her prospects also all the temporal interests of my family. I am thus ordained in terms of an ordination vow. This vow is not an instrument special in my case, not peculiar to me. It is the vow taken also by all my brothers who in this Church are exactly my peers. It has been already taken by all the brothers who in this transaction of exacting and accepting my vow represent to me and act the part to me of the Church. Not to mention that they are thus bound by the self-same vow already, taking into account merely that they exact and I render this vow in my ordination, is it conceivable that speaking of this one ordination merely, I alone became bound by it? Is it merely a pact on my side without being a compact between me and the Church? . . . Do I, then, come under obligation to the Church without the Church coming under obligation to me? Who would make an assertion so outrageous? The idea of a vow between creatures of God binding only one party in the transaction is a sheer paralogism. The vow entails very weighty obligation on my side, and on the side of the Church the obligation is as great. The obligation is manifestly reciprocal. That inheres in the idea of it. Laying out of view the contingency of my convictions as to the subject-matter of my vow coming to be changed and my leaving the Church accordingly, I am bound by it, aye, and until the Church shall release me. Is it conceivable that all this time the Church should have been silently reserving a right to release herself what time she may be able to outvote me? Is it possible that on what are actually called 'general impressions' and considerations of good sense it is proposed to regulate anew our Church Communion and I am to be—by a dispensing power, we presume—set free from my Ordination vow and the Church from her reciprocal, and another is to be substituted in its stead? Has a majority power to do this? Yes, if I have power to change my vow and still continue in the Church.

And yes, if the Church was not bound to me by prescribing and accepting my vow. . . . A majority may prove treacherous to a vow, just as an individual may : nor is it in the power of the multiplication table to settle a question of morals. Our Ordination vow taking us bound to our Confession settles that we have a Constitution, clearly enough defines it, renders us answerable to it and pledges the Church reciprocally as amenable to it also."

X.

Dr HUGH MARTIN

Dr Martin, who could write with such vigour in defence of the sacred nature of the engagements undertaken at an Ordination, was in respect of sheer intellectual and spiritual power in the very first rank of the Scottish Reformed Church during all the course of its history. He died in 1885 at the age of 63 after a broken ministry of 42 years. His work was interrupted by recurrent spells of serious indisposition which unfitted him for doing what might have been looked for from one of his pre-eminent gifts and his gracious character. He was one of the foremost home-bred and original mathematicians that Scotland has produced. But what survives as the fruit of his pen marks him out as a masterly exponent and a singular ornament of the Reformed Faith. His volume on the Atonement lets us see the kind of work that he was fitted to do. As a reasoner he was remarkably clear, cogent and powerful; and his handling of Broad Church perversions of a true Atonement is distinguished by its vigour and conclusiveness. Robertson of Brighton, in particular, came very limp indeed out of his grips. This work was not professedly one that went over the whole field. Indeed, its title page styles it—" The Atonement in its relation to the Covenant, the Priesthood and the Intercession." It has seen more than one edition, but it is not known as well or as widely as it ought to be. For it is a most convincing treatment of its theme, the work of a man who felt intensely the power of the doctrine that he taught. In distinction from his friend Smeaton's great treatment of this subject it shows more vigour and originality, while Smeaton's volumes are the work of the mature and eminently erudite theologian. The two men were comrades in arms and the best of friends.

Hugh Martin's other works are well worthy of being sought out and studied with care, for he was a theological genius.   One of them is *Christ's Presence in the Gospel History*.   This has run through two editions.   It won the warm approval of his fellow-townsman, Dr John Duncan, who speaks of it as fitted to promote " both the doctrine which is according to godliness and the godliness which is according to doctrine."   Then, also, there is his exposition in Lectures on the Book of Jonah which has run through more than one impression and which Spurgeon welcomed as " rich with good matter," calling it, as he well might, " a first-class exposition." Another of his works which is harder to get is his *Shadow of Calvary*, in which he deals with our Lord on the verge of the thick darkness into which He went to crown His service of atoning love.   The teaching of this volume is of a very profound character.   It reminds one of his handling of the Atonement.

A good deal of Martin's best work was of a fugitive kind. It is to be hunted up in periodicals and journals and single sermons and pamphlets.   We have seen that his pen was busy in *The Watchword*.   He was often a contributor also to *The British and Foreign Evangelical Review*.   As a Polemic he wielded a trenchant pen.   His *Letters to Dr Marcus Dods* and his *Westminster Doctrine of Inspiration* have been repeatedly issued.   The latter of these pamphlets is as valuable, lucid and convincing a presentation of its subject as one can find in a work of its compass.   The former was written to check, if it might be, the downward theological career of the son of one whom the writer revered and admired beyond most of the theologians of the century.   The pity is that the effort was futile.   The son took his own way and in his devious orbit he reversed his father's course.

XI.

Dr JOHN KENNEDY

There was one of Martin's intimate friends that we cannot at all pass by without a special notice. He was the great preacher of his generation in Scotland. This was John Kennedy of Dingwall. He remained to the end of his ministry in the charge which first called him. This was in the county town of a Highland shire far from the busy cities of the country. It was his own choice to stay where he began his work until his sun went down. He was repeatedly approached with a view to taking city charges. Though he laboured in a provincial town his reputation was national. Dr Kennedy was a truly great divine. In doctrine he was clear and powerful and at the same time practical. He was tender and judicious in his application of his message and he was an experimental divine in the best sense of the word. The great Puritans had no more eminent successor in the Scottish ministry in the 19th century. There is a book of his sermons to tell of the quality of his preaching. It is a massive volume and has been issued more than once, but it is exceedingly scarce. In it there are over 50 of his discourses. Almost all of these were written in the last year of his life when he was labouring under the malady that cut him off. His old hearers as a rule insist that the written sermons would not compare with his preached ones. Of course, when they were preached there was to be taken into account the impact upon his hearers of the preacher's striking personality and style and the reflex impact of his audience upon the preacher. But the written discourses, set down with the deliberate judgment of his fine mind, give us the doctrine, practice and experience that the preacher meant to lay stress upon. The English style has a decided distinction of its own. The inversion of sentences and the epigrams that often occur are marked features of it. The preacher was a special master in the realm of delicate spiritual analysis. In this respect he was even more striking than was his contemporary and friend, Dr Moody Stuart, who,

with Dr Charles J. Brown, was looked upon as the most
outstanding preacher of the introspective school in the
contemporary Edinburgh pulpit. To say that they belonged
to this school does not at all mean that they were one-
sidedly subjective in their themes. They were eminent
Evangelical and exegetical preachers who gave, however, a
considerable place in their preaching not only to the doctrines
of grace, but to the discussion of the inward work of Divine
grace; and thus it fell to them to handle cases of conscience
that their hearers might have in regard to the reality and
value of their experience of the Gospel. They were men sent
to bind up the brokenhearted, but they probed the cases with
which they dealt.

The fact that Dr Kennedy was critical at the same time
of the type of doctrine preached by Mr D. L. Moody and
of the enquiry room methods in dealing with the anxious
to which he gave vogue told against his own popularity. He
himself, however, was clear as to his duty to sound a warning
note. For his criticism was aimed at what he felt convinced
was an undesirable novelty in Scottish religious life. Yet
as the time was one of unusual excitement this criticism
created prejudice, and nothing could well be further from
the mark than the counter criticism which it elicited that
dared to say that he himself did not preach the offer of the
Gospel. This charge was without a foundation, for no man
in his generation made conscience more than he did of
proclaiming as the Gospel a message that was as full as it was
free and as free as it was full. It was, however, the day
of ebb-tide and the definite out-and-out Calvinism of another
day was going out of fashion and yielding place to a
presentation of the Gospel which, without being pronouncedly
Arminian, avoided the emphasis which the older Evangelicals
laid on the New Birth as a Divine intervention. This modified
message put its emphasis on the need the sinner has of
forgiveness to the eclipse of the equally urgent need that
he has of regeneration. It stressed the rectifying of his
standing and did not give sufficient prominence to his need of
a change of heart. In this connection the newer Evangelicalism

said less of the Spirit and His work and of the provision
made in Christ for a walk in newness of life than did the
fuller message which brought home as equally urgent the
need of having a man's nature renewed with that of having
acceptance for his person. With this change of emphasis or
balance there came to be an insistent demand for such
Conventions and Conferences as that of Keswick which sometimes wisely and sometimes unwisely set forth the provision
that the Gospel has made for believers in Christ that they
may have needed strength and power for a life and walk
becoming the name that they profess.

Like his friend Hugh Martin, Dr Kennedy was a man of
the Maclaurin type. Only he was much more richly endowed
with the gifts of the orator which enabled him to play upon
his audience almost at his will. He was the greatest of them,
yet only one of the succession of the Evangelical worthies
to the north of the Grampians. In his generation there was
a galaxy of great Evangelists, who were also good divines,
in the Highlands of Scotland. The life of some of these
has been sketched by friendly hands, yet no satisfactory
detailed account can now be given of their services in the
Gospel. The men of that generation in the northern region
were in the succession to a series of excellent predecessors
who were champions of the Reformed Faith there during the
ascendancy of the Moderates and even before the time of that
regime from the days of the Covenanter, Thomas Hog,
downwards.

In the 18th century the northern counties produced an
outstanding divine in the person of James Fraser of Alness,
whose work on Sanctification is one of the classics of our
Scottish Theology. It is a very thorough discussion of the
teaching of Paul in Romans vi. to viii. 4. In so far as he
is critical of John Locke's paraphrase of the Epistle, he deals
with what is now an extinct volcano, though in an environment
of 18th-century Legalism and Moderatism it may have been
needful to controvert it in his own day. But in his positive
Exegesis he shows himself a very solid and sensible interpreter
and in his statement of doctrine a judicious and masterly

divine. In some copies of this work one will find bound up
with it a few of Fraser's Sermons. These were first edited
by Russel of Kilmarnock, who had been in his early days
a teacher at Cromarty. The Sermons were first published
at Kilmarnock. One of them runs to 53 closely printed pages
or to 99 pages in the first edition. Isaac Barrow would find
it hard to beat this discourse for length. As a Sermon it
is a thorough and detailed treatment of Hebrews ix. 13, 14.
Dr Cunningham, on reading what was called Fraser's great
Sermon, said that what was a wonder to him was not the
excellence of the Sermon, good as it was, but the fact that
a congregation should be so schooled in divinity as to follow
with patience and appreciation such a full discussion of deep
Theology. Those were the peak days of Gospel power in his
Synod. Fraser had eminent friends and contemporaries.
They were his yoke-fellows and even his compeers such as
Macphail and Porteous and Calder, whose labours were
richly blessed and were the means of giving a dominance
in the Synods of Ross and Moray to the purest strain of
Gospel preaching. Of these other worthies, the only extant
memorial from their own pen is Mr Calder's Diary. It gives
a picture of a truly holy and diligent pastor who was as
active in seeing to the catechetical training of his flock as
he was competent in his preaching and crowned with success
in his labours. His sons worked on his lines. The Frasers
of Kirkhill, the Kennedys, the Macdonalds, the Stewarts, the
Mackintoshes in successive generations carried on the strain
of a pure Evangel, so that from the 17th century downwards,
from Thomas Hog and Angus Macbean, the sound and
powerful message of the Reformed Faith was well known in
the northern parts of the country. What survives in published
form of their work is worthy of the reputation of the leaders
of the northern Evangelical school. That reputation, however, and the circulation of the fragments of their teaching
were both provincial rather than national. It is in the north
of Scotland and mainly in the Gaelic area that the message
of such men is still to be heard as the regular theme of the
pulpit. The revolution in doctrine has not yet affected the

northern counties as it has the greater part of modern Scotland.

At bottom, the difference between the present and the past lies between the Rationalistic and the Reformed attitudes towards Holy Writ. The latter of these is the traditional one for Scotland as an Evangelical land; the former, which has been so powerful in the last generation, is but like a recurrence of the eclipse of the Evangel which took place in the Moderate age. As then the eclipse was due to the prevalence of an inimical tendency in philosophy, the Rationalism of the present day, largely an exotic, is in its own way the offspring of the spirit of the age which is swayed by tendencies that are on the one side Gnostic and on the other side Agnostic. There has emerged in recent years a movement, which is more or less of a Barthian character, to return to a message of salvation by sovereign grace. This, however, has yet to clarify its controlling principle by a repudiation of the type of critical treatment of Scripture that has wrought such havoc on the loyalty of Scotland to the Evangel. It is for the future to show the possibilities of this movement and the course that it will take. In regard to that course, the friends of the Evangel and the Reformed Theology would rejoice to see its supporters taking sides definitely with the undiluted witness of Scottish Reformed teaching and so coming under the offence of the Cross and the reproach of its message. When it does so it will pay heed to the word that says : " Whosoever therefore shall be ashamed of Me and of My words in this adulterous and sinful generation; of him also shall the Son of man be ashamed, when He cometh in the glory of His Father with the holy angels."

INDEX

350 INDEX